# Barack
## *and* Joe

ALSO BY STEVEN LEVINGSTON

*Kennedy and King*

# Barack
## *and* Joe

THE MAKING OF AN
EXTRAORDINARY PARTNERSHIP

## STEVEN
## LEVINGSTON

hachette
BOOKS

NEW YORK BOSTON

Hachette Books
Hachette Book Group
1290 Avenue of the Americas
New York, NY 10104
hachettebookgroup.com
twitter.com/hachettebooks

First Edition: October 2019

Hachette Books is a division of Hachette Book Group, Inc.
The Hachette Books name and logo are trademarks of Hachette Book Group, Inc.

The publisher is not responsible for websites (or their content) that are not owned by the publisher.

The Hachette Speakers Bureau provides a wide range of authors for speaking events. To find out more, go to www.hachettespeakersbureau.com or call (866) 376-6591.

Lyrics from "Keep On Pushing" by Curtis Mayfield © 1964 Warner-Tamerlane Publishing Corp. Used with permission.

Print book interior design by Six Red Marbles, Inc.

Library of Congress Control Number: 2019946919

ISBNs: 978-0-316-48786-3 (hardcover), 978-0-316-48788-7 (ebook)

Printed in the United States of America

LSC-C

10 9 8 7 6 5 4 3 2 1

*For Suzanne, Katie, and Ben*

# Contents

# Foreword

## Renegade and Celtic

### By Michael Eric Dyson

The buddy film is an American staple that mostly portrays the virtues of male bonding and rejects stereotypes of men as unemotional and uncaring creatures. The genre often pairs men of clashing styles and conflicting worldviews, and in the last few decades, it has brought together men of different races to combat the belief that we can't get along in the real world. There was surely progress in getting black and white men together on screen, but that didn't keep stereotypes from melting the celluloid. Black men were, at best, adjuncts to the white world or its convenient facilitators, as long as they were subordinate to the white star. At worst, black men were fall guys in a cinematic alchemy where history was reversed and black accomplishment was deceitfully turned into white heroism. The buddy film occasionally careened into "magical Negro" territory where the black male foil transformed the white protagonist in a quest for salvation, that is, if the white man didn't turn out to be the savior himself.

Near the end of the first decade of the new century, we watched a political version of the biracial buddy film play out in the nation's capital for eight years. It might even be argued by their followers that a dynamic duo took up revolutionary residence in Washington, DC.

Barack Obama and Joe Biden swept into town as an interracial Batman and Robin out to vanquish the harmful specter of George W. Bush and Dick Cheney and to bring light to a land languishing in darkness. This is where the buddy film adopted a superhero script and substantially upped the stakes of their partnership. Unlike most buddy films, the black guy was the biggest star; unlike most magical Negro films, the black guy was not only the source and symbol of salvation but the savior himself; and unlike most superhero films, at least before *Black Panther*, the black guy was the swashbuckling lead.

Barack and Joe were important to the nation's politics because they embodied an edifying symbiosis—let's cheekily call it an "Obidenosis." Obama was the country's first black president, a tall, brilliant, charismatic slice of Americana whose blended racial pedigree lent credence to his claim that we didn't live in a black or white America, but—and his mixed genes proved it—the *United* States of America. Biden had been a commanding force in the nation's dealings for decades, a sui generis political prodigy who won a Senate seat at twenty-nine and a proud Irishman who quoted Seamus Heaney and backslapped his way into the hearts of large swaths of the American people. Obama's superior political ingenuity spilled from his sophisticated brain and his nose for uncanny timing, for knowing what was needed when. Biden, despite his extraordinary run in the Senate, failed twice to leave the chamber in unsuccessful presidential runs, depending on Obama's choice of him as vice president to boost his standing in the political hierarchy. In this buddy film it was clear who was the man and who was the man next to the man, reinforcing his sublimely subordinate position by occasionally massaging the boss's shoulders.

Obama and Biden's spectacular partnership thrived because both men agreed to swap out meaningless duties and trifling symbolism in the vice presidency for substantive engagement and hearty brotherhood. When Obama came calling—and at first, it didn't seem likely, since Biden's proclivity to commit gaffes included an impolitic and racially charged assessment of Obama's "clean" and "articulate" status as a black presidential candidate when they both vied for the Oval Office in 2008 before Biden dropped out—Biden, though honored, insisted that, among other things, he get weekly private time with Obama and that he be in on every major presidential deliberation. And, perhaps most important, Biden wanted to be able to tell the truth as he saw it. Obama ate it up, and for the most part, despite Biden's predictable stumbles and unpredictable missteps, the two men flourished as a model of political fraternity in service of the nation's highest good. (Plus, one of Biden's most high-profile "mistakes," getting out ahead of Obama in support of gay marriage, proved that Biden's courage and honesty forced a reticent head of state to take the sort of stand he had already privately affirmed. While Obama enjoyed a fictional "anger translator" on television's *Key and Peele*, Biden, if not quite an Obama whisperer, may have been, on occasion, his sturdier public conscience.)

Steven Levingston, a gifted diviner of our political ethos and an eloquent chronicler of our national tendencies, delves purposefully into the relationship between Obama and Biden, showing how it was the magical melding of two forceful personalities who were quite dissimilar in many ways but capable of turning their differences into national benefit. If Obama was a bookish introvert, Biden was a literate extrovert, yet together they read the national mood, combining Barack's scholarly pensiveness and Joe's emotional intelligence to lift the country from a seemingly intractable recession.

Levingston helps us to see how much of what drew Obama and Biden to each other—both were athletes who sprinkled their speech with sports metaphors, both loved their kids (and Biden his grandkids), both fawned over their wives, both eagerly deflected acclaim for their achievements and instead heaped praise on their numerous collaborators and staff—existed off the books and beyond the stage. Yes, Obama and Biden shared an incurable love for the dreams and ideals of America, but they found in their mutually supportive ideas of empathetic manhood a portal to true intimacy and genuine camaraderie. They weren't afraid to openly root for each other, admire each other, and, rather quickly in their luminous fellowship, to love each other.

Still, Levingston isn't afraid to show the uglier side of things too. Obama, like all good or at least effective politicians, could be calculating and strategic. When Obama stood for reelection in 2012, he let concern about his political fortunes fuel behind-the-scenes discussions about whether Hillary Clinton should replace Biden as Barack's running mate. There appeared to be real teeth to the consideration, and yet, ultimately, Biden prevailed, and so did Obama, winning reelection and preserving their friendship. When Biden was weighing a run for the presidency in 2016 as Obama left office, Barack steered him clear of the field and discouraged him from running, a development that hurt Joe. He believed that Obama was understandably looking out for his own legacy, feeling that Hillary, given the political landscape, could best protect it and carry it forward. But it still stung.

And even now, as Biden has entered the 2020 presidential race, Obama has met with other hopeful candidates and touted the need for new blood in the Democratic Party, all while playing it cool on endorsing Biden—or even embracing him as the heir apparent to his presidency. Similar to how he publicly loved the black people who overwhelmingly supported him, Obama could on occasion be less enthusiastic about those who adored him and fail to return in equal measure the love that was given to him.

As long as they were in the White House, Obama gave Joe royal treatment and, for the most part, remained resolutely loyal to his second-in-command. Since they've flown the coop, Obama, while still warm and friendly, has been noticeably different, a cooler, less demonstrably supportive partner to a man whose cheek he kissed at the funeral of his son Beau, a man around whose neck he placed the Medal of Freedom eight days before they left office. As was true with black folk, Obama could be heavy on symbolism but, when it counted, sometimes faulty in the delivery of substance, such as public love in the form of policy or vigorous advocacy from his bully pulpit.

While the Obama presidency lasted, and as its meaning continues to unfold, the connection forged between Barack and Joe is one for the history books, even the first run at that history in the book you hold in your hands. This is as fine a reading of a unique and consequential political relationship—a partnership, a friendship, a brotherly affection sealed by genuine love—as we are likely to find. Steven Levingston has written a lovely and important book that touches on race and manhood at the heart of American politics. This buddy-film-come-to-life is a magnificent story told with poetic verve by a writer who sets his study up like a thriller and crafts it with the pace and surprise of a first-rate novel.

The only way the story can get better is if Biden lives out one of Obama's rare gaffes—something that might be read later as a Freudian slip that revealed a hidden truth. When he was first introducing Biden to the public as his vice-presidential choice in 2008, Obama blew the line: "So let me introduce to you the next president," Obama said before quickly revising his line after catching his error and proclaiming his running mate the next vice president of the United States.

As Biden's quest for the Oval Office heats up, all of his previous experiences come back not only to haunt him but, in some ways, to aid him, even the gaffes. After all, the present occupant of 1600 Pennsylvania has so precipitously lowered the presidential bar that Biden's errors—even his huggy, kissy, "embraceable you" rituals of social intimacy, which must be adapted for the #MeToo era—may lose their menacing repercussions or, at least, may not be viewed nearly as badly now as they were then, especially since Biden, as a plainspoken politico who calls it as he sees it, is Trump without the bile, Trump without the viciousness, Trump without the hate, Trump without the unapologetic ignorance, Trump without the racist and misogynist furor that hugs his presidency to death and squeezes from it most displays of humanity and compassion.

Perhaps Obama's faux pas might be, instead of an error, an unintended prophecy, and thus, this book is even more than the considerably insightful study that it manages to be. It will be, too, one of the first, and finest, passes at assessing a man who not only holds a venerable role in history as arguably the most important vice president ever but may one day play Batman to someone else's Robin. For these reasons and more, *Barack and Joe* is a beautiful book about two beautiful men who tried to make this country beautiful again.

Michael Eric Dyson
May 22, 2019

Michael Eric Dyson is the *New York Times* bestselling author of *Tears We Cannot Stop: A Sermon to White America* and *What Truth Sounds Like: Robert F. Kennedy, James Baldwin, and Our Unfinished Conversation About Race in America,* as well as an ordained Baptist minister and professor of sociology at Georgetown University.

# "Don't you miss these guys?"

It was just like the old days: Barack and Joe out for lunch, yukking it up together.

Except everything was different now.

It was July 30, 2018, a year and a half since Donald Trump had bullied his way into the White House and started breaking the china. Now chaos, darkness, and ineptitude reigned. After eight years of a scandal-free Obama presidency, Trump had populated the White House with criminal cronies. He had rejected facts and science, cozied up to despots, denigrated the news media, emboldened white supremacists, and turned our national discourse into gutter speak.

Yet suddenly there was a reminder of hope.

When former president Barack Obama and former vice president Joe Biden walked into Dog Tag Bakery in Georgetown on that Monday afternoon, all smiles, a bounce in their steps, nostalgia broke out. Their presence revived a national memory of cheerfulness, competence, and everyday civility. Barack and Joe, casual and friendly, in khakis and open-collar button-downs, with their sleeves rolled up, let America see itself as it was—not so long ago.

\*    \*    \*

Out of a sense of protocol, Barack and Joe had stayed mostly offstage since Trump's inauguration and had rarely been seen out together. There were glimpses: in September 2017, they attended the Invictus Games in Toronto as guests of Prince Harry, with Barack tweeting that he was proud to cheer on Team USA with his "friend Joe."

On their birthdays, they sent best wishes to each other on Twitter. Joe to Barack on August 4, 2017: "Your service has been a great gift to the country, and your friendship and brotherhood are a great gift to me. Happy birthday, @BarackObama." Barack to Joe on November 20, 2017: "Happy birthday to @JoeBiden, my brother and the best vice president anybody could have."

In February 2018 Joe witnessed the unveiling of Barack's and Michelle's official portraits at the National Portrait Gallery, a dignified postpresidential ceremony, not the place for two buddies to ham it up together.

Now, after a considerable absence, here they were at Dog Tag Bakery showing off their enduring friendship. But this was more than a good-time lunch. When Barack and Joe descended on the bakery in their black SUVs, they showered attention on this small nonprofit that helped disabled service members carve a path to civilian life; the bakery provided fellowships for veterans and their spouses to set up and run their own businesses.

Chief executive Meghan Ogilvie said she had just a six-minute warning before the former president and vice president walked in. Making their way through the place, Barack and Joe shook everyone's hand, "hugged them and listened to their stories," Ogilvie said. When Barack discovered that one fellow hoped to open a yoga studio, he performed a Tree Pose with her, balancing on one leg, his hands pressed together at his chest in the prayer position. The photo rocketed through cyberspace.

At the counter, Barack and Joe deliberated over their sandwich order. "Hold on. Hold on," Barack interrupted Joe as he was making his decision. "What'd you get here?"

Joe, holding up a plate and peering at something wrapped in white paper: "I got one of these—whatever the hell they're called." After studying the plate closely, he declared: "It's ham…and cheese."

"That's looks pretty good," Barack agreed. "I think I gotta have one of those too."

"Give the boss one of those too," Joe said, flicking a thumb in the direction of Obama, in case anyone wasn't perfectly clear on who the boss was.

And the boss quipped: "Joe's paying."

In Joe's hand was a fistful of cash.

The visit lit up the internet.

"Don't you miss these guys?" groaned @MillenPolitics.

"Miss them so much," agreed @skenigsberg, with a sad-face emoji.

America was in full flashback. During the White House years, stories and images of Barack and Joe at work and at play on the campaign trail, in the Oval Office, at a diner, on the White House putting green, had whipped across the digital universe. The media played their story huge, stoking the excitement around the pair. A vast number of Americans adored this relationship, and social media allowed them to share whatever they saw about it with friends. Obama-Biden fans intensely watched this buddy team, rejoiced in it, and identified with it. What Barack and Joe had established with each other, admirers across the country wanted to have in their own lives. The friendship became a favorite national storyline, and the public added its own chapters to it by creating touching or humorous memes. "We loved this story," observed Kate Leaver, author of *The Friendship Cure: Reconnecting in the Modern World*. "We helped write this story."

Now the media celebrated the duo's reemergence into the spotlight. The headline on the *Cosmopolitan* website read: "Barack Obama and Joe

Biden Went to Lunch Yesterday and It Was Cuter Than Your Last Date." The subhead added the detail: "They got matching sandwiches, guys."

In *Cosmo*'s view, America still pined for these guys and their friendship: "Yesterday, your two favorite bromance members of all time (Joe Biden and Barack Obama) took a break from being the retired cool humans they are to grab a quick lunch in D.C....The love between these two? Still 100 percent alive."

As *Travel and Leisure* put it, "The former president and vice president proved they are still the definition of friendship goals."

The *New York Daily News* took the opportunity to repost a retrospective of the pair's "bromance through the years." In a series of seventeen photos, the president and vice president were seen over their tenure crying, hugging, laughing, whispering, walking arm in arm, eating ice cream, backslapping, dining at a lunch joint, and strolling contemplatively on the White House grounds.

Introducing the photo gallery, the *Daily News* wrote: "Their terms as President and Vice President are over, but one thing will never come to an end—the heartwarming bromance of Barack Obama and Joe Biden."

This book is the story of how this extraordinary partnership got started, took shape, and evolved into a friendship of profound depth, a kind never before witnessed in the history of the American presidency. The odds were long. Barack and Joe were two very different men who never expected to be friends. There was no gravitational pull, one man toward the other, no instantaneous clicking of like personalities.

Here was a young, cerebral African American who sweated over the precision of his words, and an older, chummy white guy given to impulsively speaking his mind. In 2005, during their first encounters, Barack was an impatient freshman senator and Joe a veteran of thirty-two years in the chamber. Barack disdained the Senate's pace and grandstanding. Joe honored its traditions. The two men circled each other warily.

## "Don't you miss these guys?"

In 2008, they were political rivals, competitors for the 2008 Democratic presidential nomination. After Barack secured the nomination and brought Joe on as his running mate, the two men began a rocky process of accommodation. Their styles clashed. Obama's aloofness resisted Biden's gregariousness.

"Obama had the remoteness of an introvert who didn't pretend affection," observed author George Packer in his book *Our Man: Richard Holbrooke and the End of the American Century*. "He saved his warmth for the few who really generated it—his family, his old friends."

Early on Biden recognized the distance between him and Barack. "It was clear from the outset to everyone who knew him that President Obama did not easily place his trust in others," Joe wrote in his memoir. "He 'travels light,' one staffer said of him."

But no one ever fought off Joe's in-your-face exuberance for long. Barack and Joe not only grew to admire and respect each other; they developed a sense of true companionship. As vice president, Joe was Barack's sought-after general adviser and an expert in foreign affairs and Congress. No president and vice president had ever worked so intimately together, and no White House duo had been as close personally. Even their families embraced each other.

Through their two terms, through controversies that included a black Harvard professor's arrest and a general's ill-advised public comments about White House war policy, Barack and Joe operated as an effective mutual-support team. The working partnership flowered into the full bloom of friendship late in the administration with the illness and death of Joe's son Beau.

Their demonstrated affection for each other, spread by media chatter, videos, White House photos, and memes, sent a particular message to men across the country. In *The Friendship Cure*, Leaver wrote that White House photographs portrayed Barack Obama in a variety of roles: "the romantic husband, the good father, the great American. But perhaps the most adored version is best-mate Obama, walking shoulder to shoulder with Joe Biden." Barack and Joe promoted a revolutionary ethos: they showed that it was okay for men to cry, and hug, and show love to their guy friends. Leaver praised Barack and Joe's "gentle subversion" of the stereotypes of "male stoicism."

For all the apparent joy and ease of the bromance, this was a complex relationship. Many Americans, thanks to the internet, had a one-dimensional perspective of Barack and Joe's devotion to each other. We wanted to see only the beauty of two powerful men who knew how to show their love. The images fit a charming fairy tale of harmony in high places, assuring us that all was good with the world. But any power partnership, especially at the presidential level, cannot escape tremendous pressures, both public and private. Politics inevitably collided with the friendship. Ambition and political exigencies took their toll.

Strains surfaced whenever Joe spoke out of turn, and his expected presidential ambitions for 2016 were a constant backbeat. For his part, Barack had no compunction about placing his own political fortunes above the friendship. Ahead of the 2012 reelection campaign, Obama allowed his staff to ponder dumping Joe for Hillary Clinton as the vice-presidential candidate in the belief that a Clinton substitution would strengthen the ticket. As the 2016 presidential election approached, Obama failed to support or even encourage Joe as he weighed a possible run. The president contended that Joe was too grief-stricken over his son Beau's death and that a bid in 2016 would be an uphill battle against Clinton, who seemed anointed for victory. Obama didn't hide the fact that a defeat in the general election would have boded ill for his own legacy.

This book is not a history of the Obama administration. It does not presume to be an analysis of Obama policy and its successes and failures. I leave that to academic historians. (During their years in power, Barack and Joe were largely aligned on policy issues, though sharp disagreements did emerge, including Joe's opposition to the raid that killed Osama bin Laden; he feared that failure would turn Obama into a one-term president.) Readers also should not look here for a complete dual biography. My lens is narrower. What I have set out to do is to tell the story of the professional and personal rapport of a president and a vice president through a series of crucial moments. The storytelling is weighted more toward the early years when the two men were getting to know each other and working out their differences. Like any relationship, this one had to build a foundation on which to flourish, and the narrative seeks to illuminate how Barack and Joe got onto a solid footing together. In the final chapters, we witness the profound expression of a friendship realized. The arc of the Barack and Joe story reminds us that a common humanity exists in all personal relationships, even those that play out in the highest places under a glaring spotlight. It is this universality of their relationship that has moved the nation.

After their visit to Dog Tag Bakery, Barack posted a selfie on Instagram. It showed Joe and him posing just outside the bakery doors. Barack looked joyous: his smile was so wide that his eyes had shrunk to mere slits.

"My brother and friend @JoeBiden is back on Instagram," Barack wrote. "Welcome back, Joe—you'll always be one of the rare exceptions to my no-selfies rule."

Barack's post swept up nearly three million likes. One enthusiastic comment came from a guy who went by the handle Edzarco, who summed up the feelings of many: "What a real president and vice president look like. Eight years of steady management with no scandals. The good old days."

# ONE

# "Man, That Guy Can Just Talk and Talk"

Only two weeks after taking his US Senate oath in 2005, freshman senator Barack Obama was already near his breaking point. Obama, the lowest-ranking member on the Foreign Relations Committee, was seated at the outer reaches of the horseshoe-shaped table listening to fellow senator Joe Biden, a thirty-two-year veteran, drone on…and on…and on. Biden, by virtue of his seniority, was the ranking Democrat seated in his executive high-backed chair right next to the committee chairman, Republican senator Richard Lugar of Indiana.

Obama gazed across the table as Biden expounded without pause on the "God-awful" choices confronting the United States in North Korea, in Iran, and in Syria, and regaled the chamber with tales of his fact-finding journey into northern Iraq—"a seven-hour ride through the mountains." A man of few, carefully chosen words, Obama was astonished at the way Biden ran his mouth. "It's an incredible thing to see," he later confided to his adviser David Axelrod.

The committee had convened on January 18 for a two-day confirmation hearing for Condoleezza Rice, the nominee for secretary of state put forward by newly reelected president George W. Bush. For Obama, the deliberations dragged on as showboat politicians took turns filling the air. On the first day, Obama waited in silence through four hours of questions and answers during the morning session and then another forty minutes after lunch before he got a chance to speak—and then only with strict limits. When Senator Lugar finally offered him the floor, he laid out the rules: "Well, let me now call upon Senator Obama for his initial ten minutes of questioning."

Just six months earlier, on July 27, 2004, Obama had been a little-known Illinois state senator running for a US Senate seat when he stepped onto the stage at the Democratic National Convention in Boston two days before Senator John Kerry accepted the party's nomination for president. As Obama crossed to the podium at Boston's FleetCenter at about 9:45 p.m., the arena throbbed to the sound of Curtis Mayfield and the Impressions. The group's rousing civil rights tune, "Keep On Pushing," was a fitting introduction for the black man at the microphone. The lyrics blasting over the loudspeaker articulated the Obama dream.

*I've got to keep on pushing (mmm-hmm)*
*I can't stop now*
*Move up a little higher.*
*Some way, somehow.*

Under the lights, Obama looked sharp in a dark suit, white shirt, and blue silk tie. The tie belonged to an aide and had been hastily swapped for his own duller selection—a last-minute costume change demanded by his wife, Michelle. Waiting for the applause to fade, Obama waved and smiled and thanked the crowd. He was cool, full of focus; he had the calm of an athlete at the start of the championship game.

Chosen by Kerry to deliver the convention's keynote address, Obama told the story of his unique origins—a white mother from Kansas and a black father who grew up herding goats in a small village in Kenya—and his parents' dreams for him. In hypnotic cadences he urged America to welcome diversity: "I stand here knowing that my story is part of the larger American story." He invited Americans to see past bitter partisanship. "There are those who are preparing to divide us," he warned. "Well," he went on in a voice of measured challenge, "I say to them tonight, there is not a liberal America and a conservative America. There is the *United States* of America." Gracefully chopping the air with his hand, he elevated the volume of his call: "There is not a black America and white America and Latino America and Asian America. There is the *United States* of America."

His style and eloquence and story were electrifying. Stunned commentators compared him to previous standouts at party conventions: John F. Kennedy in 1956, Mario Cuomo in 1984, Ann Richards in 1988. Watching Obama, MSNBC host Chris Matthews was beside himself: "I have to tell you, a little chill in my legs right now. That is an amazing moment in history."

For Obama the basketball lover, it was as if he'd sunk a three-pointer at the buzzer to win the championship. His master strategist David Axelrod immediately understood the consequences: "I realized at that moment that his life would never be the same."

Writing in the *Chicago Tribune*, columnist Clarence Page declared, "A superstar is born. It is difficult for many of us to contain our enthusiasm for Barack Obama." In an instant, this biracial Illinois state senator had been anointed the new face of the Democratic Party. Accolades bombarded him. The public swarmed him for the remainder of the convention. The following day, when he was back at the FleetCenter riding the up escalator, a woman passing him on her way down leaned over and confided, "I just cannot wait until you are president."

Joe Biden also spoke at the convention, two days after Obama, but who remembered his twelve minutes onstage? Only one person in America seemed to hear Biden. "Barack Obama's speech at the Democratic convention drew rave reviews. So did Bill Clinton's," argued Peter Beinart in the *New Republic*. "But my nominee for best oration of the week goes to Senator Joseph Biden."

Biden, who had spent years in the Senate studying foreign affairs, spoke on America's crisis of the moment: the battle against radical Islam. He framed it not as a "war on terror"—the Bush administration's propaganda term—but as a war to defeat the ideas of Islamic extremism that were so contrary to American notions of liberty. "Radical fundamentalism," Biden declared, "will fall to the terrible, swift power of our ideas as well as our swords."

In the still-echoing din of Obama's speech, however, Biden's words were largely lost except on Beinart, a foreign-affairs expert. "On Thursday night at about eight o'clock—long before the networks began their broadcasts," Beinart contended, "Biden laid out the most compelling Democratic foreign policy vision I have yet heard."

Four months after the convention, on November 2, 2004, Obama trounced his Republican opponent, Alan Keyes, in the US Senate race, capturing 70 percent of the vote. His decisive victory sent two clear messages: one, that Keyes was a terrible candidate, and two, far more important, that Obama was a formidable new political figure—his margin of victory was the largest ever in a US Senate contest in Illinois.

The hoopla around him only intensified. He joked with David Letterman during an appearance on *The Late Show* and was invited for lunch with billionaire investor Warren Buffett. Before Obama took his Senate oath, *Newsweek* plastered his smiling image on the cover of its "Who's Next" issue. *Vanity Fair* celebrated the young senator over two pages in its January 2005 edition. The February issue of *Savoy* featured a glamorous, arm-in-arm cover portrait of Obama in a suit jacket and open-collared dress shirt and Michelle in a low-buttoned white blouse, chartreuse jacket, and blue jeans, with the headline, "Camelot Rising."

The senator-elect even earned billing as a national sex object. When the conversation on the NBC sitcom *Will & Grace* turned to butts, Grace suddenly was reminded of the junior senator from Illinois. "Speaking of butts," she confessed, "I had another sex dream last night. This time I was in the shower with Barack Obama." Throwing back her head, she cooed: "*Oh* 'Bama . . . He was Baracking my world!"

His portrayal on *Will & Grace* underscored how the freshman senator stood apart from his more senior colleagues. He represented a youthful shift in American politics. His convention speech, his landslide victory, and his media stardom made him the coolest member of the staid Senate.

He tried to fit in. On the night of his Senate election, Obama gave his victory speech in a dark suit, gray tie, and crisp white shirt. In the words of *Washington Post* fashion critic Robin Givhan, "He looked ready for the boardroom or the courtroom, rather than a rousing late-night party."

But he chafed against the Senate hierarchy. His healthy ego did not take kindly to his lowly status. His arrogance was often sympathetically described by admirers as self-confidence. One of his closest friends, Valerie Jarrett, meaning to highlight his brilliance, inadvertently painted a portrait of a man who had no trouble flaunting his superiority. "I think Barack knew that he had God-given talents that were extraordinary," Jarrett told David Remnick of *The New Yorker*. "He knows exactly how smart he is. . . . He knows exactly how perceptive he is." She described a man in his prepresidential days who was a quick study, an excellent reader of people, a synthesizer of viewpoints—all aspects of himself that Obama did not hide. "I think that he has never really been challenged intellectually," Jarrett observed.

Acknowledging a certain swagger, Obama traced it to his upbringing. As he explained to *Tribune* reporter David Mendell, his mother had feared that as a biracial kid with an absent father, her son would have a damaged self-image. To counter it, she amply inflated his ego. "As a consequence," Obama told Mendell with a wry smile, "there was no shortage of self-esteem." In his book *The Audacity of Hope*, Obama acknowledged that a healthy dose of self-admiration was essential to political success. Discussing his run for the Senate, he observed that "few people end up being United States senators by accident; at a minimum, it requires a certain megalomania, a belief that of all the gifted people in your state, you are somehow uniquely qualified to speak on their behalf."

Having arrived in the Senate upon a pedestal, Obama had to adjust to his freshman role. Sometimes humor helped. "I'm so junior," he quipped to the *Chicago Tribune*'s Jeff Zeleny early in his term, "that when I arrived in Washington, they handed me a toothbrush and said, 'Go clean the latrines!'"

For all his star power and confidence, Obama had landed in an incomprehensible, sometimes hostile terrain, and he needed help navigating the world of the Senate. He courted a consummate insider named Pete Rouse, who had served as chief of staff to Senator Tom Daschle of South Dakota until his unexpected defeat in the 2004 election.

Rouse had spent thirty years on Capitol Hill and was looking forward to collecting his government pension. But he recognized Obama's spark. He had no doubt the young senator would play a role in the future of the Democratic Party. "He had the magic," Rouse recalled. "You can tell he had the magic."

In a two-hour meeting Obama sold Rouse on his intelligence, insight, and willingness to learn. "I know what I'm good at," he told the longtime politico. "I know what I'm not good at. I know what I know, and I know what I don't know....I know policy. I know retail politics in Illinois. I don't have any idea what it's like to come into the Senate....I want to get established and work with my colleagues and develop a reputation as a good senator."

Rouse set aside his retirement. Coming on board as Obama's chief of staff, he drew up a three-part plan to guide his Senate years. First, Obama had to prove he was serious about being a senator for Illinois, and he had to deliver. Second, he had to show his Senate colleagues that he was a team player and not, as Rouse put it, "a headline hunter." Third, he had to craft a vision of the future and then, far into his term, raise his profile to realize his potential.

With Rouse at the helm, Obama wasted no time seeking to tame any suspicions on the part of his Senate colleagues. He tamped down his lust for national attention. He declined invitations to appear on the Sunday talk shows. During his first nine months in office, he accepted only one out-of-state speaking engagement and held thirty-nine town hall meetings in Illinois.

He sought the counsel of wise Democratic elders, including Edward Kennedy and Hillary Clinton, who had entered the chamber in 2001 under a similar cloud of renown and was now regarded as a respected senator. He sat with her for an hour in early February amid the daffodil-colored walls of her spacious fourth-floor office in the prestigious Russell Building. Her suite, with its photos of her and her husband, President Bill Clinton, in the Oval Office and of her heroes Robert Kennedy and Eleanor Roosevelt, was a testament to an already-full career. By contrast, Obama's dank digs in the basement of the unglamorous Hart Building underscored that he was barely in the game.

From Clinton, Obama learned that the rules for success in a stuffy institution guided by seniority were the obvious ones: keep a low profile, work hard, always be prepared, land good committee roles, and look after your constituents. Both Clinton and Obama were known to be disciplined and driven and to dig into details to the point of wonkiness, but it was uncertain whether he could emulate her patience and steady commitment to a long-term plan.

Among other senators, Obama found a mentor in the five-term Republican Richard Lugar; the men, both soft-spoken, bonded over a mutual quest to rein in the spread of weapons of mass destruction, with Obama gaining a coveted spot on Lugar's Foreign Relations Committee. "I like Lugar," Obama told Axelrod. "He's not a showboat."

On his rounds paying respectful visits to the Senate's distinguished elders (the average age of his colleagues was sixty), the forty-three-year-old Obama spent time with eighty-seven-year-old Robert Byrd. From Byrd, "a living, breathing fragment of history," as Obama described him, the newcomer got a lesson in Senate tradition. "Learn the rules," Byrd told him. "Not just the rules, but the precedents as well." Byrd escorted him through his own years in the chamber and the presidents and legislation that had crossed his path. "He told me I would do well in the Senate," Obama recalled. But Byrd warned that he "shouldn't be in too much of a rush—so many senators today became fixated on the White House, not understanding that in the constitutional design it was the Senate that was supreme, the heart and soul of the Republic."

Another member of the old guard had already issued words of warning to the rising star. When Obama hit the celebrity stratosphere after his convention speech, virtually assuring victory in his Senate race, Senator Biden thrust up a hand like a traffic cop. He saw the momentum hurtling Obama along and sensed the young man's impatience. "He's a good man," Biden told an Obama aide, "but tell him he needs to go slow when he gets to the Senate."

For his part, Biden hadn't yet proved himself to the new senator as anything more than a windbag. Obama described Biden as a "decent guy," but there was always a caveat: "Man, that guy can just talk and talk."

During his three decades in the Senate, Biden had come to deeply value the institution and its members; he expected newcomers to respect its hierarchy, it consultative style, its traditions. And, as was well-known, he was no stranger to speaking his mind on any subject at whatever length he deemed necessary. It was his blessing and his curse from his earliest days as a politician. Back on March 20, 1972, a young Joe stood before a crowd in the du Barry Room at the Hotel du Pont in Wilmington, Delaware, and passionately espoused his views for more than forty minutes—the gist of which came down to one brash declaration: "I am announcing today my candidacy for the United States Senate."

He was twenty-nine years old, a New Castle County councilman. By the rules of the US Constitution, he couldn't even take his seat in the Senate, if he won, until his thirtieth birthday, two weeks after the November election. More pertinent to Joe's candidacy, however, was his formidable opponent. Joe was squaring off against Republican Cale Boggs, a likable sixty-three-year-old who had served two terms in the Senate and had been in public service for over twenty-five years. Boggs was unbeatable; everybody knew him. Hardly anyone knew Joe.

"Boggs!" Biden's friends told him. "Joe, you're fucking crazy."

"He's tired," Biden replied, unfazed.

Like Obama's thirty years later, Joe's rise coincided with a political moment. Young people were waking up; they wanted to change the world and along the way rock to T. Rex, David Bowie, and Chicago. In this election cycle, eighteen-year-olds were allowed into the voting booth for the first time.

Boggs had served loyally but without stirring anything up. Biden promised to deliver a liberal, activist agenda on voting rights, civil rights, and water and air quality. He called for a national health-care program and, already turning his attention to foreign policy, opposed the Vietnam War. Delaware knew the tragedy of Vietnam up close. "Every week young American men were being shipped to the mortuary at Dover Air Force Base in body bags," Biden recalled. "How many mothers lay awake at night wondering how their own sons might return, and wondering what exactly they were risking their lives for?"

But Biden was no hippie rebel. He was respectful, witty, and well groomed. He showed up for his announcement at the Hotel du Pont in a dark pinstripe suit, matching vest, and brown wing tips. He was running against not only Boggs's ready recognition among voters but the strength of President Richard Nixon; the president was seeking a second term against a weak liberal opponent, Democratic candidate George McGovern.

Biden barnstormed the state with blind fervor, going door to door in the suburbs and at the shore, supported by his sister Valerie, who served as campaign manager; his brother Jimmy, his chief fundraiser; and his wife, Neilia, who was the Joe Whisperer. With his masterful touch, journalist Richard Ben Cramer captured Joe and Neilia's relationship in his book *What It Takes*. "It was Joe who called the shots—Joe and Neilia," Cramer wrote. "She was still the only one who could slow him down, or shut him up. He'd get all hot and bothered [about] something someone said...and Neilia'd tell him: 'Joe, you don't say *anything* about that. That will pass. Don't make an enemy of him.'"

Joe had met Neilia on the beach in Nassau during his spring break in 1964, when he was a junior at the University of Delaware. He was dazzled by her green eyes and long blonde hair and her confidence. The following weekend he showed up at her dorm at Syracuse University and sat in the lobby waiting for her in a white shirt, flashing that blazing smile of his. "You know what he said," Neilia revealed afterward to a friend. "He told me he's going to be a senator by the time he's thirty. And then, he's going to be president." They married in 1966.

By Joe's 1972 campaign, he and Neilia had three kids, three-year-old Beau, two-year-old Hunter, and baby daughter Naomi, or Amy, as the family called her. Early polls showed Biden getting clobbered. Only 20 percent of voters even knew his name.

But as the months wore on, Boggs's lead shrank. Whether he was tired or poorly advised, Boggs failed to accurately measure Biden's challenge. Remarkably, little more than a week before the election, the race was a dead heat.

On November 7, when the votes were tallied, Biden had eked out a victory on a margin of less than 3,000 votes out of a total of 228,000 cast. It was a stunning upset. Biden had captured not only the youth vote but also older voters of both parties. Celebrating at the Hotel du Pont that night, the victor was gracious and respectful of Boggs and his long career of public service, calling him "a real gentleman."

\*     \*     \*

Biden was riding high: he couldn't believe his good fortune. He had a stupendous wife and family, and in a few months he was going to be the youngest member of the US Senate.

But he worried. Everything was too good. The day after the election, he and Neilia were riding in the car when he turned to her: "Something's gonna happen," he fretted. "I don't know....But it's too perfect. Can't be like this. Something's gonna happen."

As the Thanksgiving and Christmas holidays approached, Biden spent time in Washington getting to know his way around, interviewing candidates for his staff positions, making courtesy calls on the old lions, and soaking up attention as the novelty figure in town: the underage freshman.

On November 30, Joe was back home for his big thirtieth birthday party at the Pianni Grill in downtown Wilmington. To mark his birthday and his eligibility for his Senate seat, he and Neilia stood side by side to cut a cake, a ceremony that reminded Biden of his wedding.

He had another momentary panic. Maybe it was just nerves over what lay ahead, and a feeling that he wasn't quite prepared for it. As he wrote in his memoir, "I'd always remember the funny feeling I had standing beside Neilia, cutting that cake."

Before he was sworn in, his premonition turned to tragic reality. On December 18, 1972, a week before Christmas, Joe was in Washington while Neilia, still in Wilmington, was preparing for the move and for Christmas. In the late morning, she piled the kids into the station wagon—Hunter, now three, in the front seat; Beau, four years old, and Amy, thirteen months, in the back—and they were off to do some shopping, including buying a Christmas tree.

After halting at a stop sign, Neilia pulled into an intersection as a tractor trailer packed with corncobs bore down on the station wagon. The truck smashed into the driver's side, knocking the car 150 feet down the road and into a ditch. The demolished station wagon came to a rest against some trees.

\*　　　\*　　　\*

The phone rang in Biden's campaign office in Wilmington, and his brother Jimmy picked it up. He then phoned Joe's office in Washington and asked to talk to their sister Val. "When she hung up," Biden wrote in his memoir, "she looked white. 'There's been a slight accident,' she said. 'Nothing to be worried about. But we ought to go home.'" Joe heard a catch in her voice and felt something in his chest. "She's dead," he said, "isn't she?"

Neilia and baby Amy were dead on arrival at Wilmington Medical Center. The boys had survived but were in bad shape. Beau had many broken bones and was put in a full body cast. Hunter had suffered head injuries. For Joe, the shock was staggering. As he put it, "I could not speak, only felt this hollow core grow in my chest." Though a devout Catholic, he raged at God. "All my life I'd been taught about our benevolent God," he wrote. "This was a loving God, a God of comfort. Well, I didn't want to hear anything about a merciful God."

Serving in the Senate suddenly meant nothing to him. All that mattered were his boys. He only wanted to be with them, care for them, never leave their side. He was on the point of giving up his seat as Delaware's new senator before he even started.

His Senate colleagues, among them the majority leader, Mike Mansfield, and Senator Hubert Humphrey, the former vice president of the United States, called him constantly, checking in and trying to keep him from being "sucked inside a black hole," as Biden described his emotional chaos. They embraced him, wanted him to join them, dangled plum committee assignments in front of him.

Torn, Biden finally agreed to give it a shot for six months to honor Neilia, who had worked so hard to get him elected, and to see if he could maintain his balance. His sister Val moved into his house to look after the boys, who would fully recover. Joe planned to live in Delaware and commute by train each morning, an eighty-minute ride, and he'd be home at night to tuck the boys in as often as possible.

Beau told journalist Jules Witcover that his earliest memories were of his father coming in to see him and his brother at night no matter the time and "jumping in bed with us, being held and kissed." In the mornings Joe dropped the kids off at school before catching his train to Washington. "I remember his entire focus was us and everything else was second," Beau told Witcover. "Never in my life did I doubt it for one second."

Biden took his Senate oath of office on January 5, 1973, in the chapel at Wilmington Medical Center, in front of Beau, who was lying in a wheeled bed, a leg in traction, and Hunter, who had been released, as well as other family members.

As he took up his duties in the Senate, Biden made it through a fragile time thanks to the compassion of his colleagues. A group of Democratic and Republican senators and their wives who dined together fairly regularly insisted that Biden join them. The Senate became his family; lasting friendships were formed, shaping Biden's love of the institution. "When I look back," he wrote years later, "I realize how lucky I was to work in a place where so many people went out of their way to watch over me."

Senator Ted Kennedy often showed up and dragged a reluctant Biden from his office to the Senate gym to relax in a steam bath and meet other senators. One day Senator Humphrey stopped by Biden's office to brighten up his new colleague. But Biden remembered that their roles were suddenly reversed. After Humphrey asked how Joe was doing, the former vice president, sensitive to the young senator's anguish, started crying himself. "He'd end up on my couch," Biden recalled, "and I'd be consoling him."

Biden acquired an abiding fondness for the majesty of the Senate, a sentiment born long before he had arrived as a member. In 1963, Joe visited Washington at age twenty-one. Heading to the Senate, he stopped in a hallway behind the chamber and poked his head into the office of the vice president and gazed into the Marble Room, where senators lounged in leather chairs and smoked and read newspapers.

Nobody was around, so Joe took himself along the hallway, through a set of doors, and then through another door and onto the Senate floor. Awestruck, he strolled up to the podium, plopped down in the vice president's chair, and looked out over the chamber. He fell into deep contemplation until he was startled by the voice of a Capitol cop, who led him to the basement for questioning. After taking his name and address, the cop released him.

A decade later, as Biden walked onto the Senate floor as a newly elected member, a Capitol cop stopped him.

"Senator Biden," he asked, "do you remember me?"

Biden apologized that he didn't.

"Well, I'm the fellow that stopped you ten years ago," he said with a wide smile. "I'm retiring tomorrow. But, Senator, welcome. I'm happy you're back."

Over the next three decades Joe Biden evolved into a quintessential man of the Senate. Wherever his journey took him, it was the Senate that had a claim to his heart. Even in his farewell speech before taking up his job as Obama's vice president, Biden declared, "I will always be a Senate man. Except for the title 'father,' there is no title, including 'vice president,' that I am more proud to wear than that of United States senator."

Barack Obama entertained no similar feelings. Though he respected the institution, he soon realized the Senate could never be a home for him the way it was for Biden and his veteran colleagues. In the words of David Axelrod: "It was clear that Obama would not be comfortable growing old in the Senate." The energetic freshman complained about the Senate's slow pace. In the state legislature, he was fond of saying, "we could get a hundred bills passed during the course of a session. In the Senate it was maybe twenty."

The endless floor debates and the posing and puffery of bloviating senators exasperated Obama. "It was his general critique of the institution that there was a lot of talking and not enough action," Axelrod explained. Obama would burst through the chamber doors at the close of a session flapping his thumb and fingers to mimic yapping lips. Even his own performances bored him. Axelrod recalled Obama leaving the chamber in a foul mood after delivering a floor speech. "Blah, blah, blah," he groused. "That's all we do around here."

Six months into Obama's term, a close Chicago friend and Democratic operative, Rahm Emanuel, picked up on the freshman senator's discomfort. "Does he look happy to you?" he asked journalist David Mendell. "I think the job looked better on paper to him."

The signs were evident in the first weeks of Obama's Senate term as he sat impatiently waiting for his chance to speak at Condoleezza Rice's confirmation hearing before the Foreign Relations Committee. The hearing had opened on the day after the commemoration of what would have been Martin Luther King Jr.'s seventy-sixth birthday. That date, and Condoleezza Rice's appearance before the panel, gave Obama a chance to highlight for all present his own achievement. Before the proceedings began, as the committee room was filling up, Obama, looking lean in his charcoal pinstripes and gray tie, and secretary of state nominee Rice, in a trim black suit and pearl necklace and earrings, had sought each other out behind the empty panel chairs; they shook hands warmly, smiled, and chatted briefly, two African American political stars who had broken racial barriers.

More than five hours later, when Senator Lugar finally gave him the floor, Obama prefaced his public remarks with a nod toward the history that allowed him and Rice to come together in this chamber to discuss the world's weighty matters. "Since it's the day after King's birthday, obviously, twenty or thirty years ago," Obama said, his freshman words a bit jumbled, "it's unlikely that I'd be sitting here asking you questions. And so I think that's a testimony to how far we've come, despite how far we still have to go."

Afterward, his moment in the limelight having passed, Obama

had to once again sit and listen as Biden's voice thrummed in his ears. Biden, that creature of the Senate, reared on its conventions, was a symbol of all that Obama found frustrating about the institution. Antony Blinken, who was Biden's staff director on the committee, observed that a gulf existed between the fleet-footed freshman and the rooted veteran. "They weren't in sync," Blinken recalled. "Obama would listen to Biden holding forth in the committee and roll his eyes."

In those early days, the two men saw only each other's surfaces: their differences in age and personal style, Obama's celebrity sheen and Biden's clubbiness. Obama was a man on the make and largely ignored Biden as an old-school politician without much to offer him. During their days together in the Senate, Axelrod observed, "I would not describe them as close in any way."

And on that afternoon of the Rice hearing, as Biden droned on and on, Obama could barely listen. Here was the Senate at its worst, noise that substituted for action, in the form of Joe Biden: "Now, when I said about—I don't know—six, eight months, maybe longer ago, I said..." For Biden, jabbering around the committee table was like yammering with family over the turkey and pumpkin pie at Thanksgiving. The Senate was his home; these men and women were his people. Though Obama bucked at the notion, he, too, was now part of the family; but he was the malcontented youth waiting for a chance to run away.

From his perch, Biden rolled on: "You've heard a thousand times the analogy that was given about, you know, when Acheson went to de Gaulle and said, you know..."

Finally Obama had had enough. In the midst of this cascade, he grabbed a sheet of paper and jotted a few words. Setting down his pen, Obama swiveled his chair around and handed the note to his adviser Robert Gibbs, who was seated behind the committee table. Gibbs gazed down at the page. There, Obama had scrawled his reaction to Biden's ad nauseam babbling in three single-syllable words: "Shoot. Me. Now."

# TWO

# Competitors

A question stood between them, and it wouldn't go away. Would Barack run?

It swirled around him from the moment he concluded his rousing speech at the Democratic National Convention in 2004. Why wouldn't the party's new political heartthrob leap into the presidential sweepstakes?

The presidency was never far from Joe Biden's mind, either. Ever since his ill-fated bid in the 1988 election—even earlier, in fact—Biden always had one eye cocked toward the White House. In late 2004, as Obama's star was rising, Biden already was seriously contemplating a second run in 2008. Though Obama adamantly discounted the speculation, a bet on him bounding into the 2008 race was not misplaced. Before Obama even set foot in the Capitol, he and Biden were potential competitors for the biggest political prize in America, each driven by raw political ambition and his belief in his own superior fitness to sit in the Oval Office. It was not a fertile ground for friendship.

After his convention speech—and before he was even elected to the Senate—Obama had stirred the hopes of a cross section of Americans. At one of his Senate campaign events in mostly white Macoupin

County, Illinois, an older white woman gushed to a reporter after listening to Obama: "This young man is going to be president of the United States someday. I just hope I live long enough to vote for him." In Denver, while campaigning on behalf of Democratic Senate candidate Ken Salazar, Obama prompted an African American woman to stir a dream in her children: "Look hard, honey," she told them. "That man might be your president someday."

Some wanted him to press forward immediately. While campaigning in Tuscola, Illinois, a retired farmer urged Senate candidate Obama, "You need to run for president in the next election." Black students pleaded with him to jump into the 2008 competition.

While Obama sought to keep the focus on his Senate candidacy, talk of a presidential run tapped into a wish he'd nursed for nearly two decades. As far back as 1987, when the twenty-five-year-old Obama was in a significant relationship with a "bright, beautiful, and intense" half-Dutch, half-Japanese woman, Sheila Miyoshi Jager, he discovered what she described as his "calling." He had come to see his destiny as shaped not by his earlier view of himself as a multicultural internationalist of Kenyan-American descent but rather by his identity as an African American. Obama's epiphany would drive him into politics and shatter his relationship with Jager.

As David Garrow recounted in his book *Rising Star*, Jager felt that the "resolution of [Obama's] 'black' identity was directly linked to his decision to pursue a political career," and it led to the "drive and desire to become the most powerful person in the world." That goal was possible only if he were married to an African American woman, especially in the political environment of Chicago, where he intended to launch his career.

Jager told Garrow that by 1987, Obama "already had his sights on becoming president." She added, "I remember very specifically that it was then he began to talk about entering politics and his presidential ambitions and conflicts about our worlds being too far apart." Though the couple saw each other off and on over the next several years, the relationship eventually crumbled.

Obama didn't waver from his determination to enter politics with an African American wife. By 1989, he was dating Michelle Robinson and was still consumed by the desire to be leader of the free world. When Michelle's brother Craig took Obama out to shoot hoops as a kind of family vetting process, Barack passed the basketball test but raised some red flags about his political ambitions. As Craig told journalist David Mendell, "Barack was like, 'Well, I wanna be a politician. You know, maybe I can be president of the United States.' And I said, 'Yeah, yeah, okay, come over and meet my Aunt Gracie—and don't tell anybody about that.'"

Some fifteen years later, while campaigning for the Senate, Obama again had to be cagey about his ambitions or risk appearing to overstep. But his handlers understood that it was never too early to build a national following. His appeal across the country was so strong that the Senate candidate traveled outside of Illinois—mostly on the sly—to raise funds and speak at political events. His ability to attract crowds and pull in cash out of state was a sign of possible broad support for an early presidential bid.

Lynn Sweet, an aggressive *Chicago Sun-Times* reporter constantly on his tail, took Obama to task for failing to tell the press about his many out-of-state visits. She noted in an article that appeared a month before the 2004 election that in the previous few weeks, Obama had traveled to "Ohio, Texas, Massachusetts, Mississippi, Alabama and Minnesota for fund-raisers and speeches." She groused that "Obama's manipulative, cagey campaign...has a passion for secrecy when it comes to raising political money or traveling to another state for a public appearance." While his campaign filed all the required Federal Election Commission fund-raising reports, its blog for the most part displayed only his Illinois events.

"Obama is doing nothing differently than any other major candidate would do," Sweet observed. "He is just being more sneaky about it."

The morning after his election landslide, Obama confronted a gaggle of reporters in his campaign headquarters. He was bleary-eyed from two hours of sleep, struggling with a cold, and weary from twenty-one months of campaigning; his exhaustion had been evident in his flat victory speech the night before. He needed to summon his strength to deflect the inevitable hammering on one question: Are you going to serve out your six-year Senate term, or are you going to run for president in 2008?

His ambition for the White House quivered within him like a concealed twitch, and only the timing of his bid was in question. But it served no purpose to offer anything but absolute denials. Besides, seasoned politicians were convinced that Obama was too inexperienced to consider a run as soon as 2008.

However strong the impulse was in his heart and his mind—and his political guru David Axelrod insisted that the presidency was beyond all calculation at this point—Obama wanted to dispense with any gossip that would detract from how seriously he took his senatorial duties. Before taking questions, he insisted to Axelrod, "We've got to tamp this shit down. It's way over the top."

True to expectations, the reporters were single-minded in pursuing the question, and the senator-elect swatted it away again and again until exasperation set in. As if condescending to children who had trouble understanding him, Obama recited the same answer in three different ways: "I am not running for president. I am not running for president in four years. I am not running for president in 2008."

During the proceedings, the persistent Lynn Sweet of the *Chicago Sun-Times* interrupted Obama several times, unsatisfied by his rote denials. She wanted a little substance from him to fill out his remarks. "Lynn," a testy Obama shot back, "you're dictating the answers as well as the questions. Let me move on to the next question."

At the close of the press conference, he let Sweet know in no uncertain terms that her hounding him on the issue displeased him. "This is like the fifth time you've done this," he complained. Then he led her into another part of the headquarters to continue their conversation in private.

For his part, Axelrod at the same time summed up what he and Obama wanted the world to know about the senator-elect's presidential ambitions. "I don't think we're trying to dampen expectations," he told a reporter. "We're trying to douse them. We're trying to pour as much water as we can find on them. We don't want even a smoldering ember when it comes to this. It's just not healthy for him."

Always keenly attuned to what was most politically expedient for himself—and at this moment, his acceptance in the Senate depended on his utter silence about his presidential ambitions—Obama and his handlers also understood that success in politics depended on timing. His keynote address had swept him to victory in his Senate campaign and turned the hot spotlight on him. A political ascent depended on momentum: you have to hit while you're hot. What if he passed up the chance in 2008 to cash in on his newfound celebrity? Would America still see him as the shiny new kid in a later campaign for the White House? Recognizing the fleeting nature of political fame, Obama had mused to a reporter a few days after his wild acclaim at the convention, "This is all so, well, interesting. But it's all so ephemeral." He knew that he was a novelty and also that novelty wore off. "It can't stay white hot like it is right now."

While Obama kept his true thoughts about a presidential run to himself, Joe Biden was honest about where his heart lay. As soon as John Kerry went down to defeat in the 2004 presidential election, Biden turned his mind toward winning the Democratic nomination in 2008.

The shame of his unsuccessful 1988 bid lingered. That campaign had ended ignominiously after Biden admitted that he had plagiarized from a speech by British Labor Party leader Neil Kinnock. But that campaign had suffered from something perhaps even worse: while Biden had an abundance of ambition, he didn't have a message. He hadn't established who he was and why exactly he was running.

Some fifteen years later, Biden had a clear motive for seeking the nomination: his disgust with the foreign policy of President George W. Bush and the neoconservative Republicans guiding his decisions, particularly the waging of war in Iraq. Now Biden stood out as a foreign policy expert, speaking with authority.

Nonetheless, Biden was a long shot, and another run for president posed fresh risks to his political persona. Already Hillary Clinton seemed the anointed Democratic nominee, and an Obama challenge, if it happened—and if it took off—was another hurdle. Biden's wife Jill, who had come into his life in 1975 and married him in 1977, five years after the death of Neilia, was keenly aware of the anguish Joe had experienced in his last campaign; she wanted to protect him from another foolhardy adventure that could leave him defeated and embarrassed.

Even as his dream for 2008 swirled in his head, Biden managed to keep his mouth shut during the family's 2004 Thanksgiving gathering in Nantucket. But around Christmas, Jill had heard enough from him privately that she called for a family meeting at their home in Delaware a few nights before the holiday. She didn't reveal to Joe what was on the agenda. Before they turned in for bed the night before, she simply told him that the family was gathering in the library the next morning. "We need to talk to you about something," she warned him.

Expecting that the family would shut down his 2008 ambitions, Joe paced the night away. The meeting would include his sons Beau and Hunter, Jill and their daughter Ashley, his sister Val, and his longtime friend and political consultant, Ted Kaufman. All night Biden heard their pleas playing in his head: "Why invite more pain and heartache? Why take the risk?" And from his kids: "You can't do this, Dad. We don't want you to go through this again."

With the clan assembled the next morning, Joe sat in a wing chair next to the fireplace to hear the dreaded verdict. Jill began by explaining that everyone had weighed in on the question and together they'd come to a decision on what they believed was best, not only for him but also for the country. Bracing for the worst, Joe heard Jill declare: "I want you to run."

Biden was stunned—so much so that, unusually, he had only a one-word response: "Why?"

Jill believed the time was right for Joe. She had been devastated by the reelection of George W. Bush and the continuation of his disastrous and divisive Iraq war policies. "We think you can unite the country," Jill told Joe.

With the blessing of his family, Biden dove into strategizing. Far in advance of what was usual for a potential presidential candidate, he let it slip publicly over the next couple of months that he was considering a run at the nomination. Then on Sunday, June 19, 2005, appearing on CBS's *Face the Nation*, Biden was blunt about his plans.

Host Bob Schieffer opened the show by declaring that, for the Democrats, Delaware senator Joe Biden was "emerging as one of their main spokesmen" on a variety of issues; among them was the situation in Iraq, where, Schieffer said, "the US is bogged down." Schieffer noted that Secretary of State Condoleezza Rice had offered an optimistic portrait of progress in quelling an Iraq insurgency and ridding the country of terrorists. In a nod to Biden's credibility on the subject, Schieffer pointed out that the senator, who served on the Foreign Relations Committee, had made five trips to Iraq and had just recently returned from his latest; he then asked the senator for his assessment of conditions on the ground there.

Biden, in a dark suit, white shirt, and bright red tie, the triangular point of his white handkerchief peeking out of his jacket pocket, laid out his view. The number of car bombs exploding each month was up sharply, he said, killing and maiming scores of people. This evidence,

Biden contended, highlighted "a gigantic gap...between the rhetoric here in Washington and the reality on the ground." Biden asserted that the Bush administration was lying to the nation. "Why would Secretary Rice characterize it the way she says it when I don't know anybody who believes that to be the case? 'The last throes.' 'We're almost there.' 'Great progress.' Only thing I can figure is they don't trust the American people."

Biden was building his case as a straight-shooting leader—and possible president—who could resolve the mess in Iraq. Toward the end of the interview Schieffer gave Biden his opening. "A lot of people are saying that—well, you yourself have said you're thinking about running for president," the host said. "Are you—how far along are you on this idea of running for president?"

Though the election was still more than three years away, Biden dropped all pretense to the caginess that clipped the tongues of Obama and other politicians when discussing their White House ambitions. "I've proceeded since last November as if I were going to run," he told Schieffer. "My intention is to seek the nomination. I mean, I know I'm supposed to be more coy with you. I know I'm supposed to tell you, you know, that I'm not sure. But if, in fact, I think that I have a clear shot at winning the nomination by this November, December, then I'm going to seek the nomination."

Schieffer, recognizing the importance of Biden's early admission, closed out the interview with a veteran journalist's appreciation for a scoop: "Well, I'll say one thing, I think you made some news today, Senator."

While Biden held forth early on his ambitions, Obama and his advisers plotted his potential run in secret. His first year in the Senate, he played the role of the good senator focused on his own constituents. But his chief of staff, Pete Rouse, put in place a careful plan to have Obama reemerge on the national stage in 2006. "It makes sense for you to consider now," he wrote in a memo, "whether you want to use 2006 to position yourself for a run in 2008." There were many discussions Obama should have and decisions he should make "below the radar" in 2006 if he wanted to make a bid in 2008, according to Rouse. Obama jotted on Rouse's memo, "This makes sense."

The seriousness of the strategy soon emerged. "Now we set in motion our plan to expand Barack's trips to include meetings with key political players, donors, and local media," adviser Axelrod said. "We also moved to enhance his political and policy teams, increase his personal fund-raising goals, and seize timely opportunities to spell out an alternative vision for the Democratic Party."

As Obama quietly undertook this effort and weighed his options, he made none of his private ruminations public; rather, he stuck steadfastly to his avowed promise not to run in 2008. While going through the outlined steps, he also cloaked his true feelings even from the advisers guiding his efforts until well into 2006. His remarks convinced his closest advisers that the presidency was not an immediate personal need for Obama. "People can believe me or not," Rouse said, "but I can testify to the fact that he never seriously considered, at least with me and others around him, running for president until, I'd say, if you want to take the most liberal definition of running, maybe you start thinking about—maybe it's a long-shot possibility in the summer of 2006."

On January 22, 2006, NBC's Tim Russert probed the senator about his plans. Russert, the host of *Meet the Press*, had asked Obama after his election to the Senate in November 2004 about his presidential aspirations. At the time, Obama had said he would "absolutely" serve out his six years as a senator.

When Russert this time asked again about his political future, Obama replied, "I can't speculate....What I have said is that, you know, I'm not focused on running for higher office, I'm focused on doing the job that the people of Illinois just sent me to do."

"But there seems to be an evolution in your thinking," Russert persisted. "This is what you told the *Chicago Tribune* last month: 'Have you ruled out running for another office before your term is up?' Obama answer: 'It's not something I anticipate doing.'"

Obama countered Russert's inquiry with no hint of budging. "I will serve out my full six-year term," he answered. "You know, Tim, if you get asked enough, sooner or later you get weary and you start looking for new ways of saying things. But my thinking has not changed."

"So," Russert asked, seeking a definitive response, "you will not run for president or vice president in 2008?"

"I will not," Obama replied.

As the year drew on, media hype only deepened the public's fascination with Obama, a torrent of acclamation that was hard to resist for a potential candidate. Ellis Cose, a black journalist writing in *Newsweek*, said Obama was "a political phenomenon unlike any previously seen." Lynn Sweet of the *Sun-Times* captured Obama's inflated image and sensed the impact of the acclaim on his thinking. "The charismatic Obama is now on a pedestal," she noted, adding that his responses to press inquiries suggested "the thought of running for president has crossed his mind."

America was still living under the shadow of 9/11 and its repercussions, particularly the quagmire of Iraq, and the highly questionable tactics of the Bush administration's fight against terrorism. Americans nursed a lingering shame after US soldiers tortured and sexually abused Iraqi prisoners at Abu Ghraib prison. Compared to the brutality and dishonesty of the Bush coterie, Obama represented intelligence and idealism and the hope of change. He was "a breath of fresh air," as a voter in the white northwest side of Chicago put it on the night of Obama's Senate victory in Illinois, a perception that was now spreading across the nation. Hillary Clinton, while a worthy alternative to Bush, represented the world as it was, the politics of old. And Joe Biden registered barely a blip in the discussion.

Though he was still largely undefined as a candidate, Obama appeared to many as a man who offered a new vision for America. If the vision lacked contours, voters filled in the details for themselves. Writing of Obama, *Chicago Tribune* reporter Don Terry explained, "He's a Rorschach test. What you see is what you want to see." *Newsweek*'s Cose underscored how people found their own dreams in Obama. The young black politician was, in Cose's words, "the perfect mirror for a country that craves to see itself as beyond race, beyond boundaries, beyond the ugly parts of its past."

If his popularity wasn't hot enough already, his book *The Audacity of Hope* set it to a boil upon its release in October 2006, well into Obama's planned reemergence onto the national stage. The book, which strove to be a manifesto of new politics, was measured by critics as largely a campaign book. *Publishers Weekly* panned it, saying it dished up "muddled, uninspiring proposals." The *New York Times*'s Michiko Kakutani witheringly complained that it "read like outtakes from a stump speech."

Nonetheless, *The Audacity of Hope* rocketed to number one on the *New York Times* best-seller list. Obama crisscrossed the nation on a book tour that put him in front of enthusiastic readers and on all the major media outlets: NPR's *All Things Considered*, NBC's *The Today Show*, CNN's *Larry King Live*, and *Oprah*.

On one program, when he was asked whether a presidential run was in the works, he tried a new way to deflect the question, even if the ambition was rising in his heart: "I don't think Michelle is going to let me do this." Yet he heard the cries for his candidacy and felt the momentum. Clarence Page of the *Chicago Tribune* was one of the many voices Obama had to reckon with inside his head: "Seize the day," Page urged. "You may never again see this many people who are this eager for you to run."

In private, Obama allowed himself to step closer, acknowledging that he heard the chorus from his supporters. "With so many people talking to me about running," he told Axelrod, "I feel like I have an obligation to at least think about this in a serious, informed way."

Yet in public he gave nothing away. He pretended in an interview with *New Yorker* editor David Remnick that he hadn't even considered the kind of candidate he'd face in Hillary Clinton. When Remnick asked, "How would one run against Hillary Clinton?" Obama's casual reply was, "Oh, I don't know."

Remnick found that hard to believe. "You never gave it any thought?"

"I haven't," Obama answered.

"You sure?"

"Positive."

Through the midterm elections in November and the Christmas holidays, Obama kept any decision to himself. After a family vacation to Hawaii, Obama, wearing blue jeans and a White Sox baseball cap, surprised Axelrod in his office. He spoke of his deep soul-searching over his readiness for the presidency and the impact a campaign would have on his family. He made no promises yet.

But, as Axelrod tells the story in his book *Believer*, on his way out of the office Obama ran into Forrest Claypool, an associate of Axelrod's, who wondered about the status of a possible presidential run. "It may not be exactly the time I'd pick," Obama explained, "but sometimes the times pick you."

Chief of Staff Rouse recalled seeing Obama two days later. "Well, I've decided to do it," Obama told him, "but I want to go home just this one last weekend to make sure I don't have buyer's remorse."

A few days after that, Obama called Axelrod and told him, "It's a go....Michelle and I have talked about it and we decided this may be as good a time as any for our family." The Obamas had determined that the campaign—and, if he won, living in the White House— would be less disruptive to their daughters, Malia and Sasha, at nine and six years old than it would be if they were older. Barack's major hurdle—running for president without wrecking his family or losing crucial support of his wife—had been resolved.

On January 16, 2007, Obama revealed his decision to the nation in a three-minute video on his website. "I will be filing papers today to create a presidential exploratory committee," he divulged. "And on February 10...I'll share my plans with my friends, neighbors, and fellow Americans."

On that Saturday in February, he took the stage in a dark overcoat and scarf in front of the Old State Capitol in Springfield, Illinois, with his wife and daughters. His speech hewed to the Axelrod playbook: this campaign was to be driven by the candidate's story as much as by his take on the issues. As journalist Ben Wallace-Wells described it, Axelrod saw "campaigns as an author might, to understand that you need not just ideas but also a credible and authentic character, a distinct politics rooted in personality."

Speaking before a large crowd bundled against the cold, Obama fashioned himself as a newcomer seeking to change American politics and society. He brushstroked in his character and the arc of his journey: from young community organizer in poor neighborhoods to civil rights lawyer and constitutional law instructor and from there to state legislator and ultimately to United States senator. He lifted his voice in praise of American decency; he offered himself as a change agent for improvement in schools, health care, wages, and he promised to bring troops home from Iraq. His refrain: "We can build a more hopeful America."

And with a flourish, he made his declaration. "In the shadow of the Old State Capitol, where Lincoln once called on a divided house to stand together, where common hopes and common dreams still live," he told the crowd, "I stand before you today to announce my candidacy for president of the United States." His admirers roared their approval, eager to find in his style, and grace, and generalities their own dreams.

\*     \*     \*

Though Obama's announcement stirred widespread excitement, his candidacy was still considered a long shot. The clear front-runner for the 2008 Democratic presidential nomination was Hillary Clinton, and all challengers to her—Obama, Biden, and anyone else—had to leap enormous hurdles. As far back as November 2, 2004, the night President George W. Bush was reelected, the British betting firm Ladbrokes had placed Clinton at five-to-one odds of capturing the White House in 2008.

With far less symbolism and little hoopla, Joe Biden had announced his candidacy during an appearance on NBC's *Meet the Press* on Sunday, January 7, more than a month earlier than Obama. His chief selling point was his foreign policy experience and his determination to clean up the mess President Bush had made of the war in Iraq.

Biden had coauthored a five-part solution that called for the creation of a federation of autonomous ethnic regions in the country, a proposal that was criticized for its impracticality and weakening of the central government. He opposed Bush's plans for sending thousands more troops to Iraq, instead favoring a gradual drawdown of American forces. And Biden now had a more prominent voice in his role as chairman of the Foreign Relations Committee since the Democrats had gained control of the Senate in the 2004 elections.

On *Meet the Press*, Biden and host Tim Russert spent some time discussing foreign policy, and Biden's expertise was amply on display. Russert then turned to the big question.

"Are you running for president?" he asked.

Biden replied bluntly: "I am running for president."

"And you're going to take on Hillary Clinton, Barack Obama, and all other comers?" Russert asked, implying that Biden's road to the nomination was a tough one.

No doubt Biden had to surmount enormous obstacles. But he was clear on one thing: he was not going to be the ill-focused candidate of his doomed earlier presidential campaign. He asserted that he knew exactly how he would run this time. "I'm going to be Joe Biden," he told Russert, "and I'm going to try to be the best Biden I can be. If I can, I got a shot. If I can't, I lose."

Barack Obama and Joe Biden were now rivals vying for the biggest political trophy in the world. No one was looking for friendships. If contestants admired the qualities or beliefs of an opponent, little or nothing was said about it, or at best the praise was given grudgingly. Every word was calibrated with great care—a skill that came naturally to one and less so to the other.

After his appearance on *Meet the Press* where he publicly announced his plan to run for president, Biden made it official by releasing a video declaration of his candidacy on Wednesday morning, January 31, on his campaign website. But no sooner had Biden jumped in than he made a verbal stumble. As the *Chicago Tribune* put it in a headline the following day: "Biden Tosses Hat in Ring, Puts Foot in Mouth."

Biden got himself into trouble in an interview he gave to the *New York Observer* over a bowl of soup at a diner in Washington. Casually dressed in a blue shirt and red cardigan, he had come in carrying a notebook with talking points. But he soon shoved the notebook aside and, following a dangerous instinct, spoke off the cuff. He laid into his presidential rivals on their Iraq war proposals. On Hillary Clinton's plan: "Nothing but disaster." On John Edwards, who had announced his candidacy in December: he didn't know "what the heck he is talking about." And on Barack Obama: "I don't recall hearing a word from Barack about a plan or a tactic."

Those statements could be called typical contender sniping, but things then took a troublesome turn. The reporter, Jason Horowitz, wrote in the *Observer* article that Biden was as "skeptical" of Obama as he was of Clinton, but Biden expressed it in "a slightly more backhanded way." Now Biden dropped his foot-in-the-mouth bombshell. "I mean," he said, "you got the first sort of mainstream African American who is articulate and bright and clean and a nice-looking guy. I mean, that's a storybook, man."

In the article, Horowitz didn't pause over the remark; there was no discussion, no commentary, and no light was shone on it. It lay there on the page like a trip wire. Biden's troubles erupted, however, on the very day he announced his candidacy when the offending snippet from the recorded interview was publicly released, and the media swarmed. On *NBC Nightly News with Brian Williams*, White House correspondent David Gregory informed the nation, "Senator Biden has launched his bid for the White House on the issue of Iraq, but...today the campaign was sidetracked over the issue of race."

On ABC's *World News with Charles Gibson*, correspondent Jake Tapper sounded off: "Obama today refused to tell ABC News whether he thought Biden was complimenting him." Viewers then heard a partial utterance from Obama: "I'm not gonna force his words..." (the rest trailed off inaudibly). Tapper elaborated, revealing that Obama had told a fellow senator he didn't take the remarks personally. In another few seconds of tape, Obama sounded confused: "I mean it was—he, he just said—he didn't mean it."

Looking for a pattern of behavior, journalists dredged up earlier indelicate remarks by Biden. The previous year Joe had been captured on video moving through a crowd when he shook hands with an Indian American man who expressed his support of the senator. Biden told the man, "In Delaware, the largest growth in population is Indian Americans, moving from India." Then, trying to show how much the Indian American community had contributed by operating small businesses, Biden added, "You cannot go to a 7-Eleven or Dunkin' Donuts unless you have a slight Indian accent....I'm not joking." He later walked back the comment by saying he had meant to convey his enthusiasm for the vibrant Indian American community in Delaware. Reporting on his latest stumble, the press also resurrected the plagiarism debacle that had ended his earlier presidential bid.

Never expecting his announcement day to be so fraught, Biden had committed to join Jon Stewart on *The Daily Show* to kick off his campaign with a little fun and humor before a friendly television audience. But suddenly Joe was now the joke. Rising to the occasion, however, he bounded onto the *Daily Show* set in his dark suit, all smiles, waving to the cheering crowd, and sat down across from Stewart.

Stewart greeted his guest and, with a wide grin, an open palm extended in welcome, he asked, "How's your daaaay been?"

When Stewart turned to the Obama matter, he noted that Biden had told the *Philadelphia Inquirer* just a day earlier, "One thing I learned from my previous presidential run is words matter."

"That's right," Biden agreed, nodding his head, smiling large, his eyes wide, knowing where Stewart was heading.

"And you can't take words lightly," Stewart continued. "And then you came out with this one." The audience burst into laughter.

"Well, let me tell you something," Biden said. "I spoke to Barack today."

"I *bet* you did," Stewart chimed in.

Stewart, closing out the conversation, offered his unsolicited advice. Leaning close, he told Biden confidentially: "When you're about to say one of those things, here's what I always do." Stewart lowered his voice and spit the words out in staccato: "I—take—a—deep—breath. I—count—to—ten."

To some, Biden's offense did not seem monstrous. The political writer Richard Ben Cramer noted that the remarks reflected an old-fashioned—not racist—mind-set, just "an old way of talking." Cramer found something appealing in the spontaneity of Biden's language. "He doesn't lawyer his own comments, and it happens to him not just in reference to African Americans—it happens on all kinds of things. That willingness to just speak is one of the things that I love about him. I can see him getting in trouble fifty times before this campaign is over."

An important voice in the black community came to Biden's defense. "It was a gaffe," Jesse Jackson said on *NBC Nightly News*. "It was not an intentional racially pejorative statement." Jackson tilted his head thoughtfully and added, "It could be interpreted that way. But it was not what he meant."

In his own statement, Obama seemed less than pleased. The relationship between him and Biden, already a bit stifled, suddenly seemed starved of air—now much like Biden's hopes for the White House. Responding to the gaffe, Obama said, "I didn't take Senator Biden's comments personally." But he scolded Biden for the racial insensitivity of his words. "Obviously they were historically inaccurate," Obama pointed out. "African American presidential candidates like Jesse Jackson, Shirley Chisholm, Carol Moseley Braun, and Al Sharpton gave voice to many important issues through their campaigns, and no one would call them inarticulate."

Biden's bid for the White House was in crisis as soon as it began. Hoping to wriggle to safety, Biden rushed out a statement expressing regret over "any offense" his remark "might have caused anyone." He added: "That was not my intent, and I expressed that to Senator Obama."

But a sense of doom now shadowed the campaign. Larry Rasky, who had been Biden's press secretary for his failed 1988 presidential run, was back as communications director in 2007. Before he launched his bid, Biden had many deep-pocket contributors eyeing him as an alternative to Clinton and Edwards. But everything was changed now. As Rasky recalled to journalist Jules Witcover, "The day the campaign ended was the day it started."

As donors fled, a bloodied Biden gamely fought on. Polling in the single digits, with Clinton the steady leader and Obama closing in on her, Biden joined the eight Democratic hopefuls for a televised debate in late April. Onstage, Obama gave an inconsistent performance, at times halting and at others eloquent. An instant poll by SurveyUSA at the close reflected more the candidates' popularity than their presentation that night. Among 403 South Carolina respondents, 31 percent said Obama had won the debate, 24 percent favored Clinton, 14 percent went for Edwards, and next in line was Biden, with just 6 percent.

But pundits saw a different outcome. Many recognized Biden's strength onstage, particularly in foreign policy, even calling him the top performer of the night. His answers were focused, not verbose. On CNN's *Larry King Live*, the network's chief national correspondent, John King, declared, "If I had to pick a winner tonight...I would pick Senator Biden." *Newsweek*'s senior editor and columnist Jonathan Alter opined, "Biden did a brilliant job of playing against type and that's the kind of thing that makes you stand out in these debates, when you do something a little unexpected."

Obama, too, was struck by Biden's understanding of the quagmire in Iraq and his skill on the debate stage. "They mostly didn't see each other during the campaign except at debates," Axelrod explained. Having seen him blather at committee hearings, Obama had been skeptical of how Biden would perform during the debates, but he saw something he didn't expect: a disciplined Biden. "I think he was really impressed by the way Biden handled himself in the debates," Axelrod observed. "Biden was consistently one of the better debaters."

The Iowa caucuses in January stood as a crucial test. They often gave shape to the primaries and allowed the winner to step into the spotlight, though in some cases only briefly. Leading up to the caucuses, Obama had to fend off attacks targeting his inexperience. The one opponent out front making the charge was Joe Biden. Playing off his vast advantage in years and in public service, Biden had suggested in the media that Obama was not yet ready for the presidency.

Clinton also encountered resistance as the caucuses approached. Her once-substantial lead had eroded. On caucus day, in freezing temperatures, Democrats voted in massive numbers: 239,000 came out, nearly doubling the turnout of 125,000 in 2004. And on that day, Obama changed the race: he captured 37.6 percent of the vote to Clinton's third-place finish at 29.5 percent, just behind Edwards at 29.7 percent. "In the language of American commentators," the *Guardian* wrote, "Iowa will provide a bounce that could in turn give him momentum. In short, he is on a roll." David Gergen, a longtime adviser who had served in both Republican and Democratic White Houses, suggested that the Illinois senator had indeed reshaped American politics. "For Barack Obama, this is a personal triumph," Gergen observed. "For an African American to go into a state that's 95 percent white and win against Mrs. Clinton is an absolutely remarkable victory."

Biden had nothing to celebrate in Iowa, coming in a distant fifth behind New Mexico governor Bill Richardson and collecting barely 1 percent of the vote, his support a mere speck on the frozen tundra.

Along with Connecticut senator Christopher Dodd, who also had a dismal showing, Biden ended his bid for the presidency that night. At about 11:15 p.m. he took the stage at the Science Center of Iowa in Des Moines, surrounded by fourteen family members, some teary, and looked out at his supporters, many also with watery eyes, hugging each other. As he announced the end of his campaign, only one cable channel broadcast a few moments of it.

If Iowa—indeed, America—was uninspired by Biden's candidacy, one of his rivals was watching him closely and liked what he saw. Barack Obama burst out of Iowa with a powerful push toward the nomination. Though it was far too early to think seriously about vice-presidential candidates, Obama had his eye on certain attractive qualities in Joe Biden. Beyond his foreign policy expertise, Biden had demonstrated a virtue highly prized by voters and by Obama, even if it got Joe in trouble from time to time. Bluntly speaking his mind, sometimes without thinking, Biden came across as authentic in a world of political calculation.

Barack and Joe, no longer opponents, were now able to move into a new phase with each other. Their competitive attacks on the campaign trail were a given and did not seem to mar the emergence of mutual respect.

Their path toward each other was still complicated by politics and ego. But one bright sign of a possible future relationship was the way both men negotiated their first serious conflict, early in the campaign. Biden's eagerness to atone for his ill-chosen words about Obama being "clean" and "articulate" showed he was willing to admit his mistakes. And Obama, after his initial stiff-backed response, softened up.

After the gaffe, Biden phoned Obama to apologize privately, then held a conference call with reporters. "So I called Barack," he recounted, "and he said, 'Joe, you don't have to explain anything to me.'"

After an early hesitation, Obama came to regard the comments, as Richard Ben Cramer had pointed out, as a generational way of talking that did not, in Biden's case, reflect the racism that many people sought to attach to it. Adopting his usual measured approach, Obama chose to absolve Biden. As Obama adviser David Axelrod explained: "I think Obama's reaction was an important benchmark because he could have turned the screws and he didn't."

On the call with reporters, Joe hoped to end the controversy. "Barack Obama is probably the most exciting candidate that the Democratic or Republican Party has produced," he said, "at least since I have been around. And he is fresh, he is new, he is insightful, and I really regret that some have taken totally out of context my use of the word 'clean.'" Explaining his usage of that word, he said: "My mother has an expression: 'clean as a whistle, sharp as a tack.' That's the context."

Though the stumble was to remain a ready example of Biden's

unruly tongue, the dustup proved to be a stepping-stone toward a partnership. In this instance, Obama and Biden showed they could work out their differences with graciousness and understanding, essential qualities for the building of trust. Biden was forthcoming about his mistake, and Obama demonstrated decency in the face of language that could have been taken as an insult. "Obama didn't go to a darker place in his interpretation of what was said," Axelrod said. Instead, Obama accepted Joe as Joe and looked past his mangled way of expressing himself. "I understand what Joe meant," Obama explained. "I know what's in his heart."

# THREE

# "A Click Moment"

The controversy hit the Obama campaign with a megaton force. "It was one of those moments that went from zero to a hundred in a second," said campaign manager David Plouffe. And soon the uproar had magnified into "an existential threat" to Obama's candidacy.

Barack had been looking invincible. After strong showings in New Hampshire and Nevada, he scored a solid victory in South Carolina, followed shortly afterward by endorsements from Caroline Kennedy and her uncle Senator Edward Kennedy, who rejected appeals from the Clinton campaign to at least remain neutral. Writing in the *New York Times*, Caroline Kennedy compared Obama to her father, President John Kennedy. "I have never had a president who inspired me the way people tell me that my father inspired them," she wrote. "But for the first time, I believe I have found the man who could be that president—not just for me, but for a new generation of Americans."

After Super Tuesday in early February 2008, when Obama won more states than Clinton and more pledged delegates, Plouffe told the candidate at around two in the morning that "all things being equal, the nomination was ours. We were no longer the plucky underdog." In early March, Clinton managed to stop her string of losses, riding to a resounding victory in the Ohio primary and squeaking by with a win in Texas.

Then in mid-March came the oxygen-sucking blow to Obama. ABC News aired its explosive report at 7 a.m. on Thursday, March 13, 2008, on its breezy wake-up show *Good Morning America*. The show's news anchor, Chris Cuomo, introduced the three-and-a-half-minute segment with some ominous language: "We want to turn now to an in-depth look at a very important figure in Democratic front-runner Barack Obama's life, his longtime pastor, the Reverend Jeremiah Wright."

Chief investigative correspondent Brian Ross began his piece by noting that Obama had been a member of Wright's Trinity United Church of Christ on Chicago's South Side for twenty years, that Wright had presided at the Obamas' wedding, and that the title of Obama's book, *The Audacity of Hope*, had come from Wright's lips. The screen filled with congregants on their feet in raucous and joyous song as Reverend Wright bobbed and weaved and called out, "The angels in heaven were singing. God never fails!"

Obama's controversial pastor had hovered largely at the edges of the campaign, despite conservative efforts to make an issue of him. But now he burst onto center stage after Ross had viewed videos of more than a dozen of his sermons, which the church sold to congregants or anyone else interested. Ross discovered incendiary examples of Wright's critique of America's failures on the issue of race. Viewers of the ABC News report saw Wright condemn America as a Ku Klux Klan nation and criticize black Republicans for selling out; he also accused America of bringing the September 11, 2001, attacks on itself with its own history of racial terrorism. In an angry voice, Wright cried, "We bombed Hiroshima, we bombed Nagasaki, and we nuked far more than the thousands in New York and the Pentagon." With a broad sweep of an arm, he concluded in a low voice, "And we never batted an eye." In a soft tone, he said, "We have supported state terrorism against the Palestinians and black South

Africans," then, building to a shout, "and now we are indignant because the stuff we have done overseas is now brought right back into our own front yard!" He twirled, flapping a hand, and delivered his final punch: "America's chickens are coming home to roost."

Ross's early-morning sensation brought into sharp focus an issue that hadn't yet been realistically addressed: the nation's racial tensions that were highlighted by a strong presidential bid by a black American. The country suddenly asked itself: What are the implications of a black American sitting in the Oval Office? With Obama's surge toward the nomination, the state of race in America gained renewed resonance. How was America to reckon with one of its thorniest social and political conditions?

In his report, Ross asked parishioners of Trinity if they believed Reverend Wright's views were radical. And the answers revealed the crux of the nation's racial divide: if you were a black American, your experience and perception of life in the United States were vastly different from those of a white American. Speaking of Wright, one female parishioner told Ross: "No, I wouldn't call him radical. I'd call it being black in America. It's not radical. How radical is that?" Obama was shown saying, "I don't think that my church is actually particularly controversial."

Obama's advisers couldn't stop thinking that the report was instigated by the Clinton campaign, a roundhouse kick aimed at the surging Illinois senator, though her people denied it. "By then," Axelrod remembered, "we were en route to the nomination and the question was: Would we be knocked off that path?"

Obama had wanted to address the race issue for some time to eliminate any public unease over his candidacy, but he hadn't found the appropriate moment. Now the moment had found him. As the media trumpeted the controversy, Obama went on television to condemn the pastor's remarks. He said he was never in church when Reverend Wright expressed such sentiments. "What is undeniable is that, you know, these are a series of incendiary statements that I can't object to strongly enough," he told CNN's Anderson Cooper. "Had I heard those in the church, I would have told Reverend Wright that, you know, that I profoundly disagreed with them. They didn't reflect my values, and they didn't reflect my ideals." He acknowledged that he had heard about Wright's extreme remarks once he started campaigning for president and, when a reporter asked about them, he condemned them.

Turning professorial, Obama explained that Reverend Wright had grown up in another era, the 1960s, during a period of racial awakening and anger, and that a good measure of African American frustration still lingered. "And that's part of what our campaign has been about, is to surface some of these issues and to be able to move forward and get beyond them," he told Cooper. "But some of these things are still there. And they're things that I have to deal with, you know, and these are things that America has to deal with as well." In Obama's trademark conciliatory manner, he suggested that the controversy presented an opportunity for him and the nation. "It's something that I think is hopefully going to offer me a capacity to teach and to talk about some of these issues," the former law professor said. "And I think it's important, because it's real."

But a TV interview wasn't enough. Obama realized he had to reconcile the scorn for America that Wright conveyed and the hope and promise of change that he promoted. His campaign hinged on it. "I want to do a speech on Wright and the whole issue of race in America," Obama told Axelrod on Friday night. "We have to try and put this in a larger context or it's just going to go on and on." He set a deadline of Monday or Tuesday for delivering the speech, which gave him only days to craft his message.

On Saturday morning at ten o'clock, Obama phoned his young speechwriter Jon Favreau. "I'm going to give you stream-of-consciousness

thoughts and then hopefully you can turn them into a draft," he proposed. Obama obviously had been thinking about the issue for a long
time and had quickly processed years of thought into a detailed discussion of the matter at hand. He ticked off the many points carefully
assembled in his head, constructing a highly detailed outline, and then
asked for a draft from Favreau by the following night. Working furiously,
Favreau delivered his first shot only to receive a much-revised version
in return. "He emailed me back a draft that was all Track Changes,"
Favreau remembered. "You couldn't see too much of mine."

Obama crafted an eloquent argument that was in many respects the
culmination of his long journey toward understanding and accepting
his own identity and his place as a black man in America. As he had in
front of the crowd at the Democratic National Convention in 2004, he
told his story. He wanted America to know that he didn't accept Reverend Wright's harsh words but also that he wasn't going to renounce the
man himself or deny the truth of racial hardship in this country.

On March 18, the Constitution Center in Philadelphia was packed with
Obama supporters. A line of eight American flags stood in a row across
the stage. No issue struck more deeply at American ideals than race,
and no location symbolized the Founders' vision more than Philadelphia. Just a short walk away from the Constitution Center stood the
hall where the Founders had gathered to sign the Declaration of Inde-
pendence. Now, some 230 years later, America was as close as it had
ever been to nominating a black presidential candidate, and in keeping
with its tortured history on race, it was also on the point of throwing
him aside.

A CBS poll over the previous two days had shown that a majority of Americans had heard at least something of Wright's inflammatory remarks, and a third of the respondents said they now had a less
favorable view of Obama. A Gallup poll over the same period put Hillary Clinton ahead of Obama for the first time in nearly six weeks,

49 percent to 42 percent. A week earlier, before the Wright imbroglio, Obama had led Clinton 50 percent to 44 percent.

Obama was among the calmest of his team waiting in the green-room. He turned to Axelrod and laid out the stakes: "I'll give this speech, and people will either accept it or they won't. And if they don't, I won't be president. But at least I'll have said what I felt *needed* to be said. And that, in itself, is worth something."

Harris Wofford, the first white student to study at historically black Howard Law School and a friend and adviser to Martin Luther King Jr., stepped onto the stage to introduce Obama. Then it was time for the candidate to speak for himself. "Barack Obama had some explaining to do to white America," observed Professor T. Denean Sharpley-Whiting, director of Vanderbilt University's Program in African American and Diaspora Studies. "Who was this seemingly affable, African American man who had lulled the white electorate by virtue of his tangled ancestry into believing that he too identified with them? Who was the Reverend Jeremiah Wright?"

Speaking from a podium in a dark suit and blue tie, his chin raised with pride and a touch of defiance, Obama declared of Reverend Wright, "I can no more disown him than I can disown the black community. I can no more disown him than I can my white grandmother— a woman who helped raise me, a woman who sacrificed again and again for me.... These people are a part of me. And they are a part of America, this country that I love." In a few clear, sharp seconds, he linked his black and white ancestries in a way that said to any black or white person: *Just try to discard your own ancestry.* These two strains— black and white—were inherently part of him and were in a larger way part of the composition of American life.

But Obama made it clear that he rejected Wright's divisive words. "They weren't simply a religious leader's effort to speak out against perceived injustice," he told the audience. "Instead, they expressed a profoundly distorted view of this country—a view that sees white racism as endemic, and that elevates what is wrong with America above all that we know is right with America."

He wasn't shy, however, about telling the country it needed to confront the issue of race boldly. "Race is an issue that I believe this nation cannot afford to ignore right now," Obama continued. "The fact is that the comments that have been made and the issues that have surfaced over the last few weeks reflect the complexities of race in this country that we've never really worked through—a part of our union that we have yet to perfect."

He spoke of the legacy of slavery, and Jim Crow, and the persistence of inequality. He called on Americans to recognize their shared obligation to address the country's unbroken history of discrimination in the search for a more perfect union. "The profound mistake of Reverend Wright's sermons is not that he spoke about racism in our society," Obama declared. "It's that he spoke as if our society was static.... What we know—what we have seen—is that America can change. That is the true genius of this nation. What we have already achieved gives us hope—the audacity to hope—for what we can and must achieve tomorrow."

After thirty-seven minutes, Obama left the stage, uncertain whether he had salvaged his candidacy. In a phone call to speechwriter Favreau, he said, "I don't know if I can be elected president saying the things I did about race today, but I also know that I don't deserve to be elected if I was too afraid to say them in the first place."

Reaction to the speech veered between extremes, both approving and dismissive. In the immediate aftermath it was unclear whether Obama's overture would dispel the doubts that had arisen around him. Peggy Noonan, a former speechwriter for President Ronald Reagan, said on *Good Morning America* the following day that "the speech was a breakthrough for [Obama] as a candidate for president." She praised him for taking on a big issue in a serious and thoughtful way that forced people to consider their own views. "I think it breaks through for him as a leader," she observed. "I was glad a grown-up American politician was talking to the other grown-ups about this fact of our country."

The *Augusta Chronicle* in Georgia didn't believe Obama went far enough. "Instead of completely cutting the cord with the Rev. Jeremiah Wright, Obama went through the odd contortion of simultaneously denouncing the Rev. Wright's words—then embracing the man himself: 'As imperfect as he may be, he has been like family to me.' But having 'family' like this doesn't mean you have to keep inviting those odious people back to the reunions year after year," the paper wrote. "Is this how Obama would level with the American people as president?"

The same day as the speech, *The Daily Show*'s Jon Stewart distilled the controversy with his trademark blend of humor and insight. He opened his late-night segment on Obama by noting the existence of an "undercurrent to his candidacy, a whisper, if you will," that the candidate was "not of this nation: a foreign name, perhaps a Muslim background." But now America had some clarification. "The good news," Stewart told his viewers, "he's a Christian!...The bad news: this is his pastor."

In the nearly six-minute segment, Stewart showed clips of Reverend Wright hoarsely hollering about American perfidy, interspersed with several comic asides. Stewart concluded the bit with a simple approbation of Obama's speech: "And so at eleven o'clock a.m. on a Tuesday, a prominent politician spoke to Americans about race as though they were adults."

Other politicians, of course, have met public prejudice head-on. In one of the most famous examples, candidate John Kennedy confronted bias against his Catholicism in a paid television speech to overwhelmingly Protestant West Virginia just two days before the state's Democratic primary. "If his religion was what they held against him, Kennedy would discuss it," wrote Theodore White in *The Making of the*

*President 1960*. "And by exquisite use of TV, he did indeed discuss it. There remains with me now a recollection of what I think is the finest TV broadcast I have ever heard any political candidate make." Kennedy had been trailing Hubert Humphrey by twenty points. On election day, he won a resounding victory in West Virginia, taking nearly 61 percent of the vote.

Like Kennedy, Obama faced intense pressure and spoke with grace and wisdom. "Those moments give people an insight into what kind of president someone will be," David Axelrod observed, "and so what looked to be a moment of peril for him turned into a moment of triumph." Axelrod argued that the speech was one of the most meaningful orations ever delivered during a presidential campaign.

Beyond its historical legacy and its impact on the electorate, the speech played a role in directing former rivals Obama and Biden toward each other. After leaving the presidential race in Iowa, Biden hadn't developed any special affection for Obama. In late January, Obama had sought his support in the remaining primaries. Though Biden was sitting on the sidelines, he was still an important voice in the party. But Biden had balked, citing his firm friendship with the Clintons. Reflecting on their closeness, Hillary once quipped, "I think you and Bill were separated at birth." Unwilling to tilt, Biden told Obama he intended to remain neutral through the rest of the campaign. He vowed to privately consult with both candidates and to throw himself fully into the campaign of the eventual nominee.

But after the race speech, something changed. Obama's performance altered Biden's perception of the man he'd once pegged as an impatient freshman senator. Right after the speech, Biden was among the first people to speak out, telling reporters that Obama had delivered "one of the most important speeches we've heard in a long time." As a man who appreciated bluntness, Biden admired Obama's courage in tackling the race issue. He said of Obama: "He told the story of

America—both the good and the bad—and I believe his speech will come to represent an important step forward in race relations in our country."

The day after Obama's tour de force, Biden asked his adviser Antony Blinken, "Did you hear that speech?"

Blinken remembered seeing Biden palpably excited.

"Yeah, as a matter of fact," Blinken replied.

"That is maybe the best speech I've heard a political leader give," Biden raved.

The whole presentation—Obama's delivery, his language, and the substance of the speech—floored Biden. "I think there was a click moment there," Blinken recalled. "Biden saw Obama in a different light than he'd seen him before, and there was a newfound respect and admiration."

Something else was also at work. The speech gave birth to an imperceptible bond between the two men. Barack and Joe were linked by their separate journeys toward the same goal: to understand and improve the plight of African Americans. Obama had lived it as a black man early in his career as a community organizer in poor neighborhoods in Chicago, and he had deeply ruminated on the racial inequities in America. Biden had witnessed it as a white man with a conscience. Having taken sharply different paths, Obama and Biden had arrived at a shared belief in the hopeful, and much-quoted, Martin Luther King Jr. maxim: "The arc of the moral universe is long, but it bends toward justice."

Biden discovered the stark difference between the black and white worlds in America in the summer of 1962, when he was nineteen. After his freshman year at the University of Delaware, he took a job as a lifeguard at a public swimming pool near a housing project. He was a suburban kid who didn't know any blacks. "I wanted to get more involved," he recalled. He was the only white lifeguard among a dozen inner-city African Americans who were all students at historically black colleges. "I actually got pulled into their lives a little bit," Biden reminisced. "I'd play on the same team with them and be the only white guy of all ten guys on the basketball court."

The experience opened his eyes, and theirs. "I came to realize," Joe recalled, "I was the only white guy they knew." Biden and his lifeguard buddies were so foreign to each other, he explained, "it was almost like we were exchange students." They asked him all sorts of questions. They wanted to know about his life and the lives of people in the white community. They asked where he lived, what kind of things white girls did. Sometimes the questions startled Joe. One guy asked if Biden owned a five-gallon gasoline can.

"No, I don't," Joe told him. "But what do you need it for?"

Joe learned that African Americans couldn't take a simple road trip without suffering discrimination and humiliation. "I'm going down to see my grandmom in North Carolina," the lifeguard told him. "We can't stop at most gas stations. They won't let us stop at most gas stations."

From his lifeguard experience Joe gained a passion for civil rights. "It was a real awakening for me," he explained. "Every day, it seemed to me, black people got subtle and not-so-subtle reminders that they didn't quite belong in America. It was a dozen small cuts a day."

Biden participated in marches to desegregate movie theaters in Wilmington. But he was not a rabble-rousing, get-out-in-the-streets protester. Like Obama, he was measured in his responses to racial inequities. As a law student at Syracuse University, he came to believe in fixing grievances through the system.

When riots swept Wilmington in 1968 following the assassination of Martin Luther King Jr., Biden, who was in his last year of law school, arrived home to see the ruins of downtown Wilmington. "The city was in turmoil," he recalled. "The National Guard was on every corner with drawn bayonets, and the state police were in the city, all white and over six feet tall....I mean they were just establishing they were in charge."

After law school, Joe took a job with a corporate law firm defending big businesses, but the work wasn't right for him, and soon he quit. As journalist Jules Witcover explained in his Biden biography, Joe "decided he needed to handle cases more suited to his temperament and objectives." So he became a public defender whose clients were nearly all African Americans from Wilmington's East Side.

Biden carried his civil rights fervor with him as he moved into the political world. When he arrived in the Senate in 1973, he paid a visit to Mississippi senator John Stennis, chairman of the Armed Services Committee, and spoke from the heart when responding to a question from the staunch segregationist.

As Biden told the story, he was in Stennis's imposing office when the senator asked him, "What made you run for the United States Senate?"

"Civil rights, sir," Biden blurted out without thinking.

He panicked, fearing a lecture from the powerful veteran. But Stennis let it pass, saying, "Good, good, good," and pressed on to another subject.

Throughout his career Biden supported black judges, rejected judges who weren't progressive enough, and defended strong civil rights legislation. In the words of state representative Fletcher Smith Jr., a member of South Carolina's Legislative Black Caucus, "Senator Biden was for civil rights when civil rights wasn't cool."

After the race speech, Biden found a sense of fraternity with Obama. Though still smarting from his resounding loss to him in Iowa, he was able to set aside those wounds and envision a closer relationship with the Democratic front-runner. Biden adviser Antony Blinken had a front-row seat as the two men crept slowly toward each other. "Having watched the arc of this thing," Blinken concluded, "the race speech was one of the pivotal moments."

# FOUR

# Subtle Similarities

In May 2008, with the primary season winding down, Barack Obama's nomination was a near-mathematical certainty. The Democratic candidate was now able to turn his sights fully toward the fall campaign against his Republican challenger, John McCain. That meant getting serious about a running mate. He planned to cast a wide net, with as many as thirty prospects coming under scrutiny.

But the first name off his lips after his victory in North Carolina's primary on May 6 was the senator on the Foreign Relations Committee he'd once ridiculed for his long-windedness. "You know, I'm thinking Joe Biden might be a good choice," Obama told Axelrod as they traveled back to the campaign's Chicago headquarters.

Having sparred with him on the hustings, Obama respected his former rival's political finesse and depth of experience. Though Biden had quit the 2008 race early, his aide John Marttila told his boss that his passion, authenticity, foreign policy judgment, and legislative expertise had left a mark. "People agree," Marttila accurately observed, "that your stature has been enhanced."

Obama's aides sensed Barack's early preference for Joe. Chicago adviser Rahm Emanuel, who had worked on Bill Clinton's 1992 campaign, told Obama he wasn't going to put forward any candidates for consideration as vice president because it was clear Obama's mind was already made up: Joe was his favorite. Clinton had been the same way about Al Gore when reviewing dozens of prospects for his vice president—Gore's name was always on Clinton's lips.

But Joe was far from certain he even wanted the shackles of the vice presidency. He loved his role in the Senate; he was his own boss, a free man with senior status that gave him the space he wanted to be independent and outspoken. Playing number two to Barack's number one was certain to constrain a man who was known to tug on his bridle.

After his loss in Iowa, Biden was asked about the chances that he'd accept a spot as vice president. He laughed off the proposition. "No," he said. "If we have a Democratic president, I can have much more influence, I promise you, as chairman of the Foreign Relations Committee than I can as vice president."

After dropping out of the race—and while remaining neutral as Obama and Clinton fought for the nomination—Biden made a promise to Obama. "If you win," he told Barack, "I'll do anything you ask me to do."

"Be careful, because I may ask you a lot," Barack replied.

Obama's regard for Biden only grew. The next month, he told Biden, "The only question I have is not whether I want you in this administration," he said bluntly. "It's which job you'd like best."

Biden presented a host of political assets as a running mate. For Obama, a key consideration—as was often the case with vice-president selections—was the candidate's appeal to voters in November. As Obama's aide Pete Rouse put it: "Barack's focus was on someone who would help him win the election. His view was, 'If this person doesn't help me win the White House, it's kind of a moot point.'"

Obama was weak with white working-class voters, those in Rust Belt states like Pennsylvania, where he got thumped by Clinton.

Biden had strong appeal in those states; his roots in Pennsylvania, for instance, went back to his childhood growing up in Scranton as the son of a car dealer before his family moved to Delaware. He was a favorite among labor unions and cops; he had won police support for his work on the massive and controversial 1994 crime bill. Biden conveyed an understanding and sympathy for the struggles of the middle class—a fundamental talking point of the Obama campaign.

But what Obama valued most in a vice-presidential pick wasn't always clear. He sent mixed messages to his staff: he didn't want only a vote-getter. According to campaign manager David Plouffe, Obama sought a vice president with strong skills for navigating the politics of the White House. "I am more concerned and interested in how my selection may perform as an actual vice president than whether they will give a boost to the campaign," Obama told Plouffe and the rest of the vice-presidential vetting team, which included adviser Jim Johnson, Caroline Kennedy, legal adviser Eric Holder, and David Axelrod.

Obama fully realized his position as a relative newcomer to the national political scene and Congress. As a presidential candidate, he had a change of heart about Biden's devotion to the Senate and its hierarchy. After having dismissed Joe for his slavish acceptance of the ways of Washington, the novice candidate now regarded Biden's experience as an asset; Joe, he realized, could provide a guiding hand on legislation and on matters of governing. Obama's regular phone calls to Biden on the campaign trail after Iowa underscored his openness to the veteran politician's counsel.

Biden's foreign policy credentials, in particular, were important to Obama, who was notably short on experience in that arena. His aides acknowledged that "when he took his seat in the Senate...he was coming to foreign policy questions 'relatively cold,'" reporter Ben Wallace-Wells wrote in *Rolling Stone* in 2007. During his brief time in the chamber, he took on the role of a student learning the history and subtleties of foreign policy and American prospects overseas.

Despite their initial distance from each other, Senators Obama and Biden often saw eye to eye on matters of international import. In a speech before the Chicago Council on Foreign Relations in 2005, Senator Obama called for a gradual reduction of troops in Iraq, mirroring the approach favored by Biden and some other Democrats but rejecting the demand of a Pennsylvania Democrat, Representative John Murtha, a former marine who insisted on an immediate withdrawal of all troops from the country.

As he pondered his vice-presidential pick, Obama faced a crucial question: Was Biden's personality the right fit? Joe was a brilliant politician, and his success stemmed in part from his sociability—his gift of gab. Obama's aides, particularly Axelrod and Plouffe, initially saw red flags: Would Biden blabber too much on the stump? Would his gaffe-prone tongue cause unnecessary distraction for the campaign? Biden's free-flowing words certainly got him into trouble, but it was part of his easygoing manner, his likability, his instinct for connecting with people on a personal level.

"Joe Biden doesn't just meet you, he engulfs you," wrote Mark Bowden, an author and national correspondent for *The Atlantic*. "There's the direct contact with his blue eyes, the firm handshake while his other hand grasps your arm, the flash of those famously perfect white teeth, and an immediate frontal assault on your personal space....If he's in a chair, he'll scoot it closer; when the furniture's not portable, he'll lean forward, planting his elbows on his knees, gesturing with both hands while he speaks, occasionally reaching over to touch your arm or leg for emphasis."

Bowden described once joining Senator Biden on his daily commute home from Washington to Wilmington. The pair sat across from each other at a table in an Amtrak car. "The space was knee-to-knee intimate—perfect for his purposes—and Biden held forth animatedly for the entire seventy-minute trip," Bowden recalled. "When he stepped off at Wilmington station, the sudden silence in the car seemed like a physical presence, the onset of a vacuum. When I described the experience to a friend who'd taken the same ride more than once, he nodded knowingly and said, 'We call it getting "Bidened."'"

If some people knocked Biden for his verbosity, others found in it a source of his strength. When critics lambasted him for carrying on too long during committee meetings, conservative *New York Times* columnist David Brooks came to Biden's defense. "Some have concluded that Biden is a blowhard," Brooks began, "though I assert he is thoughtful, just at Wagnerian length." Brooks described Biden's orations as "senatorial arias of immense emotional range." In Brooks's telling, Biden did what few politicians allowed themselves to do: reveal their unfiltered self. "Biden's emotive vitality is his greatest weapon in the war all successful politicians must wage, the war against the public self," Brooks explained.

Sure, Joe rambled on at length, Brooks acknowledged. "It is true the man has no speed bumps between his brain and his mouth. But this only makes him more candid. And by making candor the core of his self-image, he has preserved the ability to think independently and to be honest with himself....Biden, sometimes sarcastic, sometimes profane, always overlong, is still a real person, and a genuinely nice one."

If Barack and Joe were moving toward a partnership, one trait tied them together: both men were athletes. As with many men, sports helped lay a foundation for friendship. As athletes, Barack and Joe instinctively understood each other, observed Arne Duncan, Obama's longtime close friend and education secretary.

While both Barack and Joe were deeply competitive, they also appreciated sportsmanlike teamwork, an essential quality for a winning presidential campaign and running an effective White House. Craig Robinson had noticed Barack's team spirit years earlier when he took him onto the basketball court for a more-than-hour-long five-on-five game, partly to vet him as a suitor for his sister Michelle.

Robinson, a six-foot-six standout player at Princeton, was impressed less with Obama's skills than with how he expressed himself on the court. Robinson found Obama "very team oriented, very unselfish," noting that he "was aggressive without being a jerk."

Like Obama, Biden had learned through sports to honor the team ethic despite his own soaring ambitions. As a kid afflicted with a severe stutter, he had relied on sports to demonstrate his confidence and distract attention away from his impairment. At Archmere Academy, a Catholic high school for boys, he showed considerable athletic prowess, becoming a star halfback on the football team; known for his skill at reeling in passes, he earned the nickname "Hands," which replaced epithets targeting his stutter. But when Joe was passed over for team captain, he took it in stride; it didn't affect his play during the season. "He was still a leader," recalled coach John Walsh. "He had a lot of enthusiasm, he was upbeat, he was a team player."

Both Obama and Biden viewed the world through sports metaphors. After Obama upset a roster of veteran politicians in the Iowa caucuses and began to look viable as a presidential candidate, he had to fend off charges that his inexperience was a liability. Throughout his life Obama had played a lot of pickup ball, and he had made the team at Punahou prep school in Hawaii. To beat back the naysayers after his win in Iowa, he chose to express himself in a basketball analogy: "At some point people have to stop asserting that because I haven't been in the league long enough I can't play. It's sort of like Magic Johnson or LeBron James—[they] keep on scoring thirty, and their team wins, but people say they can't lead their team because they're too young."

Though a distinct underdog in Iowa, Biden turned to football terms to express his optimism. Trailing pitifully in the polls, he peered at the field through the rosy glasses of an athlete and saw only victory. "As he put it," wrote his local newspaper in Wilmington, the *News Journal*, "he was the single punt returner. The ball was about to be snapped. 'I don't think about being tackled,' he said. 'I think about scoring.'"

Politics was often framed in sports imagery. But for Barack and Joe, true athletes, their interest in sports promised something else: an underlying compatibility. Arne Duncan, a superlative athlete himself, had been cocaptain of the Harvard basketball team and later often played hoops with Obama. Over the years he had seen how sports drew players together beyond the court. The athlete's frame of mind, he believed, gave Obama and Biden a strong starting point: "That's how they were both wired."

Emerging as top candidates for vice president along with Biden were Senator Evan Bayh of Indiana, Virginia governor Tim Kaine, and Kansas governor Kathleen Sebelius. Hillary Clinton of course entered the conversations. She brought experience, intelligence, and wide appeal, as evidenced by the millions of votes she garnered in her vigorous nomination run against Obama. Despite her many attributes, she was discarded—too much baggage. She and her husband's long years in politics and their myriad controversies posed hurdles. The former president was too large a presence, and an unpredictable one. "If I picked her," Obama told Plouffe, "my concern is that there would be more than two of us in the relationship."

It didn't help Hillary's chances that Michelle Obama was less than enthusiastic about her joining the ticket. Michelle never got over Hillary's explanation to the editorial board of the Sioux Falls *Argus Leader* in May about why she didn't get out of the race as her prospects against Obama were looking bleak. Hillary tried to make the point that a candidate must keep pushing on into the late states, noting that her husband hadn't locked up his 1992 nomination until the June primary in California. She suggested that the political field can suddenly change with an allusion that Michelle never forgave. "We all remember," Hillary told the editors, "Bobby Kennedy was assassinated in June in California."

The remark touched a nerve: fear for Obama's safety ran high.

Secret Service protection had begun earlier for him than for any other presidential candidate in history, and, according to Axelrod, "agents insisted he wear protective gear under his clothes in large crowds." Hillary quickly apologized for the statement, her staff saying she never meant to imply harm to Obama or cause offense to the Kennedy family. Still, given all her complications as a potential vice-presidential candidate, she was scratched off the list.

As the summer of 2008 wore on and Obama's nomination was assured, the process for selecting his running mate moved into the final stages. Bayh and Kaine and Biden all submitted to vetting. Investigators working for the campaign dug into their pasts, their speeches, financial history, medical records—the deep recesses of their lives—looking for anything that could emerge on the trail with surprise and alarm. Each of the contenders then had secret meetings with Axelrod and Plouffe.

Biden and Obama's two advisers gathered at the home of Biden's sister Valerie in Pennsylvania, not far from Joe's home in Delaware. True to form, Biden dominated the conversation at the opening by delivering a "nearly twenty-minute soliloquy," according to Plouffe, on the campaign, on Obama, and on his own hesitance about assuming the vice presidency. "Ax and I couldn't get a word in edgewise," Plouffe wrote later.

Axelrod was even tougher in his assessment of Biden's lip flapping. He described the three-man parley as a "two-hour monologue" by Biden. "In our interview, Biden did nothing to dispel our concerns about his verbosity," Axelrod wrote in his memoir. "Even as we expressed that concern, he would respond in ten- or fifteen-minute bursts, coming up for air only long enough to inquire, 'Do you understand what I'm saying here?' or 'Am I making sense?'"

Biden was honest about his hesitation on whether the job fit him. "The last thing I should do is VP," Biden told the aides. He noted that he'd served for thirty-five years in the Senate, part of that time in top leadership positions—he'd been chairman of two committees. "It will be hard [for me] to be number two."

Biden knew the history of the vice president's limited role and was uncertain how it would fit his energetic, immersive personality. He drew up a bold portfolio that, if he accepted the job, would put him at the center of the White House action. But was Obama prepared to grant him an expansive role? Describing the overall process, Joe later told Ryan Lizza of *The New Yorker,* "I wanted to make sure we understood each other." He explained that even if he passed the vetting for the job, he wasn't necessarily going to take it. If Obama ultimately chose him, Biden said, "I needed to spend at least two or three hours with him to understand what the role would be."

Whatever his reservations, Joe was careful in his meeting with Plouffe and Axelrod to keep himself in the running for this extraordinary opportunity. He told them that he "would be a good soldier and could provide real value, domestically and internationally."

Though his inquisitors may have had their doubts about him, Biden was a man whose commitment and loyalty, once given, were ironclad. As a senator and a Catholic, Biden fully understood hierarchy and accepted his place in a pecking order. "One of the reasons why I didn't think he would have a problem being vice president, even though he had really never worked for anyone else," said his longtime friend and adviser Ted Kaufman, "was that he was very comfortable in a hierarchical organization. He felt very comfortable being nice to the chairman." And that trait would easily transfer to the White House.

By the end of the meeting, Axelrod and Plouffe were tipping toward Biden. Up close, Axelrod was able to take in Joe's many dimensions. "He was genuinely impressive, disarmingly candid, and just plain likeable," Axelrod recalled. Having vetted all three vice-presidential candidates—Bayh, Kaine, and Biden—the aides believed all were strong, but each had his own special attributes. It could go any way. As Axelrod put it, "This is a jump ball."

The two aides knew the final decision was not theirs—it rested entirely with Obama. "It'll be like the decisions he'll need to make as president—lonely and tough," Axelrod told Plouffe. "Should we tell him we oh so slightly favor Biden?"

"I think we owe it to him to put our thumb lightly on the scale for Biden," Plouffe said.

If Biden was the pick, Plouffe added, Axelrod would have to keep a close eye on him. "You're going to have to deal with him every day to make sure he stays in the corral."

Axelrod reared up in good-natured opposition, throwing that chore back at Plouffe.

"No way," Plouffe resisted. "You love talking and he loves talking. It's a perfect match. And what's a couple more hours in the day to you?"

Though Biden passed muster with the two tough advisers, he clearly left the impression that if the vice presidency eluded him, his life would not suffer appreciably. "While he would readily accept the VP slot if offered," Plouffe observed, "he was not pining for it."

On August 6, Joe Biden sneaked incognito into the Graves 601 Hotel in Minneapolis through a back entrance. No crisp suit and tie, and no glad-handing in the lobby. With a baseball cap pulled low and aviator sunglasses covering his eyes, Joe quietly made his way to a suite upstairs. On Obama's orders, the meeting between the presumed Democratic nominee and a prospective running mate was taking place in total secrecy. Obama had already held clandestine meetings with Evan Bayh in St. Louis and Tim Kaine in Indiana. Now it was Biden's turn.

Over ninety minutes, in a "spirited and pragmatic" discussion, Barack and Joe got to know each other, and they liked what they saw. Barack informed Joe that he had sailed through the vetting—no small accomplishment for a man who'd been in politics for nearly four decades. Investigators found no signs that Joe had used any shenanigans to enrich himself. He ranked low among his fellow senators in personal wealth. "All these years," Obama joked, "and you still have no money." In 2007, Joe and his wife Jill, a teacher at a community college in Delaware, had earned about $300,000, low by Senate standards but a substantial amount to most Americans.

By contrast, Obama's popularity had translated into enormous earnings from his books. His memoir, *Dreams from My Father*, published in 1995, was out of print when Obama's star started to shine. Reissued after his keynote address at the Democratic National Convention in 2004, the book took off, hitting the *New York Times* paperback bestseller list for fourteen of the next eighteen weeks. When *The Audacity of Hope* was released in 2006, it shot to number one on the *Times* hardcover nonfiction list. Barack and Michelle's tax return showed more than $4 million in royalties in 2007.

At the top of the interview agenda, Barack needed clarity: he still wasn't convinced Joe wanted the vice president's job. He was sensitive to Joe's hesitation—that Joe believed that, as chairman of the Foreign Relations Committee and a veteran senator with considerable clout, he had a fine perch to influence policy. Barack wanted Joe to view the vice presidency as a promotion in his power, not as a step backward.

He put it to Joe directly: "Will this job be too small for you?"

"No," Joe replied, "as long as I would really be a confidant."

Probing Joe's mind, Barack asked whether any other position was attractive. "You have a great interest in national-security policy, foreign policy," he said. "Would you rather be secretary of state instead of vice president?"

Having had lots of conversation with his own advisers, Joe had come to the conclusion that in an Obama administration, he could have the most power in the formulation of policy as vice president. But Obama would have to agree to his terms for the job.

If Obama were to accept Biden's demands for how he wanted to operate as vice president, Barack would be breaking with a long tradition.

Throughout most of American history, the vice presidency was little more than a standby position, unengaged with the day-to-day activities of governing or influencing the direction of the nation. In essence, the job amounted to presiding over the Senate, casting a tie-breaking vote, if necessary, and biding one's time as a president-in-waiting should any harm befall the commander in chief. Long reviled and scorned by its own officeholders, the vice presidency inspired almost no one; its occupants were quickly and easily forgotten, their impact virtually nil unless they ascended to the top job.

Until the early nineteenth century, the contender who placed second in the race for president automatically became vice president; often true rivals, the winner and runner-up had little desire or incentive to cooperate in governing. "In the first fifty-two years of the Republic," political observer Jules Witcover wrote, "every president served out one or two terms, with little interest in or concern about the identity of the vice president."

In summing up his role, a disgruntled John Adams, America's first vice president, colored the image of the office for years afterward. "Gentlemen, I feel great difficulty how to act," he complained to the Senate five days before George Washington was sworn in as the first president of the United States. "I am Vice-President. In this I am nothing, but I may be everything." He was no less frustrated after serving out his first term. Writing to his wife Abigail in December 1793, Adams protested, "My country has in its Wisdom contrived for me, the most insignificant Office that ever the Invention of Man contrived or his Imagination conceived."

The vice presidency was deemed so insignificant that Senator Silas Wright of New York declined the nomination in 1844, and for long stretches the office sat unoccupied. Between 1812 and 1900, the United States had no sitting vice president for nearly twenty-seven years because of deaths, resignations, or successions to the presidency. During that time, there was no vice president eleven different times.

"Yet," wrote historian Joel K. Goldstein, "the country survived without any discernable cry for a means to fill vice-presidential vacancies."

In 1899, the year before he agreed to be William McKinley's running mate for his second term, Theodore Roosevelt admitted he'd rather be a senator, the secretary of state, or governor general of the Philippines—any job that had "more work in it." In his view, the likelihood of a vice president doing "much of anything is infinitesimal." Yet, seven months after McKinley assumed office again in 1901, Roosevelt—to use Adams's words—went from "nothing" to "everything" upon McKinley's assassination.

In the twentieth century, vice presidents took on tasks for presidents and performed ceremonial roles. John Nance Garner, Franklin D. Roosevelt's first vice president, worked with Congress to advance New Deal legislation and traveled around the world representing America. Yet his duties still left him far from enamored of the job. The foul-mouthed Texan purportedly described the office as not "worth a bucket of warm piss."

Roosevelt's second vice president, Henry Wallace, also served as global emissary for the United States. In 1941, FDR gave him the job of chair of the Board of Economic Warfare. Yet vice presidents still did not develop strong relationships with presidents or work closely with them. Wallace eventually was booted from his leadership of the Board of Economic Warfare, and when Harry Truman became FDR's third vice president, he hardly ever conferred with the president. Only after Roosevelt's death and Truman's accession to the presidency did Truman learn of the crucial atomic-bomb-building operation known as the Manhattan Project.

As the twentieth century progressed, American power expanded, heaping the executive branch with additional duties that allowed the vice president to take on a wider and more prominent role. Richard Nixon sat in on Cabinet and National Security Council meetings, took on some diplomatic chores, helped advance President Dwight

Eisenhower's legislative agenda, and served as a spokesman for the administration.

But his efforts did not draw the two men together: the Eisenhower-Nixon relationship was never warm. Eisenhower even complicated Nixon's presidential campaign in 1960 when he was asked at a news conference to offer one idea of Nixon's that he had adopted as president. "If you give me a week, I might think of one," Eisenhower offered. Nixon's opponent in the 1960 election, John Kennedy, turned Eisenhower's slight into an attack ad.

In the Kennedy administration, Vice President Lyndon Johnson was given some minor tasks and was often sent away on overseas missions. Kennedy denied Johnson's wish to have a larger presence in the executive branch. His mostly meaningless role and his testy relationship with the president and the president's brother Robert embittered him toward the office. Ben Bradlee, then *Newsweek*'s Washington bureau chief, friend to Kennedy, and regular White House visitor, noticed that the president was a little on edge whenever Johnson was around. He observed, "LBJ's simple presence seems to bug him." The Kennedy-Johnson tensions prompted Arthur Schlesinger, a special assistant to JFK, to conclude, "With the best will in the world, the relationship between President and Vice President is doomed—a generalization almost without historical exception."

Johnson certainly felt Kennedy's discomfort and suggested that it was due to the vice president's role as a president-in-waiting. Historian Doris Kearns Goodwin helped Johnson write his memoirs after serving in his White House. In her first book, *Lyndon Johnson and the American Dream*, published in 1976, she quoted Johnson colorfully describing his sensation around Kennedy. "Every time I came into John Kennedy's presence," he said, "I felt like a goddamn raven hovering over his shoulder."

Indeed, few White House duos ever escaped the ghoulish implication of the vice president's existence. "For the Vice President has no serious duty save to wait around for the President to die," Schlesinger explained. "This is not the basis for cordial and enduring friendships."

The vice presidency was inhabited at times by ill-prepared men of mediocrity, such as George H. W. Bush's choice, Indiana senator Dan Quayle, and men given to corruption, such as Richard Nixon's second-in-command, Spiro Agnew, who resigned after he was charged with tax evasion; Agnew's departure came as he was facing possible prosecution for bribery and extortion dating back to his days as a Maryland politician and extending into his term in the White House.

The office has attracted some highly qualified individuals, and some president–vice president teams have formed strong working relationships, such as Carter-Mondale and Clinton-Gore, if still a bit at arm's length. Friendship was not part of the bargain.

Joe Biden had a lot to consider. There was not only the long, wretched history of the vice presidency but also his own future. Most important, Biden needed to know what exactly Obama was seeking out of his running mate.

In the Minneapolis hotel, Joe laid it all out.

"Barack, look," he said, "if you're going to ask me to do this, please don't ask me for any reason other than that you respect my judgment. If you're asking me to join you to help govern, and not just help you get elected, then I'm interested. If you're asking me to help you get elected, I can do that other ways, but I don't want to be a vice president who is not part of the major decisions you make."

Biden demanded to have more than an executive branch working relationship: he wanted the president and vice president's interaction to be deep and personal, even combative if necessary. Trying to understand Biden's wishes, Obama referred to a discussion he'd had with another potential running mate. "That person would be very happy if I assigned them to reorganize the government," Obama said. "They'd be very happy doing that. How about you?"

To Biden, that was too limited. "No," he replied. "That's not what I want to do."

Biden had a very clear idea of what he wanted to do as vice president: he wanted to be Obama's chief counselor, he wanted to be in attendance at every important meeting, he wanted his views considered on every crucial decision on both foreign and domestic policy, he wanted to advise and participate in legislative efforts, he wanted to be the last guy in the room whispering in Obama's ear, and he wanted a private meeting, perhaps lunch, with the president every week. Perhaps most important, given Biden's nature, he wanted to be able to speak with absolute candor. If Obama accepted having a vice president like that, then Biden was ready to take on the task.

Obama, being a supremely self-confident figure, didn't blanch at Biden's demands—he saw their merits. Directness was an attribute Obama prized. He needed a vice president who wouldn't be shy about telling him the way things really stood. "We knew Biden could be somewhat long-winded and had a history of coloring outside the lines a bit," Plouffe observed. "But honestly, that was very appealing to Obama, because he wanted someone to give him the unvarnished truth."

Though different in personality—one was reserved while the other was outgoing—they found a similarity at their core. Obama was "by his nature very buttoned-down, much more poker-faced," explained Arne Duncan. "He had deep emotions but was more closed publicly with those things." Biden, on the other hand, wore "his heart on his sleeve every day." As high-profile politicians, Duncan added, "you can't fake who you are—people see through it. The best thing you can do is just to be your authentic self. And I think both of them were their authentic selves."

"I *know* you'll be candid," Barack told Joe, stating the obvious. "Are you prepared for me to be?"

"Absolutely," Joe replied.

# FIVE

# Fat Boy and the Stutterer

On Friday, August 8, after a grueling year and a half of campaigning, Obama jetted off for his native Hawaii. He hadn't seen his ill grandmother—who had been instrumental in raising him—for at least as long, and he needed some downtime to splash in the ocean, ponder his choice of a running mate, and craft his acceptance speech for the Democratic National Convention at the end of the month.

His campaign plane, carrying seventeen family members and friends, touched down at 2:30 p.m. at Honolulu Airport on the island of Oahu. In keeping with tradition, Obama and his wife Michelle were handed leis at the airport, but neither wore them. Though on vacation in an American state, Obama had to fight perceptions that Hawaii was still too foreign in many people's eyes as a getaway destination and birthplace for a presidential candidate. So no aloha shirts either. In public, he permitted himself khaki pants and dark polo shirts, but nothing more casual. He had to project a serious look and downplay what some voters saw as his foreignness as a child of Hawaii.

On ABC's *This Week*, Cokie Roberts noted the optics of the Hawaii visit as Obama was preparing for the fall campaign against John McCain. It had "the look of him going off to some sort of foreign, exotic place," she said. "He should be in Myrtle Beach if he's going to take a vacation at this time."

Though critics disdained the "foreignness" of the location, Hawaii provided a powerful symbolic backdrop for Obama's message to a large segment of his voters. It was here that he had grappled with and nurtured his mixed heritage and his place in America. Now he returned as the presumptive Democratic presidential nominee.

From the airport, Obama went to a welcoming ceremony at Keehi Lagoon Beach Park. As he had on the campaign trail, he delivered a message of inclusion. "The ability of people from everywhere," he said, "whether they're black or white, whether they're Japanese American or Korean American or Filipino American or whatever they are, they are just Americans, that all of us can work together and all of us can join together to create a better country. It's that spirit that I'm absolutely convinced is what America is looking for right now."

After speaking for seventeen minutes, Obama set off in his motorcade with Michelle and their daughters to his eighty-five-year-old grandmother's tenth-floor apartment on Beretania Street in central Honolulu, the same apartment where he had lived in his youth. His grandmother, Madelyn Dunham, suffered from osteoporosis and was unable to endure long airline flights to visit her grandson. So he came to her. Seeing her in the modest high-rise apartment, Obama was deeply moved, especially because she had time with her great-grandchildren—seven-year-old Sasha and ten-year-old Malia. Obama visited her almost daily during his stay. She died before the year was out—just two days before the presidential election.

Before returning to the mainland for the convention in Denver, Obama allowed himself solemn moments recalling the important figures of his early life: he visited the rocky spot where the ashes of his mother, Ann Dunham, had been strewn in 1995, and stopped by the grave of his grandfather, Stanley Dunham, a World War II veteran; Dunham had been laid to rest at the National Memorial Cemetery of the Pacific, known as Punchbowl Cemetery for its location in the Punchbowl volcanic crater, with spectacular views overlooking the south side of Oahu.

Enjoying his family time, Obama snorkeled with his daughters at a nature reserve crowded with fish and took the girls for shave ice treats at Island Snow Hawaii. While golfing and indulging in some fine dining, Obama watched a top vice-presidential prospect flaunt his foreign policy prowess. The day before Obama had arrived on Oahu, Russian troops had stormed into the Republic of Georgia, igniting a war with one of the former satellites of the Soviet Union.

The conflict erupted over complicated, long-simmering territorial claims that had accompanied the breakup of the USSR. Secretary of State Condoleezza Rice condemned the Russian invasion: "We call on Russia to cease attacks on Georgia by aircraft and missiles, respect Georgia's territorial integrity, and withdraw its ground combat forces from Georgian soil."

Joe Biden, asserting himself as chairman of the Senate Foreign Relations Committee, jumped in with his own warning. "Russia should act immediately to restore calm," he said in a statement. "The world will be watching—and expects Russia to live up to its commitments." On Tuesday, August 12, the two sides agreed to a cease-fire brokered by France's president, Nicolas Sarkozy.

By Saturday Biden was airborne to Georgia to meet with the country's president, Mikheil Saakashvili, and "get the facts firsthand." On his return on Monday, he issued a long statement playing up his statesmanship, his varied meetings and consultations on the ground, his understanding of the delicate geopolitical issues and the broader danger of the conflict to Europe and the world, and his role as emissary for the Senate and as the eyes and ears reporting back to the Bush administration.

Biden recommended solutions for defusing the crisis—he called for an independent, international peacekeeping force—and once Congress reconvened, he sought approval of a $1 billion emergency assistance package for Georgia to "send a clear message that the United States will not abandon this young democracy."

By now Biden had completed his soul-searching over the job of vice president—he wanted it, and his wife Jill and his family had all agreed he should take it, if offered. The war in Georgia had arrived at an opportune moment—"fortuitously well-timed," as one aide put it. Biden's globe-trotting in the interests of peace was excellent publicity for his bid to join the ticket. An Obama aide told the *Wall Street Journal*, "We welcomed his going."

With his overseas jaunt, Biden earned the kind of media attention that distinguished him from his rivals. "While other potential vice-presidential nominees were appearing on the Sunday talk shows, Senator Joseph R. Biden Jr. spent the weekend in Tbilisi, Georgia, meeting with the country's embattled president, Mikheil Saakashvili," wrote John Broder of the *New York Times*.

Richard Holbrooke, a former ambassador to the United Nations, sounded off on Biden in the *Times* article. "He would bring to any administration a tremendous credibility and talent," Holbrooke argued. "He knows the world leaders, he knows the Congress, he knows the issues and he passes the first test—he's qualified to be president."

With Biden in the international spotlight, Senator Evan Bayh acknowledged to a confidant that his prospects as the running mate were sinking. But when Biden returned home from his trip, he seemed to cast doubt on his own chances. From his car window he shouted to reporters in his driveway, "I'm not the one." Emails flew around the Bayh camp, raising hopes until it was realized: "That's just Joe being Joe, being funny."

The man who held the contenders' fate in his hands gave Biden a big pat on the back. His vacation over, Obama addressed the national convention of the Veterans of Foreign Wars in Florida and applauded Joe's performance overseas and the action it prompted at home. "We must help Georgia rebuild what has been destroyed," Obama told the veterans. "That is why I'm proud to join my friend, Senator Joe Biden, in calling for an additional $1 billion in reconstruction assistance for the people of Georgia."

The hint wasn't lost that night on the *CBS Evening News*. Correspondent Dean Reynolds translated the message for viewers: "Obama set off a buzz today when he delivered this shout out to Biden who just returned from war torn Georgia."

As the Democratic National Convention loomed just days away, Obama made up his mind. He had given all the prospects thorough consideration. As Axelrod told the press later, "It's a very personal decision. He approached it in a very serious, sober and reasoned way." Axelrod, Plouffe, and other close advisers, including Valerie Jarrett, knew from the beginning that Obama was leaning toward Biden. Before the announcement was made, Jarrett predicted, "My guess is he ended up where he started out."

To unveil the news internally, Obama got Axelrod and Plouffe on the phone. He was preparing to move into the next phase of his campaign and initiate what was to evolve into a unique personal commitment between a president and vice president. "I've decided," he told his aides. "It's Biden."

Obama chose Biden for the reasons everyone knew: the veteran senator's experience, foreign policy expertise, and skill working with Congress. But there was something else that attracted Obama: he was drawn to Biden's personal story, his character in the face of profound setbacks. Barack, too, had pondered deep questions about the meaning of life and his place in it, and he was drawn to Biden's devotion to his family. Joe's commute every evening from Washington to Delaware to be with his two toddler sons after the 1972 car accident sent an indelible message. As Joe explained in his memoir, his boys "were hungry for assurances that I was *coming back*. And I meant to demonstrate to them that I would always be there."

His love for his boys moved Obama, whose own early life had been fractured by his parents' separation. In a Father's Day speech two months before he chose Biden, Obama recalled his father's absence when he was growing up, describing it as a "hole in your heart," and noted that his upbringing drove his commitment to his daughters. "I resolved many years ago," he told congregants at the Apostolic Church of God on the South Side of Chicago, "that it was my obligation to break the cycle—that if I could be anything in life, I would be a good father to my children."

Although Barack and Joe emerged from different backgrounds, different eras, and different personal struggles, they found commonality. Each man had been profoundly influenced by his early experiences sorting out life and the confusion it threw his way. And each was in large measure a mature portrait of the young man he had been.

Spending time both in his native Hawaii and in Jakarta, Indonesia, Barry, as young Barack was known, was a reflective youth seeking to come to terms with his mixed-race heritage. His white mother was often far from home working on her anthropology studies; he had met his Kenyan father only once. As Obama put it, the man who had deserted his family was "a myth to me, both more and less than a man." As a youth, Barry was often under the care of his white grandparents.

Further complicating Barry's self-image was his weight: until about seventh grade, he was a chubby kid and sensitive about it. Even in his early twenties, the stain lingered in his mind. While living in New York, Obama had an Australian girlfriend, Genevieve Cook, who noted, "There was still this quite raw and close to the surface aspect of himself which had to do with being the fat boy, or chubby boy, that people laughed at, that no one knew quite where to put, and who had a deeply ambivalent notion of being loved or not."

Like Biden with his stutter, Obama fought against his chubbiness even into his later years, partly by jogging almost daily, though he had outgrown his childhood physique. "One of the reasons he was maybe such a dedicated jogger was part of him still felt he was the fat boy, which I found hard to see," Genevieve remembered.

During his teenage years in Hawaii, Obama was "very, very quiet," a friend recalled, "very, very shy...just a cautious kid." As a student at Columbia University, living on Ninety-Fourth Street, he kept to himself. He read a lot. "I was...prone to see other people as unnecessary distractions," he has written. "I had grown too comfortable in my solitude, the safest place I knew."

For most of his early years Barry was on a quest for his identity. He often plunged into deep contemplation: Who was he and who should he be? Drawing on the diverse threads of his life—his relatives around the world, his several childhood locations, the complications of his mixed race—Obama became a man largely of his own self-creation. And he seemed wiser and older than his peers. As another friend in Hawaii remembered, "He would bring up worldly topics far beyond his years."

Joe Biden, by contrast, ran, jumped, and climbed through an exuberant youth and was sometimes so full of silliness that he took dangerous risks. His American childhood was, in many respects, unexceptional. He was surrounded by doting, attentive parents and extended family devoted to their Irish Catholic community: Sundays were for church, and get-togethers, and conversations about politics. But the Biden family's comfortable existence was jolted when the economy in Scranton, Pennsylvania, went on a downslide. After moving to Delaware, first into an apartment, then a house in Wilmington, the family finally recovered as Biden's father became a successful used car salesman.

What was exceptional about his early years was the way Joey, as he was called—and there always remained a touch of Joey in him—responded to his challenges. If Obama plunged deep into his private questions and applied his sharp intellect to work through them, Biden relied on sheer force of will to blast through his obstacles.

He didn't shrink in the face of his stuttering. He shouted down the bullies who gave him the cutting nickname "Dash" for the way sounds came off his lips. "I talked like Morse code," Joe explained. "Dot-dot-dot-dot-dash-dash-dash-dash." Standing up for himself, Joey hollered at his persecutors, "You gu-gu-gu-gu-guys sh-sh-sh-sh-shut up!"

He was determined to fit in. He practiced so he could speak in class without embarrassment. "Other kids looked at me like I was stupid," he recalled. "They laughed. I wanted so badly to prove I was like everybody else." He wanted to do what he loved most: chatter with his friends. He got tripped up by situations that required a quick reply, but eventually he overcame the stutter.

His struggles put the fight in him. Nothing stood in Joey's way. "I was young for my grade and always little for my age," he recalled, "but I made up for it by demonstrating I had guts."

Sometimes he went too far. In industrial Scranton, at around age ten, he accepted a five-dollar dare from a local kid to climb to the top of a culm mountain. The two-hundred-foot mountain—made up of waste material from coal mine shafts—was hot and dangerous; along its surface were invisible ash pockets that could collapse with a footstep, possibly dropping a foolhardy young kid into the burning center. But Joey took the gamble and scrambled up the side of the black mountain. As author Richard Ben Cramer told it, "By the time he got to the top, the five bucks wasn't the point anymore. It was more like… immortality." By sheer luck, Joey made it up and down unscathed.

The escapade perfectly defined the confidence Joe carried with him as a Scranton kid, a senator, and a vice-presidential nominee. Whether on a culm mountain as a youngster or in the Situation Room as a veteran public servant, Biden had the courage of his convictions.

Certainly there was a danger in selecting such an unbridled

personality as your number two. But by Obama's reckoning, the virtues of the Biden character outweighed the hazards. Days after announcing his choice, Obama explained his reasoning on CBS's *60 Minutes*. "If I'm in the room making the kinds of tough decisions that the next president is going to have to make, both on domestic policy and international policy, then I want the counsel and advice of somebody who's not going to agree with me a hundred percent of the time—in fact, somebody who's independent enough that they can push back and give me different perspectives and make sure I'm catching any blind spots that I have. And Joe Biden doesn't bite his tongue."

Little Joey was as much a part of the Obama team as was the grown-up politician he later became; indeed, Obama and Biden conducted themselves in an odd inverse manner relative to their ages. The younger Obama was the more controlled, the more mature, while the older Biden retained the impulsiveness of his childhood into his adult years, making him seem forever young.

After informing his advisers of his selection, Barack set out to give the good news to Joe. It was Thursday, August 21, and Obama wanted to announce his running mate on Saturday, two days before the opening of the Democratic National Convention.

But the man couldn't be found. Obama phoned Biden's office, but no one there could immediately track him down. It seemed strange because Biden, like Obama, was in love with electronic communications. As his wife Jill explained later, "He's on that BlackBerry and his phones constantly. I won't let him drive the car because everything's ringing." She said that amid a hail of ringing devices, she would force him to pull over. "It's too dangerous. Or we go to the wrong places."

At last Obama found Joe. "When I finally got him," Barack explained, "he said he was at the dentist's office." But Joe didn't let on what brought him there. "I realized only later that he was being a doting husband, looking after Jill during a root canal."

Informed of Barack's decision, Joe was elated and honored and, talking nonstop, declared himself ready to do everything he could for the team. He had so many questions that Obama insisted he get on the phone immediately with David Plouffe.

Before inflicting Joe on his campaign manager, Obama called Plouffe and described his conversation with Biden. "Even for Joe," Barack said, "he was going a mile a minute. He also said he was humbled and ready to do anything we ask, the way we ask it. He has a million questions, so I told him you'd call him to give him the overview of the next few days."

Plouffe filled Biden in on how his life was changing: a flurry of events were planned for the next several days, then it was to be full-scale campaigning for two and a half months, until the election. Worried about Biden's loose-cannon eruptions, Plouffe gave him an unsubtle warning: "Let's do us all a favor and make sure we reward [Barack] with a terrific, focused, and error-free ten weeks."

Later, Joe delivered the news to the family at his granddaughter Maisy's eighth birthday party. "Hey, I have something that I'd like to announce," he told everyone. "Barack called me and asked me to be vice president." Everyone was sworn to secrecy for two days.

On August 23 at 3 a.m., East Coast time, a text message whipped across the digital landscape: "Barack has chosen Senator Joe Biden to be our VP nominee." The campaign had promised to send the news first to supporters who signed up for text messages, and the list of telephone numbers had quickly grown from the low hundred thousands to more than two million. Through the use of texts, the campaign had found a savvy way to personalize Obama, and now his running mate. Text messages were more intimate than emails, and the writing style was more casual than other forms of communication. In the 3 a.m. text, the informality was evident in the way it referred to Obama: no last name, no title—just Barack.

Beginning with the intimacy of that text introducing their partnership, Barack and Joe established a digital community that took on a life of its own: soon supporters expressed their mania over the duo online and shared photos and memes of the two men during the campaign and into the White House.

By the time Barack mounted the stage later that day in the summer heat outside the Old State Capitol in Springfield, Illinois, the same spot where he had announced his long-shot bid for the presidency on a frigid morning in February eighteen months earlier, some twenty thousand to thirty-five thousand fans, depending on the news report, had flocked to the scene.

In a white shirt and red tie, sleeves rolled up, Obama gave a fifteen-minute portrait of his running mate, hitting all the themes of Joe's story and highlighting what was important to Barack himself and to the campaign. He spoke of the tribulations of Joe's early life. "As a child, he had a terrible stutter," Obama said. "They called him 'Bu-Bu-Biden.' But he picked himself up, and he worked harder than the other guy." He spoke of the Biden family's modest background, of Joe's father working "different jobs, from cleaning boilers to selling cars, sometimes moving in with the in-laws or working weekends to make ends meet."

He spoke of the devastating car accident. "Tragedy tests us," Obama said. "It tests our fortitude and it tests our faith. Here's how Joe Biden responded. He never moved to Washington. Instead, night after night, week after week, year after year, he returned home to Wilmington on a lonely Amtrak train when his Senate business was done. He raised his boys—first as a single dad, then alongside his wonderful wife Jill, who works as a teacher....Out of the heartbreak of that unspeakable accident, he did more than become a senator—he raised a family. That is the measure of the man who is going to be the next vice president of the United States. That is the character of Joe Biden."

He praised Joe's foreign policy expertise, his successes in the Senate, and his judgment, concluding, "Joe Biden won't just make a good vice president—he will make a great vice president." When he called Biden onto the stage, Obama flubbed his line, giving commentators an amusing talking point: "So let me introduce to you," he proclaimed, "the next president—" Then catching himself, he raised his arm, pointed a finger, and tried again: "The next vice president of the United States of America, Joe Biden!"

Joe, also in a white shirt with sleeves rolled up—and a blue tie—was seen far across the platform mounting the stairs as Bruce Springsteen's gravelly voice blasted over loudspeakers singing "The Rising," guitar and drums spilling into the air.

Joe jogged across the stage waving and smiling, and the two men—new teammates—gave each other a full embrace, arms extended over the other's back, the first of what would become their personalized hug, which would be photographed and videoed again and again in jubilant and somber moments and fly across the internet.

From the campaign staffers' perspective, the optics read perfectly: Barack and Joe were comfortable with each other; their warmth projected to the crowd. Advisers wanted to create an image of absolute harmony, especially heading into the rough-and-tumble of the fall campaign.

In the weeks ahead, their contrasting personalities played out in public: Obama, thoughtful and inspiring; Biden, pugnacious and down-to-earth. In this odd pairing, the young man seemed old and predictable, and the old man seemed young and unpredictable. Joe's youthful spirit on the platform in Springfield caught the admonishing eye of Gwen Ifill, host of PBS's *Washington Week*. "I'm not sure that Joe Biden needed to run across the stage," she chided on NBC's *Meet the Press* on Sunday. "I'm not sure that was the best look for a sixty-five-year-old man. But he was enthusiastic."

Campaign advisers clung to the hope that Obama's sobriety would rub off on Biden, and despite Joe's penchant for wandering astray, his performance in Springfield gave them reason for optimism. "Obama and Biden looked great together," Plouffe observed. "It seemed to be a marriage that worked."

In his Springfield speech, Biden played the attack dog, condemning the Bush administration for its mismanagement of the Iraq war and its policies that hurt jobs and senior citizens, and he blasted Republican presidential candidate John McCain for supporting Bush's policies "ninety-five percent of the time."

He set McCain and his policies in direct opposition to Obama. "Ladies and gentlemen, you can't change America," he said, "you can't change America when you know your first four years as president will look exactly like the last eight years of George Bush's presidency."

He praised Obama for his "vision," the "strength of his mind," and the "quality of his heart." He roused the crowd with calls to help the middle class. "Let me tell you something," he declared. Barack Obama has "the courage to make this a better place....There's something about Barack Obama that makes people understand, if they make compromises, they can make things better." The crowd chanted, "Yes we can!" and "Obama!"

Joe showed his age when he brought up his wife, describing her the way men talked about women in another generation and prompting rebukes from some observers. "Ladies and gentlemen," he told the crowd, "my wife, Jill...is drop-dead gorgeous. My wife, Jill, who you'll meet soon, she also has her doctorate degree, which is a problem."

Highlighting that Americans are all vastly different but have a nation in common, Biden played up his and Obama's contrasting life stories. "Folks, Barack and I come from very different places, but we share a common story," he explained. "An American story." Obama, "the son of a single mom," Biden, son of a father who "fell on hard times." And he offered what was to become a common refrain in the storytelling of his life: "My mom and dad raised me to believe—it's a saying, Barack, you heard me say before—my dad repeated it and repeated it. Said, 'Champ, it's not how many times you get knocked down, it's how quickly you get up.' It's how quickly you get up. Ladies and gentlemen, that's your story. That's America's story. It's about if you get up, you can make it."

Corny as the story may have sounded, especially after being repeated so many times over the years, it still resonated with the Springfield crowd, and it was apt imagery that captured the struggles of the two men now wedded in joint battle for the presidency. As if tipping backward into his long-ago youth, Joe unintentionally stumbled over several words in his speech. You could hear a twitch in his voice now and then, the shadow of a stutter, and a couple times he garbled his sounds, calling Barack Obama "Barackal Bama" and "Barack Obaman" and "Barack America."

Later, asked about his history of stuttering, Joe blustered through it. "I don't worry about it," he said, "but every once in a while you catch yourself and you're like, 'Oh, man.' It's not very often, but it's a humble reminder."

Now, in many ways, Joe had to watch his tongue carefully.

On Sunday, Biden went to Mass at the Church of St. Joseph on the Brandywine in Greenville, Delaware. Reverend Joseph Rebman acknowledged the Biden family in the pews toward the back, and Joe looked toward his lap and shook his head modestly. When prayers were requested in his name, he made the sign of the cross.

After church he stayed at home preparing his speech for the Democratic National Convention, which was to open the following day. A gaggle of reporters hung around outside the Biden residence. Secret Service agents, now protecting the site, arranged orange cones and put up plastic mesh fencing.

As expected, Joe fell under sharp media scrutiny, some of it silly. A *Politico* reporter surveyed stylists and hair transplant surgeons to explore whether Biden had fought baldness in the modern way: by having follicles from the back of his head grafted onto empty patches in front. The paper drew on a *Washington Post* article from 1987 that asked Biden directly whether he had had hair plugs. "Guess," Joe teased the reporter. "I've got to keep some mystery in my life."

*Politico*, for its part, believed it had solved the mystery: several hair specialists agreed that Biden had had work done to enhance his hairline, and over the years its appearance had improved. "When he had darker hair it was pretty obvious, he had larger plugs," said Dr. Michael Beehner, medical director of the Saratoga Hair Transplant Center in New York. "With the lightening of his hair, it looks much, much better now."

Another famed senator, Republican Strom Thurmond of South Carolina, had flaming orange plugs until his death in 2003. *Politico* recounted Biden's possibly revelatory remarks to Thurmond quite a few years earlier. When Biden attended Thurmond's black-tie ninetieth birthday party in 1993 at the JW Marriott in Washington, he hinted to the aging senator about his own hair transplants. "Let me tell you, I resent any reference to your hair," Joe quipped. "You've been an inspiration to me in so many ways."

The media also noticed that Biden wore no wedding band. The day after he joined the Democratic ticket, a *New York Daily News* headline shouted a provocative question: "YO, JOE, WHY NO WED RING?" Having inspected photos of Biden, the *Daily News* insisted that the new vice-presidential nominee went ringless. And it scolded the candidate: "Wedding rings are nearly mandatory among Washington's political class. It's one of the few areas where Vice President Cheney and John Kerry actually agree....Even Bill Clinton regularly wore the jewelry." The significance of its big discovery, the paper insisted, was this: "It remains to be seen if flouting that old tradition will raise eyebrows on the campaign."

The modern president–vice president relationship, David Axelrod observed, is "a little like a shotgun wedding. Sometimes they take, and sometimes they don't." As if Barack and Joe were sudden newlyweds, pundits speculated whether these two contrasting personalities, still fairly unfamiliar to each other, would meld.

*Washington Post* political reporter Dan Balz wondered how Obama and Biden would reconcile their opposing styles. "Biden's persona and political personality are in many ways the antithesis of Obama's," he wrote. He noted Obama's soaring rhetoric and Biden's blunt and plainspoken language. "Obama may seem aloof," Balz said. "Biden is always in your face. Obama offers high-altitude passion; Biden's is ground-level. Who else but Biden might have introduced his wife to the American people as 'drop-dead gorgeous'?"

The *New York Times*'s John Broder watched the unveiling in Springfield and was stumped: "It was hard to tell from their first appearance as running mates what kind of partners Senator Barack Obama and Senator Joseph R. Biden Jr. will be." Obama's speech about Biden was respectful of Joe's public service and family travails, Broder wrote. "But there were few notes of personal connection," he added, "and no anecdotes about moments they had shared in the Senate or on the campaign trail."

By most measures, the Springfield rally amounted to the standard political fare of a first joint appearance by a presidential nominee and his untested running mate.

"Chemistry?" Broder wondered. "We'll see."

# SIX

# Batman and Robin

On Friday, August 29, the day after the Democratic National Convention, Barack and Joe were headed for a weekend campaign swing together, their first, through the Rust Belt states when David Axelrod delivered some startling news. The chief strategist entered the front cabin of the campaign plane just before takeoff to announce that John McCain had chosen his running mate: the largely unknown governor of Alaska, Sarah Palin.

Obama quickly sized up the McCain strategy, surmising that a woman on the ticket was intended to counter the Obama campaign's message of change. But he wondered how a novice like her thrown into the roughest national campaign of all—the presidential race—would handle the heat.

"I guess the best way to blunt the 'change thing' is to put a woman on the ticket," Obama said. "It'll create some buzz. I get it."

To Biden, the pick was mystifying. The name meant nothing to him.

"Who's Sarah Palin?" he asked.

As a curious nation swarmed around Sarah Palin, Obama and Biden swept through Pennsylvania, Indiana, Michigan, and Ohio on a bus tour. The convention had given the campaign some momentum and a decided jump in the polls. Before the Democrats had gathered in Denver to nominate Obama, he'd been running in a dead heat with McCain. Afterward, a national poll of likely voters gave Obama-Biden a lead of 49 percent to 41 percent.

In the Rust Belt states, Biden served as the voice of the middle class, and he sprinkled the campaign trail with his easygoing levity, in contrast to Obama's more buttoned-up formality. When the duo arrived at a Pittsburgh hotel on Friday night, they were met by Pittsburgh Steelers coach Mike Tomlin.

"Hey, coach," Biden called out. "I'm Joe Biden. I'm second string."

The nominees traveled the countryside in separate luxury coaches but hung out together at stops between rallies. On Saturday morning they met up for breakfast in a booth at the Yankee Kitchen in Boardman, Ohio, Obama taking two eggs over medium, a waffle, and bacon, and Biden going with French toast. Later, hopping out at a produce stand along the road, the nominees bought sweet corn to take home. Before Barack could dig in his pocket, Joe whipped out a twenty-dollar bill to pay for both their purchases. "I'm loaded," he crowed. "I'm loaded."

Before a town hall meeting in Toledo on Sunday, Obama whipped through a rope line of supporters and landed onstage well ahead of his running mate, who took his time, as one report had it, "posing for pictures with police officers and embracing elderly women." Finally at the podium, Joe was rousing the crowd when a woman shouted, "You are gorgeous!"

"I haven't heard that in a long, long, long time," Joe shot back. "And hanging around this lean, young-looking guy is making me feel pretty old, you know what I mean?"

Obama laughed along with the audience. Joe was proving to be everything he was meant to be: down-to-earth, fun, and a draw to essential middle-class voters. When Obama stepped to the podium, another woman called out for Joe, prompting Barack to crack, "See, she thinks you're gorgeous, too."

Joe the comic was loosening up Barack the straight man. Their differences were turning into an advantage. The men complemented each other: when side by side, both were elevated. Especially attentive to the boss, Biden sometimes plucked loose threads off Obama's jacket, and the two men weren't shy about backslapping and embracing. They consulted, collaborated, and laughed together. A senior Obama aide, Linda Douglass, noted that she and Obama both were surprised by how quickly the nominees found real rapport. With Biden, Douglass said, the usual awkwardness of a political marriage was absent. "He's just this cheerful presence in the group," she explained.

The candidates and their wives, who were also on the campaign swing, had a comfortable breakfast together on Saturday. Biden's grandchildren and Obama's daughters already had become friendly and had a sleepover. The families, Barack told the *Washington Post*'s Shailagh Murray, "have just really hit it off." Murray, riding through the Rust Belt with the campaign, witnessed the early bonding of Barack and Joe. She noted that Obama had chosen Biden for the obvious campaign-worthy reasons. "But," she concluded, "it was clear that they also possessed a more elusive political quality: chemistry."

Close to the midnight hour on the first night of the Democratic National Convention, CBS had flashed a headline: "CBS News Election '08 Update." And a musical motif announced breaking news: "In a new CBS poll," the voiceover said, "voters were asked which nickname they preferred for the Democratic ticket of Obama-Biden."

Viewers then saw an outdoor campaign shot of a smiling Barack Obama, no jacket, in a starched white shirt and red tie, and a smiling Joe Biden, no jacket, in a starched white shirt and blue tie. Two buddies clapping. Two men with excellent smiles.

The poll results came on the screen, showing the preferences for an Obama-Biden nickname:

Joebama: 58 percent.

Obiden: 39 percent.

And in last place with just 3 percent, Jidenamackojoba.

It was, of course, a faux poll, a comic bit from *The Late Show with David Letterman*. But the nicknaming stunt blending the two names—scarcely imaginable in prior elections—already hinted at the merging of Barack and Joe into a unique political team.

For the next two months, the candidates hit the hustings largely on their own. Without Obama's restraining hand, Biden lost discipline. Less than two weeks after his bonding Rust Belt tour with Obama, he took the stage at a town hall forum in Nashua, New Hampshire. When a local resident said he was glad Biden was the vice-presidential nominee—and not Hillary Clinton—Biden offered a generous rebuttal in support of his friend.

"Hillary Clinton's as qualified or more qualified than I am to be vice president of the United States of America. Let's get that straight," Biden began. "Let's get that straight. She is qualified to be president of the United States of America."

Never mind that he meant to show how much he favored women achieving the highest office in the land. Never mind that he was attempting to be gracious. It all spiraled in the wrong direction.

Susan Estrich, a Democratic operative who had supported Clinton in the primaries, observed in a newspaper column what Obama and his coterie knew all along: "Sometimes Joe Biden, bless his good intentions, doesn't know when to stop."

And Joe rolled along in his nod to Hillary. "She's easily qualified to be vice president of the United States of America. And quite frankly," he insisted, "it might have been a better pick than me."

Humble, self-effacing Joe didn't reckon what those last few words implied about Obama. The McCain campaign quickly let him know in an ad rushed into circulation. Suggesting that Hillary might have been better for the ticket not only threw into question Obama's decision on his vice president—traditionally seen as the most important prepresidential move a candidate makes—but also cast doubt on Obama's commitment to women's aspirations for higher office, and that coming not long after McCain selected Sarah Palin as his running mate. A *Washington Post*/ABC News poll showed that Palin was having an effect: white women voters were fleeing Obama. They now favored McCain 53 percent to 41 percent. Three weeks earlier, Obama had had the lead with that segment of the electorate, 50 percent to 42 percent.

On other occasions, Biden slipped on a verbal banana peel. During a campaign stop in Columbia, Missouri, he called out to a state senator, Chuck Graham, in the crowd. Biden hadn't ever met Graham and only knew he was there from a reference sheet he consulted at the podium at the start of his talk.

"Chuck, stand up. Chuck, let 'em see you," Biden shouted.

Then, looking out and finding Chuck in a wheelchair, Joe realized his mistake. "Oh, God love ya. What am I talking about?" The thirty-three-year-old state senator had been a paraplegic since an auto accident at age sixteen.

Embarrassed, Joe quickly pivoted. "I tell you what, you're making everybody else stand up, though, pal," he said to Graham. "I tell you what," he instructed the crowd, "stand up for Chuck." And as people rose to their feet and cheered, Joe left the podium and went down into the crowd and shook Graham's hand, saying, "You can tell I'm new. Good to see you, buddy."

Soon after that, on Monday, September 22, Biden stumbled in an interview with Katie Couric on *CBS Evening News*. Discussing the unfolding financial crisis, Joe reached into history to describe how a president should address such an emergency. "When the stock market crashed," he said, "Franklin Roosevelt got on television." Problem was, the stock market crashed in 1929, before Roosevelt was president, and Americans at that time didn't have televisions but relied on radio as a mass communication medium.

To Obama's chagrin, Biden was living up to his billing as "a human verbal wrecking crew," in the words of the *New York Times*.

Usually even-keeled, Obama got annoyed when Joe spoke out of turn on policy positions without coordinating with the campaign; in late September Biden contradicted Obama's stance on an initial $85 billion government bailout of the giant financial and insurance company American International Group, forcing the campaign to clarify. By this time, the Republican National Committee had begun keeping track of Joe's flubs with a Biden Gaffe Clock.

But Obama still stood by his man. Conveniently, the Biden miscues didn't appear to be hurting the campaign. Toward the end of September, a *Washington Post*/ABC News poll found that voters favored Obama over McCain 52 percent to 43 percent, a strong turnaround from the dead heat two weeks earlier. Appearing on NBC's *Today Show*, Obama had no regrets about Biden as his vice-presidential pick: "I am very proud of the choice that I made."

But with a little more than two weeks until election day, Biden exhausted Obama's goodwill when he inadvertently hit the candidate in a vulnerable spot with a riff at a San Francisco fund-raiser. "Mark my words," Biden warned the audience, "within the first six months of this administration, if we win...we're going to face a major international challenge. Because they're going to want to test him, just like they did young John Kennedy. They're going to want to test him. And they're going to find out this guy's got steel in his spine."

What was meant as a solid pat on the back for Obama's toughness gave a sudden opening to the opposition. The McCain campaign rushed out an ad meant to frighten Americans into believing Obama was too inexperienced for the presidency. Biden's gift came as a CNN poll revealed that Obama's lead over McCain was expanding: voters favored Obama 51 percent to 42 percent, up two percentage points from a similar poll just the day before; but, significantly, 7 percent of those surveyed were still unsure who their choice was. In the ad, spooky music played over images of ISIS fighters marching through the streets as Joe Biden's voice reverberated in scary tones, as if he were speaking while hiding in a bunker: "Mark my words..."

On CNN's *Anderson Cooper 360°*, pundits pounded at the Biden slipup, and the show played a campaign clip of McCain setting his experience against Obama's. "Senator Biden referred to how Jack Kennedy was tested in the Cuban missile crisis," McCain began. "My friends, I have a little personal experience in that. I was onboard the USS *Enterprise*. I sat in the cockpit of the flight deck of the USS *Enterprise* off of Cuba. I had a target. My friends, you know how close we came to a nuclear war. America will not have a president who needs to be tested. I've been tested, my friends, and Senator Obama hasn't."

When Obama got on his nightly conference call with his advisers, the typically cool character was smoking mad—angrier than his team had ever seen him. "How many times is Biden gonna say something stupid?" he seethed. Obama was already so fed up that he'd exiled Biden from the campaign's nightly call, as John Heilemann and Mark Halperin reported in their book *Game Change*. "Joe and Obama barely spoke by phone, rarely campaigned together," they wrote. By now, the two teams—Obama's and Biden's—had plenty of gripes about each other. Joe wasn't happy with his treatment. On this night's call, Obama turned his attention on Biden's chief of staff, Patti Solis Doyle, who was sitting in. "Listen," he said, his composure returning. "Tell Joe I love him. I love him. But he can't be doing this."

The love, at this point, was conditional. Joe needed to acknowledge his bad behavior and apologize immediately. But no apology came, which rankled Obama. For a couple of days Obama held his fire, and when he finally phoned Biden, he let him know just how pissed off he was. Biden's job was to protect Barack, lift him, and keep the Republican hounds at bay, and he had failed at the task. For his part, Biden was miffed at the dressing-down, believing that no one seriously was able to dispute what he said—presidents often got challenged very early in office. And still Joe offered no apology.

In public, Obama played down the gaffe, but his downcast eyes and the tightness of his face showed the strain. Speaking to reporters in Richmond, Virginia, a grim Obama said, "Look, as I said before, you know, I think that Joe sometimes engages in rhetorical flourishes." He stressed that Biden's "core point" was that the next administration would be tested and it would have to send "a clear signal to the rest of the world that we are no longer about bluster and unilateralism and ideology."

By the end of the week, Joe's pratfall had become a comedy shtick for late-night television. On *Saturday Night Live* Joe Biden, portrayed by Jason Sudeikis, and Congressman John Murtha, played by Darrell Hammond, spoke to voters at an outdoor rally in Johnstown, Pennsylvania. In the skit, Biden reiterated in the most bombastic fashion his fear that Obama would be tested soon after assuming office.

"Now in this crisis," Sudeikis said as Biden, "he will have to make decisions, decisions that…ah, at first, well…they may seem to the casual observer a little ill considered. Our military may invade Pakistan, or surrender to the Chinese. We may sell Hawaii to Saudi Arabia, or just destroy it, so it can't fall to North Korean hands. But just reserve your judgment. We know what we're doing."

Worried about further gaffes as the election neared, the Obama team largely sidelined Biden from the national press and from high-profile locations. He campaigned in small towns in battleground states, doing "an estimated 200 interviews with local television and radio stations," according to the *New York Times*. He didn't hold press conferences or speak directly to reporters, and he avoided them on his campaign plane. Biden "curbed his noted volubility—or, rather, had it curbed for him by his masters at Obama headquarters, in Chicago," the *Times* reported. He raced "through his thoroughly vetted stump speech, sometimes delivering it in as few as 15 minutes—a mere throat clearing for the old Joe Biden." At his appearances, he read "from a teleprompter, altering the text only slightly to mention the place where he is speaking and the local dignitaries who are present."

Through the end of the campaign, Biden largely behaved, and on the eve of the election, Obama's prospects looked bright. The *Washington Post*'s Perry Bacon, who was following Biden on the hustings, noticed that at the last minute Biden was returning to form. "Now that the end is near, you know, Biden seems a little looser," Bacon explained on NPR's news-talk program *Tell Me More*. At a campaign stop, Biden broke from his teleprompter and joked a bit, and rambled, and resisted going back to the prepared speech, saying, "Let me just talk for a little while." Bacon observed, "So it's a little more relaxed since there's only a day left."

On that last day of campaigning, Joe suddenly became newly accessible to national reporters, speaking with them for twenty minutes aboard his flight into Columbus, Ohio. He had a superstition about hinting at victory, but he broke with it, telling reporters: "There's something in the air, guys."

Before election day, Obama and Biden had managed to smooth out their tiff over Joe's remark about Barack's inexperience. Biden's aide Antony Blinken had discovered that Barack was still irritated—not so much by Biden's loose tongue but rather his still-missing apology. Their conversations had become less frequent; a chill had invaded the warmth between the two men. At Blinken's urging, Biden got Obama on the phone and acknowledged he had messed up. He offered his apology. As they spoke, the two men realized they had missed talking with each other, and they stayed on the line for some time. The wounds were healed, and both men were energized by what looked like victory on the horizon.

With the White House seeming within reach, Barack and Joe were learning how to navigate their way to a strong partnership. For Joe, it was a matter of getting used to an entirely new responsibility: he was no longer his own boss. As a senator he'd had maximum personal freedom; he was in charge of his own life. Things were different now. He understood the inherent tug-of-war between a president and vice president and was coming to terms with his role as number two. If he were to ensure a substantial leadership role for himself, he had to accept a key dynamic of a White House relationship. As Biden later observed of the vice presidency, "The actual power of the office is reflective; it depends almost entirely on the trust and confidence of the president."

If Obama got into a snit now and then over his running mate, he also knew they were, the two of them, a perfectly matched odd couple. He was the wonk, the straight man to Biden, his endlessly entertaining sidekick. Even when Joe messed up, crowds still loved him. By the end of the campaign, 60 percent of respondents in a national poll viewed Biden favorably, according to the Pew Research Center.

With his perfectly calibrated charm, Joe knew exactly how to play to an audience. On a stop in the final week, he showed up a little late to a Saturday morning rally in Evansville, Indiana, with a solid excuse. He told the crowd that his wife had been out jogging when she happened to speak to a nun who told her about a planned special Mass that morning. Joe concluded the anecdote by saying that no doubt later he was going to be on the phone telling his ninety-one-year-old mother how the Mass was. And all at once, Joe had performed a little magic to enrapture and win over both older voters and Catholics in the audience.

His political alchemy was on display at another stop, in Titusville, Florida, where a father introduced Joe to his one-year-old son, who had the same name as Biden's son Hunter. It so happened that Biden's son was traveling with the campaign. So Joe hopped back to the motorcade and extracted his Hunter and introduced him to his toddler namesake. "Hey, Hunter," Joe said. "Meet Hunter." The father of the little Hunter burst into a glowing smile.

Obama was not as well practiced in these mysterious arts, and they did not come naturally to him the way they did to Joe. Self-controlled and circumspect, Barack spent too much time within his own head. *Los Angeles Times* reporter Peter Nicholas covered the presidential race for a year and a half. Describing Obama toward the end of the campaign, he used words like "discipline" and "steely perseverance." He added that at casual, potentially revealing moments, when tape recorders flipped on, Obama would become "more cautious."

Over the many months, Nicholas wrote, he'd "watched Obama demonstrate a soccer kick to his daughter in Chicago; devour a cheesesteak in Philly; navigate a roller rink in Indiana; drive a bumper car; and catapult 125 feet in the air on an amusement-park ride called 'Big Ben.' He has done it all with dogged professionalism but with little show of spontaneity." Unlike Biden, Obama just wasn't terribly fun. "One of the striking ironies," Nicholas observed, "is that a man who draws tens of thousands of people to rallies, whose charisma is likened to that of John F. Kennedy, can be sort of a bore."

Certainly Obama had his own charms: he offered high-minded inspiration. He was the embodiment of a political moment America had never experienced. When he spoke before a throng in his slow, purposeful way, his every word was weighed against history, and his style was utter cool, an attitude that said, "Come with me to a place you've never been." Having watched the man perform, essayist Christopher Hitchens later captured the special Obama flair. Barack in motion displayed, in Hitchens's words, "something lithe and laid-back, agile but rested, cool but not *too* cool."

Biden, too, was cool, in an older, devil-may-care way, the chum behind the aviator sunglasses. Together, Barack and Joe filled in the spaces that were missing in the other man and created something bigger than their separate parts: young and old, black and white, they melded into a whole that was brainy, goofy, standoffish, gregarious.

Taking their places in American culture, Barack and Joe were real and imaginary all at once. America had long blurred the worlds of politics and entertainment, and to many people these two stars were the latest in a long line of famed duos. America had a weakness for buddy teams. Felix and Oscar. Bert and Ernie. Buzz and Woody. To many Democrats, Barack and Joe may even have possessed a trace of Batman and Robin, swooping in to save the world from the Republicans.

On election day, CNN's *American Morning* was live as polling stations across the country were opening and voters were descending. The network zeroed in on two locations of particular interest: Barack Obama's precinct in Chicago, Illinois, and Joe Biden's in Wilmington, Delaware. As Obama showed up at the Beulah Shoesmith Elementary School in Hyde Park with Michelle and Malia and Sasha, coanchor John Roberts told viewers that second graders had put up a welcome sign for the family in the school's front window. And the gym, where the voting took place, had been painted and the floor sanded and polished for the first time since the 1950s. Then CNN ran a clip from *The Late Show with David Letterman* from the previous night. "They're saying now that weather could play a huge part in the campaign," Letterman riffed in his monologue. "Did you realize that? Weather could be a huge factor? For example, in order for McCain to win tomorrow, hell has to freeze over. I didn't realize that."

Up and out early, Barack and Michelle were among the first to cast votes at Shoesmith Elementary, in side-by-side booths. Ten-year-old Malia and seven-year-old Sasha, one smiling, the other a little impatient, stood by waiting.

Emerging after about ten minutes, Barack handed his ballot to a poll worker and kissed her on the cheek. Then came the final moment of his long run for the presidency: after twenty-one months of campaigning, Barack watched as his ballot disappeared into an optical scanning machine for tabulation. A small crowd of voters, their cell-phone cameras raised, observed the ritual in silence, then burst into applause. Displaying his validation slip—and breaking into a smile—Barack announced, "I voted."

Across the country, Joe rolled up to his polling place, the Tatnall School, near his home in Greenville, Delaware, a little after 9 a.m. He was accompanied by his wife, daughter, and ninety-one-year-old mother. Unlike Barack, who declared "I voted" in the manner of the good boy proud of his civic accomplishment, Joe played the wise-cracker. Leaving the polling station, he took his mother's hand and quipped, "All right, Mom, don't tell them who you voted for."

After voting, Barack climbed aboard his campaign plane for a last stop to cheer on volunteers working a phone bank for him at a United Auto Workers hall in Indianapolis, Indiana, a state no Democratic presidential candidate had won since 1964. The plane, which had logged 76,820 miles, then brought Barack back to Chicago to wait out the vote and to engage in his election-day tradition: a game of basketball.

With friends and staff he shot a pickup game at Attack Athletics on the West Side. Basketball was a symbol of pure competition—one side wins, the other loses, and no amount of pontificating or trash-talking changed the outcome; a small, closed session on the court served as a proxy competition to help ease the anxiety playing out on the election battlefield throughout the country.

Superstition also hovered over the hardwood. Barack had made a game of hoops an election-day ritual after he played during the Iowa caucuses and won the vote there. He didn't play during the balloting in the New Hampshire primary, and he lost to Hillary Clinton. So hoops on election day, though full of mundane sweat and physicality, took on astral significance. "Hopefully I don't break my nose for the big night or get an elbow in the teeth," he joked to syndicated radio host Ryan Seacrest.

After placing his vote, Joe left Delaware for a stop in the red state of Virginia. Then he went on to Chicago, where he spent the afternoon doing last-minute campaign interviews targeted at the battleground states of Colorado, Florida, Missouri, Nevada, North Carolina, Pennsylvania, Ohio, and Nebraska.

In the evening, Joe and Barack could do nothing more. In separate suites at the Hyatt Regency Chicago, they watched election returns with their families and staff. It was a cool and windy Chicago night. Throngs from all directions streamed toward Grant Park, where Obama was to appear after America chose its new president. The people kept coming; some estimates put the crowd at more than two hundred thousand.

In the Obama suite on the nineteenth floor, Barack sat on the edge of the couch, a tense eye on the television screen, his cupped hands almost in a prayer pose pressed against his mouth and chin. A burst of hope came early in the evening when the NBC affiliate playing in the suite announced after eight o'clock that Obama had taken the battleground state of Pennsylvania. Cheers broke out. An hour later, when Obama won Ohio, another battleground state, the room erupted, and the nervous anticipation notched up.

By 11 p.m. (East Coast time), after polls closed in California, Oregon, and Washington, history was made: Obama topped the threshold of 270 electoral votes. As the television networks announced the news, pandemonium broke out in Grant Park: people were cheering and screaming, leaping into the air, clapping and crying, waving American flags, and chanting, "Yes we can!"

In Obama's suite, Michelle's mother, Marian Robinson, then seventy-one years old, was sitting alone on the couch as the final results came in. "I sat next to her," Obama recalled, "and I grabbed her hand, and we held hands just as it was announced that the projections were I was going to win." Obama felt the magnitude of the moment through her eyes. "I could tell she just seemed like it wasn't clear how all this had happened." Holding her hand, he asked, "'How are you feeling?' And she said, 'Well, it's just a little overwhelming, isn't it?'"

Obama wondered what she was thinking: this moment must have

been even more profound for her than it was for him or Michelle. Marian Robinson, a former secretary who'd grown up on the South Side of Chicago, had lived through a time of stark segregation in Chicago when, whatever her talents were or the talents of others in her family, as Obama recalled, "there were always barriers, there were always limits, to what they could achieve." And now she sat watching as her son-in-law was elected president of the United States. "This moment [was] something she might not have ever imagined possible.... Her daughter was going to be the next first lady of the United States."

For the Obamas' daughter Malia, the moment was celebrated as it should have been for a ten-year-old. No matter that America had just confirmed its highest values. With a carefree bounce, Malia popped up and fist-bumped her dad, the president-elect of the United States.

The victory was impressive. With 53 percent of the popular vote, Obama had captured a larger percentage of the electorate than any Democrat since Lyndon Johnson in 1964, when he got 61 percent of the vote; but LBJ had ridden a wave of sympathy among a still-shocked nation in the wake of President John Kennedy's assassination a year earlier. Besides sweeping the blue states, Obama took the red states of Indiana, Colorado, North Carolina, and Virginia.

When Joe and Jill Biden walked into the hotel suite, Jill and Michelle embraced, and Joe made his way around the room, leaning down to close-talk with Sasha. Barack and Joe took a quiet moment alone, talking almost nose to nose in hushed tones while shaking hands. With familiarity and fondness, Barack placed a hand on Joe's shoulder. Their journey had begun.

Just before midnight, Obama stepped out onto the stage at Grant Park before a huge, jubilant crowd. At his side were Michelle, Sasha, and Malia. They waved and listened to the cheering and chanting; some people in the crowd had tears streaming down their faces. The new first family soaked in the love for several minutes, and then Obama bent over to chat with his kids. He kissed his daughters and his wife, and they strode off as the president-elect walked to the podium.

"Hello, Chicago!" he called out, and a roar went up. Then, in a lilting voice, he went on: "If there..." he began, then paused to set a slow-paced delivery, "...is anyone out there...who still doubts that America's a place where all things are possible...who still wonders if the dream of our founders is alive in our time...who still questions the power of our democracy...tonight is your answer." Another roar.

He praised his opponent, John McCain, and the crowd respectfully applauded and cheered the Arizona senator. Obama acknowledged McCain's long, hard-fought campaign. "He's fought even longer and harder for the country that he loves," Obama said. "He has endured sacrifices for America that most of us cannot begin to imagine. We are better off for the service rendered by this brave and selfless leader."

And he thanked many people: his family, his campaign aides, his strategists. First on his list was his vice president. "I want to thank my partner in this journey, a man who campaigned from his heart and spoke for the men and women he grew up with on the streets of Scranton and rode with on the train home to Delaware: the vice president–elect of the United States, Joe Biden." Cheers again.

On the television networks, the pundits remarked on Biden's long road to this moment placing him a heartbeat from the presidency. As NBC's Chuck Todd put it, "Joe Biden, thirty years ago, was the Barack Obama of the Democratic Party....He's probably feeling real vindication tonight. This is a guy whose career had a ton of ups and downs, and he's now vice president–elect."

The historic moment inspired a sense of awe. Former *NBC Nightly News* anchor Tom Brokaw chimed in: "I don't think we've fully caught up to the magnitude of what happened here tonight." He compared the excitement of Obama's victory across the nation to the election of John F. Kennedy, when many accomplished people were inspired to join the administration. "People are going to want to go to Washington and go to work for the government." The Obama victory was a clarion call to African Americans to take a larger role in shaping American society. "They've felt shut out," Brokaw observed. "We're in for something that we don't know yet how vast it will be, but it's going to be a profound change."

Historian Doris Kearns Goodwin, also on the NBC roundtable, sought a historical parallel in Franklin Roosevelt. "Well, you know, just listening to Barack's acceptance speech, it makes you feel that this may be one of those moments, like FDR talked about, a rendezvous with destiny, because he's really been able to make people around the country feel part of his victory," she observed. "Politics has become exciting again, it's become fun, it's become a sport again. And that's an extraordinary power for him."

Barack as president was the nation's chief messenger of hope and change. But in a way rarely seen in American history the new president had a sidekick who brought amusement, warmth, and authenticity to his administration. Joe provided the fun that Goodwin had alluded to, while his passion and experience added to Obama's sense of seriousness and purpose.

The television talking heads already sensed there was something personal in the way America watched Barack and Joe. "Look at these two families," NBC's Brian Williams said during the coverage that night, "the Obamas and the Bidens." This was a president and vice president whose families clicked, and they weren't shy about flaunting it.

Years later, reminiscing, Joe recalled that on the night of the Democratic convention, his granddaughter Finnegan, then ten years old, came to him with an idea. His kids and grandkids and Obama's daughters were all staying in the same hotel, and Finnegan wanted to have the beds taken out of one of the rooms so all the younger kids could sleep together in sleeping bags in one place. If Joe had had any doubt about having joined the ticket, it was washed away in that moment.

When he went to the room later, opened the door, and "saw them cuddled together," he said, "I knew this was the right decision."

On another occasion, after the kids had spent a lot of time together, Joe observed, "My grandchildren and [Barack's] children are each other's best friends now. They vacation together." Joe thought back to his earliest days with Barack: "I warned the president that when he got me, he got the whole family. He thought that I was kidding."

# SEVEN

# Cheney's Dark Shadow

The twelve cupcakes with candles were laid out in the Obama transition office in Chicago. By now, November 19, the president-elect and his staff were deep into putting together a White House team. So many slots to fill and so many consultations to conduct. Who was going to sit around the table at Obama's Cabinet meetings? Who would run interference between the press and the White House? Who would be the liaison with the business community? Who would look after American interests around the world from our embassies?

In the midst of all this feverish planning, Wednesday came to a halt shortly after midday and the staff gathered around the cupcakes. Led by Barack, everyone belted out "Happy Birthday" to one key member of the advisory group, Joe Biden. The following day, November 20, Joe would turn sixty-six.

Barack gestured toward the treats and quipped to his sometimes impulsive, even childlike, vice president–elect: "You're twelve years old." Joe, recognizing the reality of age pulling on him, joked: "Maybe in dog years." The president-elect's gifts to the birthday boy were aimed, with a bit of humor, at immersing Joe in the Chicago world that Barack inhabited: a White Sox cap, a Bears cap, and a bucket of popcorn from Garrett, a popular Chicago popcorn shop.

Among the weighty matters under discussion during the transition was the role Biden was to play in the Obama White House. Preliminary discussions during the vice-presidential selection process and afterward had laid out the contours of Joe's wishes and Barack's needs. And the two men largely saw eye to eye. Now it was time to fine-tune and set in motion the Obama-Biden working partnership.

In carving out his role, Joe had a mentor. Thirty-two years earlier, Walter Mondale had inaugurated a new era in the duties and power of the vice president. His vision for the office redefined the role. It was implemented by subsequent vice presidents to varying degrees and with varying success, depending largely on the characters and ambitions of the two men at the top.

Like Biden, Mondale came to the vice presidency after years as a Washington insider and US senator. Like Obama, the president Mondale served was a newcomer to Washington with minimal experience negotiating with Congress. To effectively assist President Jimmy Carter, Mondale believed he needed full intelligence briefings, the authority to command cooperation and candor from others throughout the executive branch, including the Cabinet, a strong relationship with the White House staff, a seat in key advisory groups, and private time with the president, at least thirty minutes each week, particularly when major decisions were under consideration.

Carter, a former governor of Georgia, recognized his own limitations and Mondale's expertise, and he eagerly signed on. After the victory of the Carter-Mondale ticket in November 1976, the vice president–elect outlined his thoughts in an eleven-page memo the following month. Mondale wanted to be a voice unlike any other in the administration, fully informed and unafraid to speak tough truths.

"I believe the most important contribution I can make," Mondale wrote in the memo, "is to serve as a general adviser to you." He believed he offered the president something no one else could: he was the only elected official in the nation who was not beholden to special obligations or institutional interests; his sole occupation was to serve the president and the interests of the entire nation. Because others pushed their own aims, or the ambitions of their departments or constituencies, the president often heard advice that was not impartial or comprehensive. Mondale wished to change that.

"The biggest single problem of our recent administrations," he observed, "has been the failure of the President to be exposed to independent analysis not conditioned by what it is thought he wants to hear or often what others want him to hear." In the memo, Mondale informed Carter he did not want to shield him "from points of view that you should hear."

Two weeks after Mondale presented the memo, signs began to appear publicly that this vice president was indeed breaking from the office's tradition of powerlessness. At a televised press conference at an agricultural center just outside of his hometown of Plains, Georgia, President-Elect Carter unveiled his final Cabinet appointments, with Mondale looking on. Carter told reporters that he intended to deploy Mondale as his "top staff person" with "unprecedented" responsibilities. He also revealed that Mondale would have an office in the West Wing of the White House "very near to mine."

In the past, vice presidents had been relegated to space in the Executive Office Building just west of the White House—the physical separation underscoring the vice president's traditional occupation as an outcast from the center of power. "The big breakthrough was, of course, locating the vice president in the West Wing," Mondale observed years later. "I used to say going to the EOB building was like going to Baltimore."

Two days after the press conference, the *New York Times* reported that Mondale had an "important impact" on the selection of Cabinet members and suggested that "he may become the most influential Vice President in the history of the modern presidency." In securing his powerful role, Mondale worked hard to ensure that Carter trusted him and did not feel any political threat from him.

Like Obama and Biden thirty years later, Carter and Mondale also benefited from strong personal chemistry, a crucial ingredient that Carter looked for in the partnership. As one insider told the *New York Times*, "Jimmy is always saying how close he feels to Fritz," the nickname often attached to Mondale.

When Joe Biden decided to accept Obama's offer to join the ticket, he immediately got on the phone. "The first person I called was Fritz," Biden told a crowd at George Washington University in 2015 during a forum on "The Mondale Vice Presidency and Its Legacy." Biden admired Mondale and the vision he created for the office, and he wanted to know how he'd worked it out with President Carter. From those discussions and from the memo that Mondale shared with Biden, Joe shaped his own approach to the vice presidency largely along the prototype Fritz had created. But Joe also understood the constraints of the office, as he noted at the forum: "The vice presidency is totally a reflection of the president. There is no inherent power, none, zero. And it completely, thoroughly, totally depends on your relationship with the president."

As Biden discussed his expectations with Obama, it became clear that the Mondale model appealed to both men. Biden wanted to speak his mind honestly to the president, and the president needed to hear from someone who had the courage to do just that. Biden asked to join Obama's intelligence briefings, to have scheduled time with the president each week, and to be granted authority to work among competing groups in the White House; he wanted to be included in the paper flow, to be allowed to speak his mind and spur debate in meetings, and to be the last person in the room after advisory sessions.

Obama was fully on board. "The President likes to listen to argument and decide," said Ron Klain, Biden's first chief of staff. "It helps the President get to better decisions if the Vice President is stirring things up and he is hearing different points of view."

While Biden and Obama met regularly during the transition period to discuss personnel and major administration initiatives, Joe stayed largely out of the public spotlight, prompting speculation in the media. "And then there's the incredible shrinking vice president–elect, Joe Biden," *Washington Post* columnist David Ignatius wrote. "Where is he these days? Do they have him in a box?"

In December, Biden reappeared in an interview from his home in Wilmington, Delaware, on ABC's Sunday morning show, *This Week with George Stephanopoulos*. "You know, you've been fairly invisible since the election," Stephanopoulos reminded Biden. "Can you lift the veil a little bit on what else you've been doing during the transition?"

Joe took the opportunity to lay out how his role as vice president was taking shape. With his usual enthusiasm, he told Stephanopoulos that his job was to give the president "the best, sagest, most accurate, most insightful advice and recommendations" he could so the president could make "the very, very important decisions that have to be made." He recounted for television viewers his initial discussion with Obama during the campaign, a meeting that Joe claimed lasted three and a half hours. "I want a commitment from you," he'd told then-candidate Obama, "that on every important decision you'll make, every critical decision, economic and political, as well as foreign policy, I'll get to be in the room."

Stephanopoulos asked, "Has he kept it?"

"He's kept it," Joe affirmed. "Every single solitary appointment he's made thus far, I've been in the room, and the recommendations I have made in most cases coincidentally have been the recommendations he's picked. Not because I made them but because we think a lot alike."

Joe also told Stephanopoulos where he drew the line on the job. "I don't want to be the guy that goes out and has a specific assignment," he said, referring to Vice President Al Gore's task of reinventing government.

To highlight the breadth of his work, Biden then foreshadowed an Obama announcement coming later in the day. "I have been asked—the president is going to announce today the formation...of a middle-class task force that I will chair."

Picking up on the inconsistency, Stephanopoulos asked, "So isn't that a specific responsibility?"

"Well," Biden offered, "it is a specific responsibility in terms of—but it is—it is a discrete job that's going to last for only a certain period of time."

Though a generalist, Biden did take on leadership of a series of defined duties at Obama's urging. He oversaw not only the task force on the middle class but also the effort to aid the economic recovery. Joe also served as point man on building congressional support for legislation on health care, the economy, and gun control, and he won Senate backing for international agreements.

In January, before the inauguration, Biden joined a Senate trip to Iraq, Afghanistan, and Pakistan, setting him up to flex his foreign policy muscle in the White House. Biden's role was vast and multifaceted, a sign of how much the president not only leaned on Joe's managerial and political skills for specific tasks but also turned to him as an all-purpose counselor. The trust that developed between them on the professional side encouraged a blossoming personal commitment to each other.

At the heart of the relationship lay fundamental agreement on most issues, from managing the war in Iraq to the importance of family. During the 2008 primary campaign, Obama and Biden squared off against each other along with the rest of the Democratic field in several debates before Joe dropped out. "If you look back on it," Joe recalled, "the only two people who did not disagree on a single substantive issue were the president and me. We disagreed on degree, but we never disagreed on a substantive issue. So it started off where I knew that I was simpatico with the president-elect....We had a genuine relationship... built on top of a genuine personal affection."

In his quest to be a different kind of vice president, Joe set out to sharply distinguish himself from his predecessor, Dick Cheney, a widely reviled figure who had grabbed and wielded power for himself in the day-to-day operations of the White House. By some estimates, Cheney was the most powerful vice president ever. He was not so much a partner with his boss, President George W. Bush, as the ruler of his own secretive fiefdom.

Though Cheney dismissed the notion, "he had command of events" in the Bush White House, according to Barton Gellman, author of *Angler: The Cheney Vice Presidency.* He masterminded and manipulated President Bush by playing to his vanity and obsessions and pretending to loyalty. He sold Bush on his theory of an abusive extension of executive power—convincing the president in the wake of the September 11, 2001, terrorist attacks that it was the right thing to do—and in the process expanded his own power.

Cheney's brief was "so wide-ranging and autonomous that he was the nearest thing we have had to a deputy president," Gellman observed. There were times "when Cheney took the helm—sometimes at Bush's direction, sometimes with his tacit consent, and sometimes without the president's apparent awareness."

Cheney derived his boldness in part from his understanding that his job in the White House was protected in a way no one else's was. Cabinet secretaries and other White House staff served at the pleasure of the president. Cheney operated in a different realm. While he often said that President Bush was his boss, he also knew the president couldn't fire him. Like the president, Cheney was an elected official whose job was inscribed in the Constitution. He took an oath independent of the president to serve in the best interests of the nation; in his mind, that freed him to act as he wished.

"I'm not a staffer," he observed. "I'm the vice president, a constitutional officer, elected same as he is." During the 2008 presidential campaign, both Republican and Democratic candidates warned that the Cheney vice presidency was "a cautionary tale." Cheney as much as admitted to his dangerous domination when he offered his own wry advice to incoming Obama staffers: "Above all else, control your vice president."

On a personal level, Cheney's arrangement with his president was nothing like the emerging Obama-Biden friendship. "Cheney didn't crave personal closeness to Bush. He merely wanted influence," wrote Jacob Weisberg in *The Bush Tragedy*. He "did not presume to be Bush's buddy."

To Biden, Cheney's conduct as vice president was abhorrent. Cheney's view of the office and his abuse of his position disgusted Biden. Before the inauguration, the two men sparred publicly over their sharp personal, political, and operational differences.

During Biden's appearance on *This Week* shortly before Christmas, host George Stephanopoulos reminded him of a cutting remark he'd made about Cheney during his vice-presidential debate with Sarah Palin in October. In the debate, Biden didn't mince words, asserting, "Vice President Cheney has been the most dangerous vice president we've had probably in American history."

A week before Biden's appearance on the show, the reclusive Cheney had spoken to ABC's Jonathan Karl and defended his tenure. He was responding to criticism from Biden and others that he and the Bush administration had pursued so-called enhanced interrogation tactics on prisoners in the war on terror, a practice regarded by many as torture and therefore unconstitutional. Cheney fired back, arguing, "Those who allege that we've been involved in torture, or that somehow we violated the Constitution or laws with the Terrorist Surveillance Program, simply don't know what they're talking about."

Stephanopoulos pressed Biden for a reaction, noting of Cheney, "He was pretty defiant."

In response, Biden described Cheney's counsel to Bush as "not healthy for our foreign policy, not healthy for our national security."

Biden rejected the Bush administration's expansion of presidential powers, calling it "dead wrong" and asserting it overstepped the Constitution and weakened US security and its standing around the world.

In an extraordinary second interview, the publicity-averse Cheney had spoken to Fox News the Friday before Biden's appearance on the Sunday talk show. The Fox interview, taped in the Executive Office Building and airing on Monday, served as a rebuttal to Biden's long-standing criticisms. Fox's Chris Wallace reiterated Biden's jab at Cheney from the debate and raised the notion that Biden was going to shrink the role of the vice presidency. "He is not going to have his own 'shadow government' in the White House," Wallace pointed out, as if that were a detriment to the nation. "Biden has said that he believes you have dangerously expansive views of executive power."

"Well, I just fundamentally disagree with him," Cheney replied. He nitpicked Biden's view of the Constitution, then gave his perspective of Biden's role in the Obama administration. "If [Biden] wants to diminish the office of vice president, that's obviously his call," Cheney chided. "I think that president-elect Obama will decide what he wants in a vice president. And apparently, from the way they're talking about it, he does not expect him to have as consequential a role as I have had during my time." Cheney's abuse of the office, Mondale noted at the 2015 forum, took the vice presidency to the dark side. His tenure even prompted some ghoulish humor. Biden recalled seeing a cartoon in which Cheney was giving him a tour of the vice president's residence, the walls of the basement outfitted with manacles and chains. "I'm standing behind him," Joe remembered of the cartoon. "And he said, 'Joe, you might want to make a few decorating changes.'"

Four days before his inauguration, Barack Obama boarded a 1930s railcar in Philadelphia for a whistle-stop tour to Washington, DC. After a campaign powered in good measure by modern technologies—email, blogs, Twitter, text messaging—the president-elect chose this old-world conveyance to deliver himself to the nation's capital.

The journey traced part of the much longer path taken by President Abraham Lincoln on his travels from Springfield, Illinois, to the White House in 1861, and in speeches along the way, Obama relied on rhetorical flourishes of Lincoln (appealing to "our better angels") and Martin Luther King Jr. (a promise to act with "fierce urgency") to underscore the long arc of American history that had delivered the nation to this day.

Inside his shiny blue railcar were luxury appointments, including cherrywood-and-brass Pullman lamps suitable for any traveling president of the past eighty years. And outside, standing on a small, covered back balcony draped with red-white-and-blue bunting, Obama rolled along the tracks waving to crowds of Americans who turned out bundled against the cold.

After Philadelphia, the vintage railcar—tugged along by a ten-car Amtrak train carrying friends, family, and staffers—rolled into Wilmington, Delaware, to pick up the vice president–elect, Joe Biden. Despite the bone-chilling, single-digit temperature, eight thousand people turned out at the Wilmington train station where, for decades, Senator Biden had boarded his ride into DC.

With Joe at his side, Barack spoke to the crowd, describing their administration as a team dedicated to improving the lives of working Americans. Then it was Joe's turn to greet his people as vice president. "Folks," he told the enthusiastic throng, "this is more than an ordinary train ride—this is a new beginning."

Joe looked as though he was just warming up before his hometown crowd for one of his long-winded rambles. Several Obama aides almost in unison glanced worriedly at their watches, one of them wondering out loud, "How long do you think he'll go?"

Enjoying the limelight, Biden told the gathering of locals that the Amtrak staff treated him like a friend. When he was running late, Joe admitted, the train conductor would delay the departure for him under the pretext that there was "some mechanical difficulty that would last a minute or two."

Thus began the Obama-Biden presidential partnership in earnest. Two men of contrasting styles, each in his own way with vast appeal: Obama lifting his followers to inspirational heights, a scripted yet charming figure defining and embodying a long-deferred dream of the American promise; Biden going straight for the heart, a man of raw emotion drawing his audience close with his in-your-face, down-home reality.

Joe passed his first test: under the uptight gaze of Obama's aides, he kept his remarks brief, and the threat of a delay passed. The inauguration express—known as "Bamtrak"—shoved onward, with a stop in Baltimore before arriving in Washington.

Celebrants converged on the capital despite the freezing temperatures— men and women of all races and ethnicities—and streamed toward the Mall and fanned out in front of the Lincoln Memorial by the tens of thousands; some estimates put the crowd at more than four hundred thousand. It was January 18, 2009, two days before Barack Obama was to be sworn in as the first black president.

The scene carried echoes of the 1963 March on Washington: decades ago a throng had gathered at this same location for speeches and music, politics and hope. Then, as now, the star of the show was a charming, idolized black man whose presence and rhetoric brought people to tears. In 1963 Martin Luther King Jr. delivered his now-iconic "I Have a Dream" speech. Gospel singer Mahalia Jackson sang, along with Bob Dylan, Joan Baez, and Peter, Paul, and Mary. A twenty-three-year-old John Lewis spoke in words that were fiery even though he had been ordered to tone them down at the last minute.

Forty-five years later, Barack Obama, president-elect of the United States, was the man pilgrims from across the country came to see. It was his preinaugural celebration—slicker, full of more pomp than the March on Washington, but occasioned by its civil rights predecessor: if not for King, there would have been no Obama. And if not for Abraham Lincoln, whose marble memorial framed the event, there would have been no King. Though the president-elect's concert brought out musical royalty—Bruce Springsteen, James Taylor, John Legend, Stevie Wonder, Beyoncé—it was King and Lincoln who cast their long shadows over the day. And Obama was deeply conscious of their hovering presence.

All eyes were on Obama, looking dignified in his overcoat and dark muffler even while on his feet clapping and rocking to Stevie Wonder. Obama was the man of history, the object of celebration. His sidekick, Vice President–Elect Joe Biden, boisterous and room-stealing as he was, had shrunk beneath the legend that was already swelling around the man soon to take the highest office in the land.

Biden, in a dark overcoat and a hint of noisiness in his red scarf, sat next to the president-elect on the platform with family and friends and staff. He was allowed a few moments at the microphone, wedged in after a joint performance by James Taylor and John Legend and just before John Mellencamp belted out "Pink Houses" with backup from a sixty-member Baptist choir.

Without referencing the March on Washington, Biden resurrected one of its motivating themes: a cry for jobs. In that earlier year, it was jobs for African Americans. In 2009, in Biden's rhetoric, it was jobs for all Americans as the nation stared into the abyss of recession.

Joe called out to the crowd, "Folks, in my family...we learned the dignity of work, and we were told that anyone can make it if they were given a fair chance. That's how I came to believe, to the very core of my being, that work is more than a paycheck—it's about dignity. It's about respect. It's about whether you can look your child in the eye and say, 'Honey, it's going to be all right.'"

Later in the program, Bono, scruffy faced, in blue jeans and purple shades, singled out the star of the show at the conclusion of his first song, "Pride (In the Name of Love)." He turned toward the VIP box and spoke directly to the president-elect: "What a thrill for four Irish boys from the north side of Dublin to honor you, sir, the next president of the United States, Barack Obama..." Gazing up at the rock star, chin raised, the rock star of politics broke into a shiny smile as Bono continued, "...for choosing this song to be part of the soundtrack of your campaign."

Obama, his smile widening, nodded.

Bono also gave a shout-out to Joe while performing "City of Blinding Lights," with a few improvised lyrics inserted for the moment. His earring glinting in the sunlight, Bono pointed a gloved hand toward the president-elect's box and called out, "Joe Biden!" And Joe smiled demurely while his wife Jill beamed at him.

As Bono performed, Obama prepared to follow him onstage to deliver a few remarks. His campaign manager, David Plouffe, was seated behind him in the VIP box. Plouffe, who was used to keeping his eye on the candidate, sensed that Obama's mind was wandering.

"The president-elect was intently gazing in the direction of Abraham Lincoln's imposing statue rising up behind and above the stage," Plouffe recalled. "Watching our first African American president look quietly at Lincoln, the Great Emancipator, before taking the steps of the memorial built in his honor simply took my breath away."

Later Plouffe asked his boss what he had been thinking about at that moment. Obama told him he was pondering the crises Lincoln had confronted—and that had led him to reflect on the historical weight that came with the office of the president.

"For all of our challenges," he told Plouffe, "we've faced greater. Lincoln had to save the Union."

In a couple days, Obama knew he'd take his seat behind the Resolute desk in the Oval Office and it would all fall on his shoulders. He confided to Plouffe, "So I asked ol' Abe for wisdom and judgment and patience."

After Bono left the stage, a female voice over the loudspeakers announced: "Ladies and gentlemen, the president-elect of the United States, Barack Obama." Amid cheers and whistles, Obama strode toward the podium, stopping to wave and gaze at the blanket of people stretching out along the edges of the reflecting pool all the way to the Washington Monument. Greeting the crowd, Obama called out, "Hello, America!"

The next day—Monday, January 19, the day before the inauguration—the Obama and Biden families edged a little closer together. Michelle Obama and Jill Biden began jointly working on what was to become a key campaign for them: helping and celebrating families of service members.

On Monday night, the Obama daughters and the Biden grand-daughters—already hanging-out buddies—joined Michelle and Jill at a raucous Kids' Inaugural concert at the Verizon Center; in the audience, among the fourteen thousand in attendance, were four thousand children of military service members. Onstage were Miley Cyrus, Demi Lovato, and Bow Wow. Things really started shaking when the Jonas Brothers took the stage and Sasha and Malia and the Biden grandkids danced at their seats before climbing onstage with the boy band.

With just a day to go before Barack and Joe became an official White House team, the murmuring over the Biden penchant for gaffes had quieted—until he and Jill showed up at the Kennedy Center to tape a special inaugural *Oprah Winfrey Show*. This time the slipup came from a different quarter. Discussing the decision whether to accept Obama's offer to be his running mate, Joe told Oprah that he and Jill went home to talk it over.

"And Jill had an interesting phrase," Biden said. "She said, 'You know, I think this is good for the family.'"

Oprah turned to Jill and asked, "Why did you say good for the family?"

"Because I think—" she began, then went in another direction. "Joe had the choice to be secretary of state or vice president. And I said, 'Joe—'"

The audience burst into laughter, stopping her.

It was an embarrassing moment on several fronts: Jill had unintentionally insulted Hillary Clinton by suggesting that Clinton was not Obama's first choice for secretary of state.

Realizing her goof, Jill shrugged her shoulders and said, "Well, okay, he did."

The camera showed Joe laughing along, being a good sport, then squinching up his face and raising his eyebrows in a "we got caught" moment.

Oprah sought a response from the vice president–elect. "Joe?"

But Joe had a frozen smile on his face, realizing: *Better to say nothing.*

Oprah pressed him. "Joe?"

Without speaking, he put his arm around Jill, as if to convey, *It's all right.*

Oprah seconded Joe's approval. "It's okay. It's okay."

The crowd swelled into cheers, supporting Jill.

Joe turned to Jill, gestured with an open hand. "That's right. Go ahead."

And Jill explained why it was good for the family that Joe chose to be vice president over secretary of state. "So I said, 'Joe, if you're secretary of state, you'll be away, we'll never see you. You know, I'll see you at a state dinner once in a while.'" But if he were vice president, she continued, he'd be around and the family could be a part of his adventure and see him regularly. "And that's what's important to us."

So just as Barack Obama was about to vault into the history books, his team scrambled to swat down a Biden family gaffe.

At 7 a.m. on inauguration day, the incoming press secretary, Robert

Gibbs, was on CBS's *The Early Show*. Host Harry Smith came right at it: "The sort of news of the last twenty-four hours is based on an event that happened on *The Oprah Winfrey Show*." He then played a clip from the show. "Robert Gibbs, what is the true story behind the story?"

"Well, you know," Gibbs began, "then-senator Obama and then-senator Biden sat down to talk about how Senator Biden could be most helpful to this ticket. They talked about a number of things, including staying right here in the Senate. But the one job that then-senator Obama offered then-senator Biden was the offer to be vice president of the United States should they win this election. That's the job that was offered and the one he accepted and the one he'll assume with President Obama today."

On NBC's *Today Show*, Meredith Vieira tried to frame the incoming administration's response as its first cover-up. "In the interest of transparency, Robert," she scolded Gibbs, "which is a word that your campaign used frequently, I was watching *Oprah* yesterday." She noted that Jill Biden "was not ambiguous at all" when she said her husband had been offered the job of secretary of state. "In fact, she reiterated it, although the campaign now says that he was only offered one job. So I have to ask you, was Hillary Clinton second choice when it came to secretary of state?"

Gibbs's short answer was, "No." And he restated what he had said earlier, nearly word for word.

The gaffe, like most of them during the Obama years, was inconsequential for policy, national security, intelligence—in almost every possible way. If anything, it was an embarrassment to Clinton, a tiny revelation that the incoming administration preferred not to own up to. Addressing it in a forthright matter was the easy and appropriate way to defuse it and quiet the press. But Obama's staff established itself from the outset as uptight and opaque, preferring to stiff-arm the media with a fortresslike approach to uncomfortable—and sometimes innocuous—inquiries. By the same token, the media—sometimes thinking it smelled a stench—scented nothing of great relevance but nonetheless pursued it anyway for the sake of drama.

With the inauguration only hours away, Barack and Joe and the media were settling into a pattern. If the mindless pack mentality of reporters was an annoyance, it was also a boon to the Obama-Biden relationship. Just as journalists in television, print, and online over-played the Biden gaffes, they also helped shaped positive public percep-tions of the partnership. The media willingly disseminated attractive images of Barack and Joe together in serious and light settings and turned the relationship into a feature of pop culture: a bromance.

The White House insisted that it did not actively participate in promoting the bromance notion, but once it realized the public was intrigued by the interplay of the two men, it put out relationship-style photos of Barack and Joe.

"Certainly there were moments when we thought, 'Okay, that pic-ture is better than the other one to feed the narrative of the partner-ship,'" acknowledged Deputy Communications Director Liz Allen. But, she added, "we were not pushing it in any way. I mean, it wasn't driven by the White House. It was driven by the mainstream media."

# EIGHT

# "Oval Newlywed Game"

Had Martin Luther King Jr. been alive to see the inauguration of Barack Obama on January 20, 2009, he would have been eighty years old, his birthday falling just days before the historic swearing-in. King was present in spirit, and his legacy shone in one longtime soldier of the civil rights movement who had been beaten and bloodied for the cause. John Lewis, who was serving his eleventh term in the House as a representative from Georgia, had a seat on the platform.

When Obama emerged from the Capitol and started on his way down the steps past the VIPs, he stopped and embraced Lewis. The men had a brief private exchange: Lewis congratulated the president-elect, and Obama asked for his prayers. "You'll have them, Mr. President," Lewis told him. "That, and all my support."

On his way to his seat, Obama greeted friends and supporters as a wave of cheers swept up from the hundreds of thousands of Americans gathered on the Mall. For Obama, the days leading up to the inauguration were almost too much to take in. "I have to tell you," he told *The New Yorker*'s David Remnick, "that you feel a little disembodied from it." The struggles of those who had battled for this day were never far from his thoughts. "Never during that week did I somehow feel that this was a celebration of me and my accomplishments," he observed. "I felt very much that it was a celebration of America and how far we had traveled."

On this brisk January day, Americans turned out bundled against the cold in heavy coats and mufflers and ski caps, and millions more watched the ceremony on television. Among the dignitaries and former presidents on the platform—Jimmy Carter, George H. W. Bush, Bill Clinton, George W. Bush—sat outgoing vice president Dick Cheney, in a wheelchair. His office issued a statement saying he had injured his back moving boxes. After Cheney was seen on television being pushed down a corridor of the Capitol toward the ceremony, a listener called in to NPR's *Talk of the Nation* the following day to draw a comparison between the outgoing vice president and Mr. Potter in the Frank Capra movie *It's a Wonderful Life*. The listener observed, "Dick Cheney in a wheelchair was the best Lionel Barrymore we've seen in decades."

Cheney's image was a public-relations gift to the incoming vice president. Joe Biden, known for his affability, stood in stark contrast to his predecessor. Joe, in his way, fostered a wish for decency in the nation's leaders, beginning perhaps with openness and amity between the president and vice president.

After a little pomp and ceremony—the US Marine Band, a children's choir, an invocation—Aretha Franklin serenaded the nation in "My Country, 'Tis of Thee" in a gray felt hat topped by a giant bow lined in glittering Swarovski crystals.

Just before noon, Obama rose and took a few steps toward Chief Justice John Roberts, who looked solemn and formal in his black robe. The long arc of the moral universe, as King wished to believe, bent toward justice on that morning on the Capitol platform. With his wife Michelle at his side, President-Elect Obama placed his hand on the burgundy, velvet-covered Bible that once belonged to Abraham Lincoln.

"Are you prepared to take the oath, Senator?" Chief Justice Roberts asked him.

"I am."

"I, Barack Hussein Obama—" Roberts began.

But before Roberts completed the phrase, "do solemnly swear," an eager Obama interrupted him: "I, Barack—"

Realizing he'd jumped in too soon, the president-elect tried again: "I, Barack Hussein Obama, do solemnly swear."

Now it was Roberts's turn to fumble. The chief justice said, "That I will execute the office of president to the United States faithfully."

Recognizing that the wording was wrong, Obama began, then stopped. "That I will execute..." And he nodded to Roberts, as if to say, *Go on.*

Roberts resumed, moving the word "faithfully" forward in the sentence where it belonged. Obama smiled as Roberts stressed the word: "*Faithfully* execute the office of president of the United States."

But then Obama recited the earlier, incorrect wording: "The office of president of the United States faithfully."

Ignoring Obama's error, Roberts plowed on: "And will, to the best of my ability."

Obama repeated, "And will, to the best of my ability..."

Roberts: "Preserve, protect, and defend the Constitution of the United States."

Obama echoed, "Preserve, protect, and defend the Constitution of the United States."

"So help you God?" Roberts asked.

"So help me God."

It was now official: Barack Obama was president of the United States.

But they had messed up the swearing-in. Misplacing the word "faithfully" raised concerns in some quarters that the oath was not properly administered and some could challenge Obama's legitimacy. Late-night comics seized on the moment. On *The Tonight Show,* Jay Leno riffed, "It was announced today they're coming out with an official Inauguration

Day DVD. And listen to this, it's going to contain a lot of extras, including the Supreme Court Justice John Roberts blooper reel."

Journalists latched on to the off-script stumble—one, for a change, involving not Biden but Obama. On CNN, senior White House correspondent Ed Henry relayed to television viewers how he played gumshoe reporter to sniff out the big first-day story of the Obama administration: that Chief Justice Roberts had come to the White House to conduct a second swearing-in of the president. It was, in fact, a minor story. But in a flood of words, Henry took viewers through the steps of his reporting, from overhearing something in the White House, then making a series of phone calls, and finally nailing down that White House counsel Greg Craig believed there was no problem but still thought that Chief Justice Roberts should administer the oath again, out of an abundance of caution.

Roberts arrived at the White House in his black robe for the do-over—as the *Washington Post* put it: "In golf, they call it a mulligan." Obama, relaxed and joking, explained to the few people gathered around that he had enjoyed himself so much the first time, why not try it again? When Roberts asked if Obama was ready to take the oath, the president said, "I am, and we're going to do it very slowly."

In the Map Room, beneath a fairly minor 1804 portrait of Benjamin Latrobe, architect of the US Capitol, the men went through the ritual in twenty-five seconds, perfectly, with no Bible and Obama's right hand raised. Only a few onlookers were present, no lineup of celebrities and distinguished guests, no throng of Americans on the Mall, just a pool reporter recording the quick recitation.

At the completion of the swearing-in, Roberts smiled and said: "Congratulations, again."

If Obama was miffed that the world focused on an inconsequential flub on the day of his historic assumption of power, his vice president only added to his annoyance. Before the redo of the president's oath, Biden had been charged with swearing in senior White House staff members in room 450 of the Eisenhower Executive Office Building. Though the ceremony was meant to be a serious affair, Joe was in a frisky mood.

President Obama began the formality by delivering a few words in a somber tone at a podium in front of an American flag; he was dressed in a crisp dark suit, brilliant white shirt, and blue tie, like a man wishing to make the best impression on the first day of a new job. He spoke in lofty terms of the duty they were all embracing on behalf of the entire nation. "For those of us who have been in public life before, you know, these kinds of moments come around just every so often," he told the staffers, his voice grave. He raised his fist and shook it gently to stress his point: "The American people are really counting on us now." He turned to Vice President Biden standing behind him and said, "Joe, you want to administer the oath?"

As the president stepped back, Joe stepped forward.

"Am I doing this again?" It seemed to be a Biden joke about Chief Justice Roberts.

But the president wasn't playing along. He responded as if Joe really wasn't sure what was going on here.

"For the senior staff," Obama said, unsmiling, looking a little tense.

"For the senior staff," Biden repeated, seeming to play along with the president. Then he tossed out his zinger: "My memory is not as good as Justice Roberts'."

Joe, who was often the butt of jokes over his missteps, had been given a rare opportunity, and it seemed he couldn't stop himself from poking fun at someone else for his slipup. The assembled staffers rode with him. A wave of laughter broke out, and a few in the crowd gasped, "Ohhh!"

President Obama, stern-faced, shook his head, took a step forward, and tapped his vice president on the elbow as if to say, *Stop screwing around, Joe, and get on with it.*

The cable news programs swarmed. By drawing attention to the chief justice's error, Biden ironically handed the media an opportunity to portray the joke as Joe's first official gaffe and to hint at tension between him and the president right at the outset of their term. CNN aired a video clip on *Anderson Cooper 360°*, with senior White House correspondent Ed Henry advising the television audience, "Look at the president's body language. He was not in a laughing mood."

It was a rocky debut for the Obama-Biden partnership, as Joe was still taming his instincts for his role as vice president. Barely two weeks later, he spoke frankly at a retreat for House Democrats in Williamsburg, Virginia, about the uphill battle to save the economy. "If we do everything right," he admitted, "if we do it with absolute certainty... there's still a thirty percent chance we're going to get it wrong."

Joe was just being honest, as he tended to be, but this was not the kind of straight talk preferred by the White House. When reporters asked Obama about the remarks at his first presidential press conference, he was somewhat dismissive of his vice president. "I don't remember exactly what Joe was referring to," he said, causing the room to erupt in laughter, and added, "Not surprisingly." And there was another wave of laughter: Joe was again the butt of a joke.

Turning professorial, Obama sought to clarify the administration's prospects in tackling a potential catastrophe, the massive financial and economic crisis hanging over the American economy. "I think what Joe may have been suggesting... I wouldn't ascribe any numerical percentage to any of this—is that, given the magnitude of the challenges that we have, any single thing that we do is going to be part of the solution, not all of the solution.... Not everything we do is going to work out exactly as we intended it to work out. You know, this is an unprecedented problem."

He outlined the enormity of the task: getting the recovery package right and focusing on a range of approaches, not only tax cuts or only investment in threatened institutions. "But even if we do everything right," he said, largely echoing Joe's appraisal of the hurdles in his own sober, reflective way instead of Joe's media-triggering short-hand, "we've still got to deal with . . . the financial system, and making sure that banks are lending again. We're still going to have to deal with housing. We're still going to have to make sure that we've got a regulatory structure, a regulatory architecture for the financial system that prevents crises like this from occurring again."

The president's snide remark in public wounded the vice president, prompting Obama to send an apology through his aides: he insisted he didn't intend any disrespect. But the put-down festered until Joe brought it up at one of their weekly lunches. Joe acknowledged the need to be more careful in his language, but he also told the president he didn't like being ridiculed by him or his staff. Through straight talk over lunch, Barack and Joe resolved their spat.

Even though Barack and Joe patched up their differences, the president's mocking of his vice president still set off alarmed speculation about the White House partnership. On its website a Fox News headline screamed: "Did Obama Throw Biden Under the Bus?" Its story began: "Ying and yang . . . or, oil and water?"

A writer for the *Christian Science Monitor* expressed shock at Barack's shaming of Joe. "Come on, is this any way to treat your wingman?" wrote Jimmy Orr. The *New York Times*'s Maureen Dowd, noting that Biden's "stream of consciousness can be impolitic" but also "bracingly honest," chided Obama for dissing his partner in public. Barack's take-down of Joe certainly was restrained, but coming from the ever-civil Obama, it rattled the house. "The new president is so elegant, and so full of comity, even to his foes, that when he is simply a tad ungracious, it jumps out," Dowd wrote. "It was the 'not surprisingly' that was surprisingly snarky."

Like any newlywed couple, especially one so high-profile and under unrelenting scrutiny, Barack and Joe were still ironing things out between themselves. As the headline on Dowd's piece suggested, the duo was caught in a kind of "Oval Newlywed Game." Making things tougher for them, reporters were climbing over each other to assess the degree of friction between the new president and vice president. Dowd portrayed Obama as putting on the "'disappointed parent' routine" with Biden. But she had spoken to insiders who said "the two men get on well": Obama welcomed Biden's candid advice, and Biden felt included in discussions.

But, in Dowd's view, there was an imbalance in this matchup. Biden, though sometimes free-spirited, would never intentionally show disrespect to the president. To Dowd, the president's allegiance to Biden was less clear. "It can't be easy for someone with a highly defined superego to be bound to the wacky Biden id, for one so disciplined to be tied to one so undisciplined, for a man so coolly unsentimental to be paired with someone so exuberantly sentimental," she observed.

Joe, for all his faults, was a prized partner, particularly in the double-crossing world of politics. "Joe is nothing if not loyal," Dowd reminded the president in her column. "And the president should return that quality, and not leave his lieutenant vulnerable to 'Odd Couple' parodies."

While the media speculated, Obama soon sent a clear message that the rumors of a rift were misplaced. He and his vice president had no time to waste on bickering. They had landed in the White House together as the American financial system was imploding. The country wobbled on the brink of its worst crisis since the Depression. Immediate action was needed to keep the economy from plunging over a cliff. Whatever gripes Barack and Joe had with each other were minor compared with the duty that lay before them to forestall catastrophe.

If Obama had any hesitations about leaning on Biden at this critical juncture, if he had any doubts about Biden's ability to manage a key feature of the nation's push toward recovery, he showed no sign of it. On February 24, barely a month after his inauguration, the president went before a joint session of Congress to outline his plan to tackle the crippled economy. "We will rebuild, we will recover," Obama promised the nation, "and the United States of America will emerge stronger than before."

Seated in the front row, right in the center, was the new secretary of state, Hillary Clinton. In the ceremonial procession of VIPs before the speech, Clinton had led the president's Cabinet members very slowly down the aisle toward their seats, hugging one Congress member after another, to the apparent annoyance of Treasury Secretary Timothy Geithner, who did all he could to stop himself from pushing by her.

When Obama began speaking, Michael Coleman, the Washington correspondent for the *Albuquerque Journal*, watched Clinton from his perch in the Capitol press gallery directly above the podium. "She gazes up at Obama, who is speaking to the nation a few steps away at a podium she thought she would occupy," Coleman wrote. "So close, yet so far away. What must be going through her mind?"

Unveiling the strategy, Obama summarized his program to create jobs, fix the banks and credit system, improve schools, institute health-care reform, foster domestic sources of energy, and—not tied directly to the recovery—end the war in Iraq. He left the specifics for later. The president was conscious of the partisan acrimony stirred by his massive expenditures. The stimulus bill Congress had just passed was huge, $787 billion, providing vast opportunity for mismanagement and squandering of money.

"With a plan of this scale," Obama continued, "comes enormous responsibility to get it right. That is why I have asked Vice President Biden to lead a tough, unprecedented oversight effort—'cause nobody messes with Joe."

Barack paused. Smiling, he hooked a thumb in the direction of Joe, seated behind him in his official vice president's spot on the dais. When the chamber erupted in applause and laughter, Obama waited. The *Los Angeles Times*, which was live-blogging the speech, offered its commentary. "Weird moment of humor because it almost sounds patronizing," the paper wrote. "Biden does not seem to mind and the crowd eats it up."

Seated next to Joe, House Speaker Nancy Pelosi shot to her feet and turned toward him, applauding. Obama looked back at Joe and called over to him: "Am I right?"

Joe, wearing a broad grin, brought both hands up open-palmed, as if to say, *Well, I guess so.*

Millions of Americans had lost their jobs, many had lost their homes and their savings, nobody could get a loan, and everyone was fearful of the future. The recovery plan was immense. Its aim was not just to save the economy but to reshape America in the process.

"It was Obama's one shot to spend boatloads of money pursuing his vision," said journalist Michael Grunwald, "a major down payment on his agenda of curbing fossil fuel dependence and carbon emissions, modernizing health care and education, making the tax code more progressive and government more effective, and building a sustainable, competitive twenty-first-century economy. It's what he meant by 'reinvent the economy to seize the future.'"

The stimulus plan had another effect: it stimulated a sharp Republican backlash that put party loyalty over the good of the nation, a symptom of the disease of dysfunctional partisanship. Ohio's Republican senator George Voinovich summed up his party's approach toward Obama: "If he was for it, we had to be against it."

In their mania to obstruct Obama, Republicans discounted any sign of success. Making their task all the more difficult, Obama and Biden and the entire White House team confronted a tricky dynamic with the American people: selling the virtue of something that didn't happen—such as a crippling depression—was tough. As Biden's chief economic adviser Jared Bernstein explained, "'It Would've Been Even Worse Without Us' is just a fruitless message."

To navigate the enormity of the task, Biden leaned on the words of his mother, imparted to him when he was a tyke in Scranton, Pennsylvania. As Grunwald tells the story in his book, *The New New Deal*, if little Joey broke a leg or bumped his head, his mother was quick to remind him how much worse it might have been: he could've broken both legs or smashed his skull.

"As the White House point man on the Recovery Act," Grunwald elaborated, "Biden felt like he was recycling his mom's talking points, trying to persuade America to feel grateful its injuries weren't fatal." Biden realized, however, it was nearly impossible to get credit for keeping a colossal disaster at bay: once the biggest threat receded, people were focused on the very real troubles left in its wake.

With his working-class roots—he was not a member of the multimillionaires' club of politicians—Biden was able to connect with people suffering the ravages of the economy. He insisted that the high-falutin financial discussions be brought down to the common man's level in understandable language. "When I brief him," Bernstein said of Biden during the height of the crisis, "his not-uncommon criticism is, 'Would you speak English and not economese?'" What Bernstein discovered from Biden was that "people are willing to work with us if we talk to them like grown-ups and explain the lay of the land, what it is we face, and how we get from here to there in honest, coherent terms."

Ever optimistic, Joe took up Obama's directive like a faithful hound barking out the administration's message of hope. "This is the exciting part of my job," he told Grunwald, his arm draped over the journalist's shoulder as if they were old friends, though they'd only met moments earlier. "We're building tomorrow!"

The day after Obama's speech before Congress, Joe stormed the morning talk shows. He laid out his plans sounding like a man empowered. On CBS's *The Early Show* he told coanchor Maggie Rodriguez that he would be calling a Cabinet meeting to learn what each department head was doing to ensure that the president's goals were met and how they were using their resources; he was going to meet with governors and mayors and leaders of industry and business.

"We're going to follow the money," he asserted. "This is a matter of discipline and getting this right, and that's what we intend to do." Joe was the sheriff now: he promised transparency, and he intended to expose impropriety. "When we find that the money isn't being used as it's intended to be used, when governors, if they were to take the money and put it in a rainy day fund instead of creating a new job, we will expose that," Joe warned.

When a caller to the show asked for details on how the stimulus package was going to help small businesses, Joe turned into a well-informed salesman. He said the assistance depended on the kind of business and its specific need: Was the business grappling with a credit obstacle, high energy costs, labor issues? "I would recommend that woman call my office directly," Joe offered, "and I will be able to guide her as to how—what pieces of this package would be directly helpful to her."

As captain of the stimulus project, Joe exuded confidence. His performance earned Obama's approval and minimized any rough patches that surfaced in their relationship. "They each had to let go of things to trust the other guy," observed Liz Allen, who served alternately on the staffs of both Obama and Biden.

On Saturday evening, March 21, a C-SPAN camera positioned just inside the Renaissance Hotel in Washington watched Beltway insiders enter the building in their white ties and evening gowns and make their way toward the down escalator. The passing dignitaries paid no heed to the camera.

Here was President Obama's cocky chief of staff, Rahm Emanuel, gesturing and talking animatedly. There was Federal Reserve chairman Ben Bernanke, striding with purpose, his expression serious, as if he were late for the nation's best-dressed meeting on the financial crisis. At the top of the escalator, giving a hug to an acquaintance, was Dana Perino, former press secretary for President George W. Bush. In came Minnesota senator Amy Klobuchar, smiling, stopping to chat with a colleague. Gliding by in brainy thought was the Nobel laureate Steven Chu, Obama's energy secretary. It was as if C-SPAN had set up a nature cam to capture the behavior of political creatures in the wilds of Washington.

Some six hundred A-list power brokers—Cabinet members, senators, governors, mayors, television celebrities—poured into the hotel and disappeared down two flights of escalators into the grand ballroom for the annual Gridiron Club dinner, an evening of satire directed at the press and the political establishment. No cameras were allowed inside the ballroom, where the nation's leaders joked, and performed, and chowed down on a $300-a-plate meal of lobster panna cotta while millions of Americans fretted over a collapsing economy.

One high-profile guest—the usual featured luminary—was missing: the president of the United States. Obama was spending the night with his family at Camp David. Members of the Gridiron Club, the oldest organization of Washington journalists, founded in 1885, weren't happy at the snub. Every president had endured a roasting at the club's annual dinner in his first year in office—except Grover Cleveland, who never showed up once; he believed he was raked over the coals enough and saw no need to submit himself to a special night of it.

Speculation swirled around why Obama shunned the dinner. The official reason was that it was the first night of his daughter's spring break and the Obama family had decided to spend it together at Camp David, the president's Maryland retreat. It also might have been that Obama was sensitive to the poor optics of dressing up in fancy attire and enjoying fine food in a time of crisis. Or, as Britain's *Telegraph* theorized, "Obama's never really been one for back-slapping socializing, small talk or going out on the town anyway."

At first journalists were led to believe the Obamas were traveling to Chicago for spring break. But now that they realized the president was only a short distance away at Camp David, they were especially peeved. "That's not exactly out of town by presidential standards," reported *Politico*. "In fact, it is about a 20-minute helicopter ride if Obama had decided the event were important enough." The publication said that Michelle Obama had decided the family's plans for the night "and no one on the senior staff was about to challenge that," a supposition that the White House flatly denied.

Dan Zak of the *Washington Post* offered his own Michelle angle with a dose of snarky humor. Suggesting that Obama had cozied up to the press to win the White House, Zak dinged the president for now turning his back. "Typical," he wrote. "String 'em along, get elected, go back to the wife. The nerve."

Club members weren't shy about expressing their disappointment over Obama's absence. "People feel uncommonly saddened, miffed and burned," said *Chicago Tribune* columnist Clarence Page. "I don't think he understands the implications of not coming to the club in the first year. It's not your ordinary state dinner."

All this speculation and hand-wringing only gave credence to a belief that Obama was avoiding the dinner because after three months in office he was already sick and tired of the goofy media coverage he'd received. The same week as the ballroom gathering, Mark Leibovich of the *New York Times* zeroed in on the media run amok in the Obama era, detailing the inanities journalists reported in the race for scoops no matter the subject.

Among the latest silliness: *Politico* beat all other news organizations to report that the president's aides had surprised Assistant Press Secretary Nick Shapiro with a chocolate cake and sang "Happy Birthday" to him. *Politico* added to its laurels by informing the world that the fiancé of White House deputy press secretary Jen Psaki had cooked dinner for her and proposed marriage—*and* the whole time she was in her pajamas. The *Wall Street Journal* revealed that Peter Orszag, head of the White House Office of Management and Budget, was a sucker for Diet Coke. The *Washington Examiner* caught Chief of Staff Rahm Emanuel using an ATM.

"While there has always been a hearty appetite for stories—and trivia—about the people in a new administration," Leibovich wrote, "today's White House press corps (competing for up-to-the-second news) has elevated the most banal doings to a coveted 'get.'" In a perfect illustration of how the news mill ground away, Leibovich then showed up on CNN's media show *Reliable Sources* to reiterate everything in his *Times* story. By sitting on television talking about what already appeared in the print media, Leibovich contributed to the endless droning of the news cycle, and, apparently unconscious of his own role, he concluded, "Frankly, the fact that Peter Orszag drinks Diet Coke, winding up in the *Wall Street Journal*, maybe does say something about where the media is these days."

Journalists complained during Obama's campaign and after his arrival in the White House that the candidate/president shunned the traditional media, preferring instead to speak directly to the American people. On *Reliable Sources*, host Howard Kurtz addressed Obama's relationship with the media. "There was some chatter before Barack Obama took office," he told viewers, "that maybe he would conduct a YouTube presidency, using his own digital channels and blowing off much of the mainstream media."

Though the media noise had grown louder, journalists' dire warnings about Obama bypassing them were unfounded, in Kurtz's view. "Well, that was dead wrong," he concluded. He noted that Obama went on *60 Minutes* for his first interview after the election, then showed up on the major networks for chats with their big-name news anchors, and sat down with the *New York Times* and the *Washington Post* and a host of syndicated columnists, regional reporters, Hispanic journalists, and black journalists. The president was about to appear on *60 Minutes* a second time.

Two days after *Reliable Sources* aired—and three days after the Gridiron dinner—Obama held the second press conference of his administration. Elizabeth Sullivan of the Cleveland *Plain Dealer* later complained that the president sent a clear message by picking certain organizations to ask him questions. He began in traditional fashion by giving the first opportunity to the Associated Press. But then, Sullivan wrote, "President Obama stiffed almost every other reporter present from the 'mainstream media,' including those from the *Post*, the *Wall Street Journal*, the *New York Times*, *Newsweek* and *Time*."

Sullivan, an editorial-page editor and foreign-affairs columnist, described the administration's various efforts to bypass the traditional press; for instance, the president asked people to vote on the White House website for what questions Obama should answer at an online town hall, and he named a director of new media to improve the website's ability to blog directly to the people. "In Obama's first two months in office," Sullivan worried, "White House press handlers have gone out of their way to convey the idea their boss cares little what big-city newspapers say or think."

If Obama's absence from the Gridiron dinner suggested his true feelings about the press, it also provided an opportunity to showcase the increasing comfort between him and his vice president. He sent Joe Biden to the event in his stead armed with a battery of jokes, some mocking the boss himself. If real tension existed between Barack and Joe, it seemed unlikely the vice president would have fired off wise-cracks with Obama as a punch line.

In a slight to the administration—and to Biden—the *Washington Post* anointed someone other than Joe as the hottest personality in the room. "Without Obama, the highest wattage belongs to California Gov. Arnold Schwarzenegger, sweeping in with wife Maria Shriver, who's seemingly shrink-wrapped in a tight shoulder-baring violet gown," the *Post* wrote. In his appearance at the podium, Schwarzenegger jabbed at the journalists' grievances of the night. "You did such lovely work for [Obama]," he told the men and women of the press. "You put your lives on hold to put him in the White House. Now you get all dressed up, the champagne's on ice, and you find out he's just not that into you." The room erupted.

Contrary to the *Post*, *Politico* named Joe the man of the hour, as seen in its headline: "Biden Steals the Show at Gridiron." The vice president took the stage late in the evening when the ceremony was already running late, offering the *Post* a chance to jab at Biden: "If your show's running long, the last thing you want to do is put Joe Biden behind a microphone."

Relishing the spotlight, Joe knew the rap about his long-windedness and poked fun at himself. He promised everyone, "I'm going to be brief," then took it back: "Talk about the 'audacity of hope.'"

Taking aim at Schwarzenegger, Joe congratulated the governor "on a really great speech," then ridiculed his thick accent: "I can hardly wait for the English translation."

With gusto, Biden leveled some comic hits at President Obama and his staff, delivering what amounted to a series of sanctioned gaffes. "President Obama sends his greetings," he told the crowd. "He can't be here tonight because he's busy getting ready for Easter." Joe lowered his voice to a whisper: "He thinks it's all about him."

Joe took aim at Rahm Emanuel's well-known penchant for loud cursing, noting that the walls between the chief of staff's office and his own were "paper thin." Hearing the language that flies off of Emanuel's lips, Biden said, was like "listening to *Sesame Street* where every day is brought to you by the letter 'F.'"

Having carved out his role as trusted counselor to the president, Joe felt comfortable joking about his place in the White House. Leaning into the microphone, he revealed how much Barack loved to hear from him. "To give you an idea of how close we are," he explained, "he told me that next year—maybe, just maybe—he's going to give me his BlackBerry e-mail address."

The White House had a serious task at hand: tackling the economic meltdown and ensuring that the Barack-and-Joe relationship caused no untoward distractions. The administration took pains to present a sense of harmony between the president and vice president, and the release of sanctioned photos helped convey an image of peace within the Oval Office.

In April and May, the White House distributed two shots that conjured the shared, serious-yet-fun-loving attitude of the two men. In one, the president and vice president, in suits, white shirts, and ties, sans jackets, knocked golf balls around on the White House putting green; the columns of the South Portico rising behind them cast an air of dignity on the playful scene.

In the other photo, Barack and Joe were captured grabbing lunch together at Ray's Hell Burger in Arlington, Virginia; as though entirely alone, they were engrossed in their conversation while awaiting delivery of order number 88, the numeral displayed in a raised clip on their table. Both men, like workers having dashed from the office, were in white shirts and ties, Barack with his sleeves rolled up. Clustered in the center of the table were bottles of ketchup, steak sauce, and mustard, and a roll of paper towels standing upright. These were just a couple of regular guys eating at a regular place.

Their relationship was firming. Obama now accepted that Biden might go off-script now and then but was still able to be an effective partner, and Biden trusted that Obama was going to maintain their close working relationship no matter what wrinkles might crop up. Holding the two together was a mutual desire to speed past the flare-ups in the daily news cycle and stay focused on their long-term goals.

"The gaffes weren't that important," White House adviser Liz Allen said. "Obama and Biden both shared a belief in playing the long game. Obama used to say he viewed his administration as his leg of a relay race, and he was just trying to get it right." Obama wanted to keep his eye on the future and not be hindered by the ups and downs of the moment. "It was the same for the relationship," Allen explained.

# NINE

# Flu Mania

All early signs indicated that Biden was becoming a key figure in the Obama White House. Besides managing the stimulus package, Joe flew to Munich, Germany, to represent Obama at a leading security conference and deliver the administration's first major speech on foreign policy. He was also jetting around the country to promote the goals of the new Middle Class Task Force.

Obama drew on a basketball analogy to portray Biden's contribution to the team. Joe, he said, was like a player "who does a bunch of things that don't show up in the stat sheet." In Obama's rendering, Joe was the guy on the court who "gets that extra rebound, takes the charge, makes that extra pass."

When Barack and Joe were both in Washington, they spent a good amount of time together, between three and five hours a day, including intelligence and economy briefings and a variety of other meetings. Biden had Obama's calendar and was permitted to join the president in any session. Sometimes Obama called Biden without warning and asked him to sit in on a discussion.

Their partnership was taking shape along the lines Biden had requested and Obama had promised. The president held true to his commitment to "always seek Biden's counsel and take it seriously even if they didn't agree," said Liz Allen, who had experience on both staffs.

One adviser pointed out that as the Obama-Biden relationship strengthened, Biden was regarded all the more as a "peer, not a staffer."

But it was always clear who was the boss—even on minor decisions. At their weekly Friday lunch together, Obama chose the menu. "The dietary bar is set by the president," explained Ron Klain, Joe's chief of staff. "Biden eats anything. He's a pretty easy guy that way."

Observers kept a close eye on how things were going between the two men. A *Christian Science Monitor* reporter noted that Barack and Joe had "settled into their own symbiosis." Allan Loudell, a radio journalist in Wilmington, Delaware, Biden's hometown, likened the relationship to a marriage of opposites. "It's like a couple who are the reverse of one another, yin and yang," he said. "And it seems to be working."

With particular ingenuity, the White House found a way to turn Joe's blunt speaking—even when it was out of turn—into a positive for Obama. Writing in the *New Republic,* Michelle Cottle deftly explained the White House strategy. "Faced with a vice president incapable of censoring himself," she reported, "Team Obama has set about turning this nuisance into a strength. Forget everything you may have heard about Senator Biden, the impolitic, self-promoting, long-winded gaffe machine. Meet Vice President Biden, the brutally frank, calls-'em-like-he-sees-'em, couldn't-be-a-yes-man-if-his-life-depended-on-it truth-teller."

If Biden slipped up, the argument went, he was only revealing the virtues of his character. In White House parlance, Joe was "authentic," "real," "honest," "blunt," "a straight shooter." "Within this framework," Cottle explained, "Biden's lack of a verbal filter is the modest price one pays for a politician of conspicuous integrity, openness, and candor—rare and welcome traits in this industry, no?"

Obama benefited from having a straight shooter as his sidekick.

Typically cautious and calculating, the president learned to loosen up by spending time with his vice president. What's more, Joe, by his nature, helped Obama establish an image as a leader who encouraged openness and debate within his administration. In private and in high-level meetings, Biden spoke the truth as he saw it, and sometimes he even played devil's advocate to provoke wide-ranging discussion. It was a role Joe had demanded from the outset, and one that Obama welcomed.

"There's, I think, an institutional barrier sometimes to truth-telling in front of the president," Obama told the *New York Times*. "Joe is very good about sometimes articulating what's on other people's minds, or things that they've said in private conversations that people have been less willing to say in public. Joe, in that sense, can help stir the pot."

The Obama-Biden give-and-take was a boon to both men. "Whatever the outcome of a particular debate," Cottle observed, "the dynamic plays to both Obama's self-image as one who encourages dissent and Biden's self-image as one who delights in providing it."

Though the White House had devised a way to rationalize the Biden style, Joe's loose tongue still had the potential to cause the president and his aides nightmares. So far, Biden's gaffes had been, at worst, embarrassing for himself and Obama: no great damage had been done. It was possible, then, in this harmless environment, to spin his missteps as the mere side effects of a truth-speaking man.

This strategy worked well as long as the slipups were minor. But, Michelle Cottle asked, "if Biden speaks the truth, the whole truth, and nothing but the truth, what happens should he eventually utter a disastrously inconvenient truth—not a run-of-the-mill gaffe but something more grave and substantive?" For now the administration was able to cover for Joe and cast a positive light on the Obama-Biden relationship. "Whether this plays out happily or ruinously remains to be seen," Cottle concluded. "But that suspense is just part of the fun of watching Joe be Joe."

\*　　\*　　\*

On April 30, Joe showed up on NBC's *The Today Show* in the midst of a severe national flu outbreak. Many communities were hard hit: scores of schoolchildren were home sick. Ten percent of students in an elementary school in Burke County, North Carolina, were knocked out; so were more than 10 percent of students in Pierce County, Washington, and 31 percent in the Perkins County, Nebraska, school system; and in Chappaqua, New York, Horace Greeley High School shut down for a day as flu symptoms felled a wave of students. Adding to fears was evidence that the common flu contained an altered gene that made the disease resistant to Tamiflu, a popular antiviral drug.

Fears of a flu pandemic led the news. Commentators reached into history to shock the public about just how bad things could get. The 1918 influenza pandemic, the nervous were reminded, killed at least 50 million people around the world and some 675,000 in the United States. Other pandemics in 1957 and 1968 each wiped out a million people worldwide and a hundred thousand in the United States.

And all that was before anyone had to face the newest, most worrying, threats: the emergence of avian flu and swine flu. Cases of these exotic strains were turning up in the far reaches of the world and had lately landed in some US cities.

Americans heard reports of bird flu striking in Indonesia—four people dead since January—and in Vietnam—three cases, with one death. The numbers seemed small, but reports suggested the contagion was growing: since 2003, Vietnam had 109 reported cases, with 53 deaths. Some 250 people had died from avian flu since 2003, according to the World Health Organization. And avian flu was sweeping through farms. In Hong Kong, ninety thousand chickens were slaughtered in 2008 because of an outbreak; in mid-March 2009, authorities in the town of Darjeeling in the state of West Bengal in India began culling as many as fifteen thousand chickens after the flu hit the flock.

Isolated incidents cropped up in America. In early April, Kentucky reported an outbreak of bird flu on a poultry farm in the western part of the state; the farm, which produced hatching eggs for Perdue Farms, was quarantined and some twenty thousand chickens were killed. Singapore announced it was banning the import of poultry from Kentucky. Whereas Americans had feared Asia's avian flu, now Asians feared America's outbreak.

If bird flu weren't frightening enough, Americans shuddered over the spread of swine flu, too. The epicenter was Mexico, where more than one hundred people had died. Other countries, including New Zealand, Canada, Spain, Israel, and Great Britain, acknowledged cases of the scary virus.

Alarm mounted as people on American soil tested positive. By late March, the number was at least forty patients nationwide, and growing. On March 28, swine flu hit Ohio for the first time when a nine-year-old boy showed the signs of infection.

Panic spread online as people turned to the web for information and to speculate on how severe the dangers were. Experts asked the public to refrain from spreading rumors and stoking fears. Nielsen Online reported that web chatter about swine flu was doubling daily on blogs, news sites, and forums. "You cannot catch swine flu by using Twitter," observed Robert Cringely on the *PC World* website. "But you wouldn't know it by looking at the swirl of misinformation."

Some newspapers tried to tamp down rising hysteria. In a column looking at five myths about pandemic panic, the *Washington Post* concluded, "The truth is that the threat is being hyped." The Associated Press, like other news organizations, put out explanatory information. In a question-and-answer format, the AP told readers that they should not expect another pandemic, if one occurred, to replicate the course of the 1918 Spanish flu and kill millions. "That's unlikely," the news service concluded. The piece explained that many treatments now existed that were not available in the first decade of the twentieth century, including antibiotics for secondary infections such as pneumonia, which struck down many victims in the 1918 pandemic.

Cable news networks, while trying to convey the latest information, indulged in their customary dramatics. On April 27, Alina Cho, CNN's coanchor in the morning, ticked off the statistics on flu cases around the world and in the United States and checked in on slumping Asian stock markets, which were jittery over a possible pandemic. The following evening on CNN's *Anderson Cooper 360°*, Anderson Cooper magnified the scare with an on-screen close-up of the microscopic virus that was causing all the havoc. Sounding like a detective in an evening radio mystery, Cooper presented the elusive murderer.

"Tonight," he said, "our first picture of a killer. Take a look. This is a photo of the actual virus taken through an electron microscope at the Centers for Disease Control in Atlanta. H1N1, swine flu. Nothing but a tiny bit of protein and genetic material, it doesn't eat or breathe or move on its own. But when it gets inside a human body, it breeds, it kills, and right now the virus is spreading."

President Obama, choosing his words carefully, sought to fight the national panic. Appearing before the National Academy of Sciences, he emphasized the crucial role of science and medicine to the prosperity, health, and security of America and announced his commitment to increase investment for research.

In that context, he noted that the Department of Health and Human Services had declared a public health emergency "as a precautionary tool" so resources would be swiftly available if needed. And in his no-drama-Obama tone, the president told the nation: "We are closely monitoring the emerging cases of swine flu in the United States. This is, obviously, a cause for concern and requires a heightened state of alert. But it's not a cause for alarm."

The same day, Wolf Blitzer, anchor of CNN's *The Situation Room*, played the clip of Obama speaking in measured terms to ease the nation's anxieties. Then Blitzer immediately raised a new alarm.

With CNN's senior White House correspondent Ed Henry on the screen, Blitzer asked, "Ed, quickly, the president was just in Mexico, and there's a lot of speculation out there he actually got a tour by a Mexican who wound up dying the next day." Blitzer was referring to the president's trip to Mexico ten days earlier to meet with the country's president, Felipe Calderón. "Is there a sense the president himself, when he was in Mexico, or his advisers, was in any serious danger?"

Reporters had raised the question with Press Secretary Robert Gibbs at a briefing. "Robert Gibbs stressed over and over," Henry told Blitzer, "that the president's health was never in any jeopardy, that his doctors feel he's healthy now. He's shown absolutely no symptoms."

Then, discounting the sensationalism around the story, which CNN fueled, Henry added, "And in fact, the person you mentioned who had given the president a museum tour in Mexico, who died, it's not clear that that person died from the swine flu."

Blitzer, after raising the concern about the president's health and batting it around with his correspondent in front of millions of viewers, then confirmed the irrelevance of the story.

"Yes," he told his audience. "And we're just getting word that according to a Mexican government official, that person who gave the president a tour died from a preexisting condition and not from swine flu."

Two days later, President Obama opened a press conference with a few words on the flu emergency. "This is obviously a very serious situation," he said. He reassured everyone that the "entire government is taking the utmost precautions and preparations." He said health officials recommended that schools consider temporarily closing if they had confirmed or suspected swine flu cases. He noted that he'd requested $1.5 billion in emergency funding to tackle and track the virus and have drugs on hand at health facilities should they become needed. "Everyone should rest assured that this government is prepared to do whatever it takes to control the impact of this virus," he said.

In the first question, a reporter asked if the president thought it was time to close the borders.

Obama reiterated, "This is a cause for deep concern, but not panic." He wanted the response to be intelligent and systematic and in accordance with recommendations from public-health officials. "At this point," he said "they have not recommended a border closing."

With his typical composure, Obama laid out a good strategy for every American: "Wash your hands when you shake hands. Cover your mouth when you cough. I know it sounds trivial, but it makes a huge difference. If you are sick, stay home. If your child is sick, keep them out of school. If you are feeling certain flu symptoms, don't get on an airplane. Don't get on any system of public transportation where you're confined and you could potentially spread the virus."

Amid this national mood of confusion and panic, Biden appeared at 7 a.m. on *The Today Show* on a split screen from Washington the day after the president's press conference. Cohost Matt Lauer began the interview with an apocalyptic warning: the World Health Organization had put the flu threat at level 5, meaning a pandemic or epidemic was now imminent over a wide area. He reminded viewers that President Obama had no plans to close the borders with Mexico or curtail air travel between the two countries. He then asked the vice president to help everyone understand what was going on.

Sounding like a voice of reason and speaking for the administration, Biden said that top health experts in the United States and around the world had advised that dramatic actions such as closing borders or restricting air travel were not necessary. Rather, it was important to take careful steps to mitigate any spread of the flu in schools and other places where people congregated. "Closing a classroom and closing a border are two fundamentally different things," Biden explained. "And so we've been operating on the best evidence we've been given by the world's leading experts on pandemics and epidemics, and that's the advice we've been given."

Lauer, not extracting the level of panic he seemed to want from

Biden, pressed the vice president. "Let's just talk as nonexperts, then, you and me," he proposed. Then Lauer offered his analogy for the crisis: it was like a water-main break that floods houses. Of course, you close down the affected houses, he said, and clean them up. The burst water main, in his telling, was located in Mexico and was sending a flood of infection into the United States.

"But wouldn't you also go back," he argued, "and turn off the water in that water main so it doesn't continue to flood other neighborhoods?"

"I don't think the analogy is appropriate," Biden countered.

The vice president pointed out that infected people were possibly crossing American borders, but they were coming from other areas besides Mexico. "Which borders do we close? Do we close the Canadian border too? Do we close flights coming out of countries in Europe where it has been identified now? We're told that is not an efficacious use of our effort, that we should be focusing on mitigation."

Still not satisfied, Lauer took another swing. "Let me ask you this," he said, "and this is by no means a gotcha type of question, I promise. But if a member of your family came to you—"

Biden laughed.

"No, Mr. Vice President," Lauer continued, "if a member of your family came to you and said, 'Look, I want to go on a commercial airliner to Mexico and back within the next week,' would you think it's a good idea?"

Biden, speaking as a husband, father, and grandfather, gave his honest answer—veering off-script from what the Obama administration would have liked to hear him say. "I would tell members of my family, and I have," he admitted, "I wouldn't go anywhere in confined places now. It's not that it's going to Mexico. It's you're in a confined aircraft. When one person sneezes, it goes all the way through the aircraft."

To emphasize that this was a personal recommendation, not his view as vice president, he added, "That's me." Then he rolled on: "I would not be, at this point, if they had another way of transportation, suggesting they ride the subway. So from my perspective, what it relates to is mitigation. If you're out in the middle of a field and someone sneezes, that's one thing. If you're in a closed aircraft—"

"Right," Lauer agreed.

"—or closed car or closed classroom, it's a different thing."

The howling arose immediately. As vice president, Biden quickly learned, he could not speak as a private citizen, as a father or grandfather. His words, honest as they may have been, inevitably amounted to an official White House stance—and, to the ire of the administration and some business groups, they misstated the president's finely honed approach to the emergency.

Before 9 a.m., Biden's office had rushed out a clarification of the vice president's words that reimagined what had actually come out of Joe's mouth. "The advice he is giving family members," his spokeswoman, Elizabeth Alexander, said in a statement, "is the same advice the administration is giving to all Americans: that they should avoid unnecessary air travel to and from Mexico. If they are sick, they should avoid airplanes and other confined public spaces, such as subways."

By 10 a.m., Homeland Security chief Janet Napolitano, in another courteous adjustment of the vice president's language, said on MSNBC, "If he could say that over again, he would say if they're feeling sick they should stay off of public transit or confined spaces, because that is indeed the advice that we're giving."

Michael Bloomberg, the billionaire mayor of New York, made a point of riding the subway to work that morning. "The bottom line is, I feel perfectly safe on the subway," he said, "and I think taking the subway doesn't seem to present any greater risks than doing anything else."

As for what Biden meant to say, the mayor, like others, reshaped the vice president's language. "I think what Joe Biden was talking about was," he explained, "it is true if you have all these symptoms, we recommend you stay home."

Others came down harder on Joe. Dr. Mark Gendreau, the vice chair of emergency medicine at the Lahey Clinic near Boston, had extensively studied the spread of diseases. "With all due respect of the vice president," he admonished, "every scientific evidence that we have contradicts everything that he stated today."

The airlines' lobbying group, the Air Transport Association, heard the sound of footsteps fleeing the airports and raced to counteract Joe's impact. The association's CEO, James May, called Biden's remarks "extremely disappointing." He asserted that the airlines were working with government officials, and none of them had advised that travelers avoid airlines unless they're sick.

"The fact is that the air onboard a commercial aircraft is cleaner than that in most public buildings," he argued.

At the regular White House press briefing, a reporter asked Press Secretary Robert Gibbs about Joe's language: "I'm wondering if you wanted to clarify or correct or apologize for the remarks that he made."

"Well, I think the..." Gibbs began, searching for the right words. "What the vice president meant to say was the same thing that...many members have said in the last few days. And that is, if you feel sick, if you are exhibiting symptoms—flu-like symptoms, coughing, sneezing, runny nose, that you should take precautions, that you should limit your travel, and I think he just—what he said and what he meant to say."

The reporter was having none of it. "With all due respect, I sympathize with you trying to explain the vice president's comments, but that's not even remotely close to what he said. He was asked about if a member of his family—"

"I understand what he said," Gibbs interrupted, "and I'm telling you what he meant to say, which was that—" The room burst into laughter as Gibbs reiterated his early statement. "Obviously, if anybody was unduly alarmed for whatever reason, we—we would apologize for that. And I hope that my remarks and remarks of people at CDC and

Secretary Napolitano have appropriately cleared up what he meant to say."

The evening of the gaffe, Ron Brownstein, the political director of Atlantic Media, appeared as a panelist on MSNBC's *Hardball* and took Biden to task. "One thing the Obama administration says is that Joe Biden is more helpful to the president in private than in public," he said. "I think that's something on which we can all agree."

Host Chris Matthews, a Biden proponent, jested, "You're so sarcastic. I'm going to take the mike away from you. Let's go to Jonathan Alter, sir. It was—I'm always sympathetic to Joe Biden. I like the guy.... What do you think?"

Matthews got no support from Alter, a national-affairs columnist for *Newsweek*. "This was just a classic gaffe and then it was bad damage control," Alter argued. "Instead of trying to pretend he didn't say something, they should have just said he misspoke or use one of their classic formulations when somebody steps on a banana peel."

Alter pointed out the sympathy Biden engendered. "People are very indulgent of Joe Biden's gaffes. Everybody would have moved on," he advised. "They should have just acknowledged that what he said was in danger of shutting down the entire transportation industry in the United States."

While Obama's fretful advisers were quick to react, the president, for the most part, took Biden's miscue in stride. Always playing the long game, he let the noise die down without directly addressing it. Gibbs noted at his press briefing that Obama hadn't spoken to Biden about his remarks.

Here was another instance when the brouhaha over Joe's ill-advised remarks outweighed their actual impact. His misstatement, though it may have stirred already-existing panic, did not alter the state of the emergency, or the government's policy or response.

For the most part, the incident again reflected Joe being Joe, honest and direct, and showed the administration moving quickly to contain any outcry over his candor while the media swarmed partly to help disseminate accurate information and partly to fill the airwaves and sweep in viewers.

Joe's place as a wise, closed-door counselor to Obama remained intact. Though still adjusting to his role as vice president, Joe was a good soldier leading the charge on the stimulus plan and a traveling emissary for American foreign policy around the world.

Discussing his role at a forum with former vice president Walter Mondale, Biden recalled his difficult transition from the Senate to the White House. "I have never in my entire life had a boss," he explained. "You get asked your opinion as a senator and my whole life I'd say, 'This is what I think.'" In the White House, he noted, "that's not appropriate. You have to demur and work out what the administration's position is."

It was a whole new world for Biden, requiring him to rein in his impulses and think a moment before speaking. Joe Biden, long a solo high-wire act, was now part of a team. He was learning, but, he admitted, it took him a little while, at least six months, to shake off the old Joe Biden. "I had to realize that anything I said would be attributed to the president," he told the forum. "And so you had to—when asked a question—you had to refrain from answering it, or modulate your answer, or make sure it was in line with the president's."

Biden turned to Mondale. "It took me a lot longer than it took you, Fritz."

In a time of pent-up anxiety, Joe gave Americans a chance to laugh, even if at his own expense. The night of his *Today Show* appearance, Jon Stewart on *The Daily Show* contrasted the styles of Obama and Biden as they spoke to the nation about the flu outbreak, one the calm and reasonable father, the other the wacky alarmist grandfather.

After playing clips of both men, Stewart summed up in his own special way the different advice from the president and the vice president. On Obama, he said, "So there you have it. Use your normal hygienic practices."

Moving on to Biden, Stewart threw up his hands in a crazed panic and screamed his interpretation of Joe's warning: "Live a life of solitude inside a sterilized prison of your own making!" Calming, Stewart gave his mocking appraisal of the White House partnership so far: "That's Joe Biden doing the vice president's job of making the president look terrific."

TEN

# The Audacity of Hops

After the votes were tallied in the 2008 presidential election and Barack Hussein Obama was headed to the White House, some Americans believed the nation had shed in an instant two hundred years of torturous racial history: We were suddenly beyond race now. America had magically crossed over into a golden age. We were a postracial nation. The *New York Times* declared across its front page: "RACIAL BARRIER FALLS IN DECISIVE VICTORY."

Following Obama's inauguration, CNN's Larry King noted the impact of the election on his eight-year-old son. "He now says that he would like to be black," the host told his guests on his show, *Larry King Live*. "I'm not kidding. He said there's a lot of advantages. Black is in." King asked his guests: "Is this a turning of the tide?"

Obama hoped his election would help America look past the divisiveness of race and move it closer to Martin Luther King Jr.'s dream proclaimed in 1963: that his "four little children will one day live in a nation where they will not be judged by the color of their skin, but by the content of their character." But Obama also was a realist. A long, tumultuous history of racial strife was not washed away by a single—albeit remarkable—election.

On July 16, 2009, for the first time since taking office, Obama spoke at length on racial conditions in America—always a controversial topic and a delicate one for him as the first black president. The occasion was the hundredth anniversary of the National Association for the Advancement of Colored People. Standing before a packed ballroom at the New York Hilton, Obama noted the strides in civil rights that had made his election possible.

"I understand there may be a temptation among some to think that discrimination is no longer a problem in 2009," he observed. "And I believe that, overall, there probably has never been less discrimination in America than there is today. I think we can say that. But make no mistake, the pain of discrimination is still felt in America." The crowd applauded in agreement.

Only hours earlier, as if foreshadowing the president's point, a scene of racial disharmony had erupted in Cambridge, Massachusetts. A Harvard professor, tired and relying on a cane, climbed out of a hired car in front of his yellow house on Ware Street, after a long journey from China. Henry Louis Gates Jr., one of the most celebrated black scholars in America and director of Harvard's W. E. B. Du Bois Institute for African and African American Research, had spent a week in Asia researching the ancestry of famed cellist Yo-Yo Ma for a PBS series, *Faces of America*.

The driver for the car service carried Gates's three bags up the stairs to his porch. As he tried to unlock the front door, Gates found it was jammed. He thought his secretary, who had picked up his mail for him, might have latched the door from the inside and left through the back of the house. Gates recalled, "I said, 'Let's just push it.'" He and his driver, a large Moroccan man in a black uniform, went to work on the door, shoving at it and tearing the screen door.

On the sidewalk, Lucia Whalen was on her lunch break from her job at the Harvard alumni magazine when she was stopped by an older woman who had noticed the activity on Gates's porch. After seeing it for herself, Whalen called 911.

"Can you tell me exactly what happened?" the male operator asked.

"Uhm, I don't know what's happening," Whalen acknowledged. She said she saw the men pushing on the door. "I don't know if they live there and they just had a hard time with their key, but I did notice that they had to use their shoulder to try and barge in. And they got in. I don't know if they had a key or not, because I couldn't see from my angle."

Whalen said nothing about the race of the men until the dispatcher asked. "Were they white, black, or Hispanic?"

"Uhm," Whalen replied. "Well, they were two larger men. One looked kind of Hispanic, but I'm not really sure. And the other one entered and I didn't see what he looked like at all."

"Okay, are you standing outside?" the operator asked.

"I'm standing outside, yes."

"All right, police are on their way; you can meet them when they get there." After he asked for her name, he told Whalen, "Okay, they're on their way."

"Okay. All right, I guess I'll wait."

Sergeant James Crowley of the Cambridge Police Department was riding in uniform in an unmarked cruiser on Harvard Street near Ware when he heard the Emergency Communications Center broadcast the possible break-in. He headed over to the house.

As he climbed the porch stairs to the front door, he heard a woman call out to him from the sidewalk. Whalen identified herself and briefly described what she had seen. Crowley asked her to wait down on the sidewalk for other officers who were on their way while he investigated the scene.

When he turned back to the door, he saw through a glass pane an older black man in the foyer. Gates and the driver had unstuck the door after about fifteen minutes of shoving it, and Gates had gone inside his home; the driver had departed. Sergeant Crowley said he asked the man in the foyer to step out on the porch to speak with him.

"No, I will not," the man said, according to Crowley's report.

Recalling the incident, Gates said, "Instinctively, I knew I was not to step outside." Gates, who was fifty-nine, five foot seven, and a hundred and fifty pounds, said the officer was in his thirties and several inches taller than the professor. The officer's tone, according to Gates, was threatening. He described the sergeant as "a big white guy with a gun."

According to Crowley, Gates demanded to know the officer's name, and the sergeant said he gave it. Crowley wrote in his report that when he explained that he was "investigating a report of a break-in in progress" at this address, Gates opened the front door and exclaimed, "Why, because I'm a black man in America?"

Crowley said he asked for a photo ID, and at first Gates refused and demanded to know the sergeant's name. In his recounting, Gates said he went into the kitchen to get his ID and Crowley followed him. "I was thinking, this is ridiculous," Gates told the *Washington Post* a few days after the run-in, "but I'm going to show him my ID, and this guy is going to get out of my house. This guy had this whole narrative in his head. Black guy breaking and entering."

The sergeant then asked Gates if anyone else was inside the residence, at which point, according to the report, Gates yelled that it was none of the officer's business. "He...accused me of being a racist police officer," Crowley wrote in the report. He believed that the man, whose identity he still hadn't confirmed, resided at this address, but he "was quite surprised and confused with the behavior he exhibited toward me."

In Gates's account, he handed the sergeant his Harvard ID and

Massachusetts state ID—both bearing his address. He asked the officer repeatedly, "'Who are you? I want your name and badge number.' I got angry." Gates claimed the sergeant never identified himself.

Crowley radioed in that he was at the address with someone who seemed like he was the resident but was "very uncooperative." According to the report, the man made a call on his cell phone and said "Get the chief" and "What's the chief's name?" and that he was "dealing with a racist police officer in his home." Crowley wrote that the man turned to him and said he "had no idea" who he was "'messing' with" and that he "had not heard the last of it."

According to the incident report, Gates continued yelling, demanding to know Crowley's name, even though Crowley asserted he'd already given it. Gates insisted later that he kept asking for the officer's name and felt humiliated when Crowley ignored his request. He said he told the officer, "This is what happens to black men in America."

According to Crowley, Gates kept accusing him of being a racist police officer and warning him that he was not someone to mess with. Crowley turned to leave, telling Gates he'd only speak with him outside. "Ya," Gates told Crowley, according to the report, "I'll speak with your mama outside."

A small crowd had gathered on the sidewalk—Cambridge and Harvard University police, Whalen, and a cluster of passersby—all looking up at Crowley and Gates as the professor stepped out onto the porch. While the sergeant went down the stairs toward the sidewalk, Gates kept yelling at him, according to the report, reiterating his charges of racial bias and warning that Crowley hadn't seen the last of him. He shouted to the people on the street, "This is what happens to black men in America!"

Crowley wrote in his report that, with the public looking on and the professor still yelling, "I warned Gates that he was becoming disorderly." Gates continued to yell. "For a second time, I warned Gates to calm down while I withdrew my department issued handcuffs from their carrying case," Crowley wrote. When he continued yelling, "I informed Gates that he was under arrest."

Crowley went back up the stairs and onto the porch and tried to cuff Gates, who resisted, the sergeant said. Gates yelled that he was disabled and would fall without his cane. When Crowley handcuffed Gates with his hands behind him, the professor complained that the restraints were too tight. So the cuffs were removed, then snapped onto his wrists in front of his body.

Crowley went inside the house to get Gates's cane. The Harvard professor was then taken in a cruiser to the Cambridge Police Department and booked and fingerprinted. He surrendered his belt, wallet, and cane, and was locked in a cell.

Gates's arrest punctured the dream that America was leaving its racial complexity behind. As the incident spread across the media, outrage flared on both sides. The facts were disputed. Gates insisted he was targeted because he was black and argued that he was not as belligerent as the sergeant reported; Crowley insisted Gates was "exhibiting loud and tumultuous behavior" and merited a charge of disorderly conduct. The truth was lost, but what emerged from the conflicting accounts was that racial discord remained a troubling reality in America—despite the election of Barack Obama.

"It took less than a day for the arrest of Henry Louis Gates to become racial lore," wrote the Associated Press. "When one of America's most prominent black intellectuals winds up in handcuffs, it's not just another episode of profiling—it's a signpost on the nation's bumpy road to equality....If this man can be taken away by police officers from the porch of his own home, what does it say about the treatment that average blacks can expect in 2009?"

Harvard sociologist Lawrence Bobo visited Gates at the police station and drove him home after Gates posted a forty-dollar bond. "I felt as if I were in some kind of surreal moment, like *The Twilight Zone*,"

Bobo said. "I was mortified." What Gates endured was "humiliating," Bobo said, adding that it was "a pretty profound violation of the kind of trust we all take for granted." Once Gates had presented his identification proving he was standing in his own house, Bobo argued, "the whole interaction should have ended right there, but I guess that wasn't enough. The officer felt he hadn't been deferred to sufficiently."

The dispute swelled into a battle over police treatment of blacks in America. In his interview with the *Washington Post*, Gates said, "I am appalled that any American could be treated as capriciously by an individual police officer," adding that blacks and poor people were "vulnerable to the whims of rogue cops." Speaking later to *Jet* magazine, Gates rejected Crowley's portrayal of the incident in his police report. "I thought I was in creative writing class," Gates said. "It's just a tissue of lies."

In a bid to defuse the controversy, prosecutors dropped the charges against Gates on Tuesday, July 21, and in its public statements the Cambridge Police Department sought to divide the blame. "This incident should not be viewed as one that demeans the character and reputation of Professor Gates or the character of the Cambridge Police Department," read a joint statement by the police, the city of Cambridge, and Gates.

Police spokeswoman Kelly Downes added, "I think what went wrong is that you had two human beings that were reacting...and cooler heads did not prevail. It wasn't Professor Gates's best moment, and it was not the Cambridge Police Department's best moment."

The controversy tested the new president, who was still gauging how far he could and should wade into the issue of race in America. He was known for his careful words on the subject, and so far in his political life, for the most part, he'd kept his commentary rather muted. His race speech during the campaign in response to the uproar over his friend the Reverend Jeremiah Wright was a notable exception.

Obama's race speech had been carefully crafted and well rehearsed, unlike his comments during a prime-time press conference on July 22. The purpose of the question-and-answer session was to discuss progress toward Obama's promised reform of the health-care system. After delving into the nitty-gritty of the reforms, the president took a final question from Lynn Sweet of the *Chicago Sun-Times*.

"Recently Professor Henry Louis Gates Jr. was arrested at his home in Cambridge," Sweet began. "What does that incident say to you and what does it say about race relations in America?"

"Well," Obama said, "I should say at the outset that Skip Gates is a friend, so I may be a little biased here. I don't know all the facts." Then he got the facts slightly wrong. "What's been reported, though, is that the guy forgot his keys, jimmied his way to get into the house." Gates had said publicly that he had his keys and the problem was the jammed door. Obama continued: "There was a report called in to the police station that there might be a burglary taking place—so far, so good, right?"

He tried to lighten the mood. "I mean, if I was trying to jigger into..." And he shot a thumb over his shoulder, indicating the White House: the East Room where he was standing, its wide red carpet and tall, polished wood doors. Reporters laughed. "Well, I guess this is my house now, so it probably wouldn't happen. But let's say my old house in Chicago," he went on, smiling, laughing, riding with the moment, and the reporters busted up again. "Here I'd get shot." More laughter, for this was a surprisingly caustic quip from a famously self-controlled leader. Obama may have been testing the limits of what he could say and used humor to blunt his frankness. (As MSNBC's Rachel Maddow observed on her show later that night, it was "a very good joke, got a big laugh, and it was also a very incisive, cutting, direct remark about racial profiling in America.")

"But so far, so good," Obama continued. "The police are doing what they should. There's a call, they go investigate....My understanding is, at that point, Professor Gates is already in his house. The police officer comes in, I'm sure there's some exchange of words, but my understanding is, is that Professor Gates then shows his ID to show that this is his house. And at that point, he gets arrested for disorderly conduct—charges which are later dropped."

The president was trying to be as careful as he could, delivering only the facts he knew. "Now, I don't know, not having been there and not seeing all the facts, what role race played in that."

It was when he veered into commentary—and skipped the humor—that Obama stumbled. Later his aides told reporters the president "was personally outraged by the arrest and wanted to speak bluntly about it." He also recognized that, this being the first major racial controversy of his term, it was a tricky moment. The president had discussed with his aides how he ought to address the matter and, as a lawyer himself, had found it significant that Gates was arrested after it was confirmed he was standing in his own home. As a black man, the president was inflamed by the apparent injustice.

"But I think it's fair to say," Obama told the reporters, "number one, any of us would be pretty angry; number two, that the Cambridge Police acted stupidly in arresting somebody when there was already proof that they were in their own home."

He then put the dispute in context. "And number three," Obama offered, "what I think we know separate and apart from this incident is that there is a long history in this country of African Americans and Latinos being stopped by law enforcement disproportionately. That's just a fact."

In conclusion, the president sounded optimistic, reminding America of how far it had come. "Race remains a factor in this society," he said. "That doesn't lessen the incredible progress that has been made. I am standing here as testimony to the progress that's been made."

*　　*　　*

The media latched on to one word Obama uttered—and it wasn't "progress." The evening of his press conference, broadcasters immediately pointed toward trouble ahead for President Obama for saying that Cambridge police, in arresting Gates, acted "stupidly."

On NPR's *All Things Considered*, senior Washington editor Ron Elving summed up the president's predicament: "We're going to hear a lot about that particular adverb."

As a conciliator at heart, the president was distressed—and not a little surprised—that his word choice had set off the media and now posed the risk of polarizing the nation over a racial incident. His aides wished he had chosen to express his view differently.

White House press secretary Robert Gibbs publicly acknowledged the consternation within the administration. "I think if he would do it again, he would change a word," Gibbs said. No one doubted the explosiveness of the issue, particularly in the hands of the all-day-and-night television news stations. "Whenever you get race and politics, it's like catnip," Gibbs said regretfully. "All you need is a spark—and cable television is happy to do that."

The two sides—Gates and Crowley—quickly hardened their positions. On his CNN show Anderson Cooper broadcast Gates's first television interview, in which the professor suggested that he expected an apology from the sergeant. "I haven't heard from Sergeant Crowley," Gates said. If Crowley admitted to his poor behavior and the fabrications in his police report, Gates offered, "I would be prepared as a human being to forgive him."

But Crowley had already ruled out any apology: his actions, he believed, were entirely appropriate under the circumstances. As he told Boston's WCVB-TV off camera, "There are not many certainties in life, but it is for certain that Sergeant Crowley will not be apologizing."

Lost amid the heated voices was the fact that Crowley had served with distinction for eleven years on the Cambridge force and that he taught other officers at the police academy about the dangers of racial profiling. As for the president, Crowley made it clear he had nothing against him; he just wished Obama had kept his thoughts to himself.

"I support the president of the United States a hundred and ten percent," he told a Boston radio station. But, he added, "I think he's way off base wading into a local issue without knowing all the facts."

Police in Cambridge and across the country made their feelings known to the president. Cambridge Police Commissioner Robert Haas said at a press conference that his department was "deeply pained" by the president's characterization of one of its officers.

The International Brotherhood of Police Officers, representing fifteen thousand public safety officials around the country, came to the support of the Cambridge Police Department. "The president's alienated public safety officers across the country with his comments," said the association's president, David Holway.

The president had unleashed a war of words on all sides. His miscue rivaled—and threatened to surpass—any of his sometimes-clumsy vice president. His political allies were surprised he had stumbled so obviously. "He rarely screws up like this," said one.

Seeking a solution, the president huddled with his aides, and the next day, as Obama flew to Chicago for a fund-raiser, Press Secretary Gibbs went into damage control. Speaking to reporters aboard Air Force One, he sought to clarify Obama's language. "Let me be clear," he said. "He was not calling the officer stupid, okay? He was denoting that...at a certain point the situation got far out of hand, and I think all sides understand that."

The escalating crisis threatened to overwhelm other issues on Obama's agenda, particularly health care. While in Chicago, the president had dinner at his home with friends, and they batted around the imbroglio. On Friday morning, Obama talked it through with his wife Michelle.

At 10 a.m. on Friday, Press Secretary Robert Gibbs informed reporters the president would have nothing more to say on the matter. Obama's staffers were divided on the best plan forward: some wanted him to move away from the issue and advised against any apology; others believed he had to head off a distracting crisis by confronting it again publicly.

That same morning, the Cambridge police union held a news conference. Sergeant Dennis O'Connor, president of the Cambridge Police Superior Officers' Association, didn't mince words. He insisted that Professor Gates had turned the confrontation into a racial incident and issued a call for President Obama to apologize to Sergeant Crowley. "The facts of this case suggest," O'Connor said, "that the president used the right adjective but directed it to the wrong party."

O'Connor's charge helped convince Obama that he had to assert his leadership. Since he had inflamed the situation, blown air onto the flames, he felt he had to provide clarification and, he hoped, placate the parties involved. A little after noon on Friday, he phoned senior adviser David Axelrod. "I'm going to call Sergeant Crowley and then I think I ought to step into the press room and address it," he told Axelrod.

At around 2 p.m. Sergeant Crowley was at a favorite lunch hangout, Tommy Doyle's Irish Pub in Cambridge, Massachusetts, munching on a burger and sipping a Blue Moon Belgian White beer, when his cell phone rang. His conversation was brief, and when he clicked off, according to Peter Woodman, a co-owner of the pub in Kendall Square, Crowley had a look of amazement on his face: "He said, 'Jesus Christ, you'll never guess who's going to ring me.'"

As the *New York Daily News* recounted the scene, everyone at Tommy Doyle's soon knew that White House press secretary Gibbs had just warned Crowley to expect a call from President Obama. Cries of "No way!" flew around the place.

Then suddenly the lunchtime clamor fell silent. Someone muted the TVs and the music. In the kitchen, there was quiet instead of the usual tumult. Crowley, seated at a table near a front window, became the pub's top attraction. A crowd stood around him, waiting. Crowley sipped his beer, his cell phone lying in view in front of him. The suspense played out for five or six minutes in the stillness of the pub.

"You could hear a pin drop," Woodman recalled. When a couple walked in from the street and asked for a table, everyone in the bar turned on them: "'Shh! Shh! Shut up and sit down!'"

Finally the phone rang. Crowley got himself ready, took a breath, and answered after three rings.

"Hello, Mr. President."

Obama, on speakerphone, addressed the cop as Sergeant Crowley.

"Call me Jimmy," Crowley said.

Obama returned the informality, saying Crowley should call him Barack.

They chatted for at least five minutes amid dead silence in the pub.

"Not a person breathed," Woodman recalled.

Waiter Kyle Shearer was over at the bar filling an order when the bartender nodded toward Crowley's table and said, "Hey, they're on the phone with President Obama." It hardly seemed possible, but Shearer made his way over. "I couldn't believe it until I got close enough to hear Obama's voice."

Barack and Jimmy discussed the uproar, and Jimmy said he'd like to get past it. In friendly, easygoing banter, Barack asked Jimmy what he was drinking, and the cop learned the president was also a fan of Blue Moon.

When they signed off, the crowd burst into cheers.

After his call with Crowley, President Obama stepped into the White House press briefing room, surprising reporters gathered for their daily session with Press Secretary Gibbs. Given Gibbs's pronouncement in the morning, reporters thought they had heard the last from the president on the matter.

Arriving unannounced at about 2:30 p.m., Obama sought to turn down the heat, saying, "If you got to do a job, do it yourself," prompting laughter from the room.

The president told reporters he'd just got off the phone with Crowley. "I have to tell you that...my impression of him was that he was an outstanding police officer and a good man, and that was confirmed in the phone conversation. And I told him that."

At Tommy Doyle's Irish Pub, all eyes were turned toward the television screen on the wall showing the president in front of reporters. Shearer, the waiter, marveled at his brush with greatness. "The president was on TV, talking about the man I was standing next to," Shearer said. "Even I felt powerful. And I'm just a lowly waiter."

In the briefing room, Obama addressed his own role in the fracas. "Because this has been ratcheting up, and I obviously helped to contribute ratcheting it up," he said, "I want to make clear that in my choice of words, I think, I unfortunately gave an impression that I was maligning the Cambridge Police Department or Sergeant Crowley specifically. And I could have calibrated those words differently."

Without offering his own apology, Obama stressed that both sides—Crowley and Gates—could have behaved better. "I continue to believe, based on what I have heard, that there was an overreaction in pulling Professor Gates out of his home to the station. I also continue to believe, based on what I heard, that Professor Gates probably overreacted as well."

The president's brief appearance ended on a light note. He let reporters know that he and Crowley had discussed a way toward an amicable resolution: Why not have the cop and the professor come to the White House and sit down together with the president over a beer?

"We don't know if that's scheduled yet," Obama grinned, provoking some laughter. "But we may put that together."

In his conversation with Crowley, the president told reporters, he and the cop commiserated over a mutual torment. Now that Crowley was in the media glare, he complained that reporters had staked out his home, and his three kids couldn't go outside to play.

The officer asked if "there was a way of getting the press off his lawn," Obama said, causing reporters in the briefing room to break into laughter. Obama told Crowley he had his own predicament: "I informed him that I can't get the press off my lawn." The reporters laughed again.

After his appearance before the media, the president phoned Gates to ask if he'd be willing to hoist a beer with Sergeant Crowley at the White House, and the professor agreed.

Over the weekend, reporters pressed administration officials about plans for the get-together, which the media dubbed a "Beer Summit." On Sunday, Bob Schieffer, host of CBS's *Face the Nation,* put the question to Obama's adviser David Axelrod. "Well," Axelrod said, "they have both expressed interest. I expect that it will happen, yes. I think the president sees this as an opportunity to get dialogue going on an issue that has...been historically troubling."

Obama knew as well as any African American the humiliations of being black in America. As a young man searching for his place in the culture, he pondered the treatment of blacks and wrote about it eloquently in *Dreams from My Father.*

In the book he recounted walking into the kitchen of his white grandparents' home, where he lived, in the middle of a morning argument. His grandmother had been accosted at her bus stop the previous day on her way to work by a man asking for money. "He was very aggressive, Barry," she told Obama. "Very aggressive. I gave him a dollar and he kept asking. If the bus hadn't come, I think he might have hit me over the head."

Obama's grandfather was shaking, he was so tormented by the incident. "She's been bothered by men before," he said. "You know why she's so scared this time?" He then answered his own question. "I'll tell you why. Before you came in, she told me the fella was *black*." Barack's grandfather whispered the word *black*. "That's the real reason why she's bothered. And I just don't think that's right."

His words hit Barack almost like a physical blow and, for a moment, he peered into the divide between white and black. Even though these were his grandparents, who loved him completely and, as he wrote, "had poured all their lingering hopes into my success," he had to face a cruel reality. "I knew that men who might easily be my brothers could still inspire their rawest fears."

Obama was no stranger to feelings of being a second-class citizen. He had read the great black authors—Baldwin, Ellison, Hughes, Wright, Du Bois—"trying to reconcile the world as I'd found it with the terms of my birth." He had studied the long history of black subjugation and ill treatment and had come to believe that the white man was in control "because of that fundamental power he held over you." As a young man, he believed that domination by whites was a collective legacy of that entire population, leaving him unable back then to make "any distinction between good and bad whites."

The Gates-Crowley incident handed Obama the opportunity to address the racial stains on American culture. If he chose to use his presidential megaphone, he had the power to lead the country toward education, empathy, and understanding. But his first statement had been a stumble, and he was scrambling to regain his footing. As Axelrod suggested on *Face the Nation*, Obama wanted to establish this conflict as a teachable moment.

Others wanted him to take the lead as teacher in chief. Also on *Face the Nation* that morning, Georgetown professor and author Michael Eric Dyson urged the president to assume an active role in a national conversation on race. "There are some big problems here," Dyson said. "If Mr. Crowley and Mr. Gates go join Mr. Obama in the White House and have a beer, that's great. But... what ails us are structural problems.

And the president, by the way, has the bully pulpit to talk about this in a more powerful way. I think he has been loath or at least reluctant to speak about it. I think he should dive right into it."

Dyson's co-panelist, Kathleen Parker, a conservative *Washington Post* columnist, agreed: "This conversation about race desperately needs to take place."

Peniel Joseph, then a professor at Brandeis University and author of a book on black power, noted in the *Chronicle of Higher Education* that "America's racial disparities remain as deep-rooted after Barack Obama's election as they were before.... The Gates incident has become a new metaphor for America's still-tormented racial politics."

Soon a date was set—Thursday, July 30—for Gates and Crowley to join Obama for a beer at the White House. Immediately the media zeroed in on the event's sillier aspects—the men's drink preferences. The *Kansas City Star* asked, "What beer's on tap for Obama, Gates and Crowley?" The *San Francisco Chronicle*'s website polled readers on what brew they believed was going to be served. Fears were raised that the White House might disrespect American brewers by providing foreign beers. And some Americans disapproved that beer was the drink of choice. Susan Bourque, a resident of Riverside, California, wrote to her local newspaper, the *Press Enterprise*, to voice her view: "Since when did it become acceptable for our president to publicize that drinking could solve problems?"

Journalists competed to coin the wittiest name for the event: "Yes, Three Cans," "Beerastroika," "A Thousand Points of Bud Light," "The Audacity of Hops," "Brew-ha-ha," "Ale to the Chief."

The afternoon of the scheduled get-together, CNN was on air previewing the coming attraction, with anchor Kyra Phillips wondering to White House correspondent Ed Henry whether it would amount to a "deep conversation or just a few brews?" Henry reported that White House spokesman Robert Gibbs had informed the media "a short while ago that the president is not going to be announcing any new policy initiatives. Not going to have any agenda.... Instead he's really going to try to make this a personal situation."

Moments before the beer summit got under way, the guest list expanded. The pre-summit speculation focused on only three men—Obama, Gates, and Crowley—raising beers around a picnic table in the Rose Garden.

But when newspaper and television cameras were permitted to move in for snapshots and video from fifty feet for about thirty seconds, they captured a fourth man at the table. If the day called for bonhomie, it made sense to open the soiree to an affable party crasher: Vice President Joe Biden.

Then–Pennsylvania governor Ed Rendell later summed up Biden's appeal around the table: "If you said to me, 'Who's the person in the administration you'd most like to have a beer with?' Joe Biden would be the guy most Americans would choose."

As White House communications specialist Kate Bedingfield noted, the four-man beer fest "was a fraught and tough situation"—the kind of circumstance that played to the vice president's social skills. "The president would have wanted him there," Bedingfield explained, "because the vice president has an uncanny ability to cut through to the real human emotion and understand where others are coming from." That Obama had Biden join the discussion "reflected the trust the two men had in each other," Bedingfield added. "It speaks to their personal relationship."

Biden's presence also balanced the look around the table. Instead of a lopsided image of two African Americans and one white man resolving their differences, the scene now projected racial equivalency: two blacks and two whites. Having Biden—a cop-friendly, blue-collar, union guy—at the table sent an administration message to law enforcement officers across the country who were disgruntled by President Obama's ill-chosen words.

The confab, even with the addition of Biden, was anything but casual. Gates and Crowley sat in the open air under a magnolia tree in suits and ties despite the heat and humidity. Obama and Biden also wore ties but were jacketless, the sleeves of their white shirts rolled up. The white oval lawn table was empty except for the four frosted mugs and silver bowls containing peanuts and pretzels. A formally attired White House waiter slid in and out, not exactly in the style of a laid-back garden party. In such a setting, the wry Alan Abelson, writing in *Barron's*, saw a special contribution from the vice president. "Joe Biden," he wrote, "was there in his role as official noisemaker to put a little zing into the party."

The conversation was by turns serious and light. Amity broke out when Obama, Gates, and Crowley all leaned across the table and clinked mugs. At one point Joe, reaching for one of the snack bowls, said something that caused Barack to break into a wide grin.

American brewers had complained about Obama's choice of beer. But the president stuck to his plan for a Bud Light, even though it was now bottled by a Belgian brewer. Crowley drank a Blue Moon Belgian White with an orange slice. Gates, who was expected to go with a Red Stripe, nursed a light beer from Sam Adams. Biden, a teetotaler, had a nonalcoholic Buckler beer with a lime.

In its reviews of the event, the print media took pleasure in scorning coverage by the cable networks. Dana Milbank of the *Washington Post* noted that "news outlets were tipsy with coverage of the 'Beer Summit.' MSNBC went with a countdown clock to the big event showing three mugs, while CNN opted for two clinking mugs on its own countdown clock."

As for the summit itself, Milbank found little in it that pushed the race conversation forward. "The big moment came out flat," he wrote. "The three had no agenda and no comment as they sat in the Rose

Garden....In the end, the sudsy summit produced little more than the peanuts the men were served—and the puns." The participants offered their own judgments. At a press conference, Crowley described the conversation as "frank," "very cordial," and "private." "What you had today was two gentlemen agree to disagree on a particular issue," he said. "I'd rather not go into the specifics of what we discussed." When asked about the presence of Biden at the summit, Crowley was quick to offer: "The vice president was just a great man." Crowley also noted that he and his wife and kids had had a few moments with Biden inside the White House. "He was very nice with the children," Crowley said of Biden. "We did share a few stories that were unrelated to the topic at hand."

Gates posted a statement on The Root, a website he'd cofounded in 2008. "The national conversation over the past week about my arrest has been rowdy, not to say tumultuous and unruly," he wrote. "But... there's reason to hope that many people have emerged with greater sympathy for the daily perils of policing, on the one hand, and for the genuine fears about racial profiling, on the other hand."

Obama, for his part, did little to suggest in his post-summit comments that he was embracing the dialogue and moving it forward. In a written statement, the president said he thanked Gates and Crowley for joining him "for a friendly, thoughtful conversation."

If Obama needed any encouragement to turn away from race to other matters, particularly his health-care plan, he had to look only as far as the latest polling. In a survey by the Pew Research Center, 41 percent of Americans disapproved of Obama's handling of the Gates incident, while fewer than three in ten approved. His job approval rating sank among whites from 53 percent to 46 percent. For Obama, playing the role of the nation's racial counselor was fraught with political danger; almost any utterance he made in a tense racial situation risked being construed as an outburst of an angry black man.

Obama's attorney general, Eric Holder, earlier in the year had

Freshman senator Barack Obama looks on in January 2005 as fellow Democratic members of the Foreign Relations Committee John Kerry, Bill Nelson, Joe Biden, and Christopher Dodd chat after confirming Condoleezza Rice as secretary of state. Obama arrived in the Senate thirty-two years after Joe Biden, and the two men were not initially close. Biden's long-windedness at the confirmation hearings prompted an exasperated Obama to write a note to an aide saying, "Shoot. Me. Now." *(AP Photo/ Dennis Cook)*

Fellow presidential contenders Joe Biden and Hillary Clinton listen as Barack Obama answers a question at the first Democratic primary debate, in April 2007. Obama admired Biden's strong, disciplined performance, which highlighted his long experience and foreign policy expertise. Biden's campaign collapsed soon after he described Obama as "articulate and bright and clean." His bid ended after the Iowa caucuses in January 2008. *(AP Photo/J. Scott Applewhite)*

Obama crosses the stage in March 2008 to address the inflammatory rhetoric of his longtime pastor, the Reverend Jeremiah Wright. Before this now-famous speech on race, Biden had regarded Obama largely as an impatient fresh-man senator eager for a bigger stage. But Obama's speech filled the veteran senator with admi-ration. A Biden aide said that for Joe, the speech was "a click moment." *(AP Photo/ Alex Brandon)*

Obama and Biden hit the campaign trail together in August 2008. Two weeks before the election Biden inadvertently highlighted Obama's inexperience by declaring that, if they won, a foreign power would likely test the young president within six months. In private, Obama flared in a rare display of anger and awaited an apology, and his team largely sidelined Biden from the national press. *(AP Photo/Alex Brandon)*

Obama and Biden developed a fondness for each other that extended to their families. Here, the candidates and their wives, Michelle and Jill, dine together in Boardman, Ohio, shortly after Joe joined the ticket. The Obama daughters and the Biden grandchildren also grew close and had sleepovers together. *(AP Photo/Alex Brandon)*

Obama and Biden take to the White House putting green a few months after capturing the White House. Sports and teamwork were important to both men—Barack was a basketball aficionado and Joe had been a star football player in his youth. Sports helped build a foundation for friendship. "That's how they were both wired," said Education Secretary Arne Duncan, former cocaptain of the Harvard basketball team. *(Courtesy Barack Obama Presidential Library/Pete Souza)*

Barack and Joe have beers in the Rose Garden with Harvard professor Henry Louis Gates Jr. and Cambridge police sergeant James Crowley after an encounter between Gates and Crowley flared into a racial incident. While Obama was sometimes reluctant to speak out forcefully on race, Biden was able to help ease tensions because of his long history of opposing racial injustice and discrimination. As Georgetown University sociologist Michael Eric Dyson said, "In one sense, the perception was that the blackest man in the White House was the white guy." *(SAUL LOEB/AFP/Getty Images)*

Obama names General David Petraeus (at his left) in June 2010 to replace General Stanley McChrystal as the commander of US forces in Afghanistan. McChrystal had publicly opposed Biden's recommendations on Afghanistan policy, and a *Rolling Stone* article had described the general's staff ridiculing Biden. The controversy strengthened the bond between the president and the vice president. They became "brothers in arms," said administration aide Kate Bedingfield. It was now understood: anyone who attacked one implicitly attacked the other. *(Alex Wong/ Getty Images)*

Their affection for each other was obvious. Barack and Joe weren't shy about grabbing each other, walking arm and arm, and laughing together. They set an example: it was okay for men to cry, and hug, and show love to their guy friends. Kate Leaver, author of *The Friendship Cure*, praised Barack and Joe's "gentle subversion" of the stereotype of "male stoicism." *(Courtesy Barack Obama Presidential Library/Pete Souza)*

In a May 2012 interview with Robin Roberts of ABC's *Good Morning America*, Obama acknowledges for the first time his support of same-sex marriage. His appearance was prompted by his vice president, who surprised Obama less than a week earlier by admitting he approved of such unions. Biden apologized to Obama for inadvertently forcing his hand, and any bad feelings between the two men evaporated. The vice president's verbal miscues, though widely criticized, were largely innocuous bursts of honesty from a man given to straight talk. Barack assured Joe that they were "in this thing together, and that can never go astray." *(Courtesy Barack Obama Presidential Library/Pete Souza)*

Obama and Biden embrace on November 6, 2012, under the gaze of Michelle, Sasha, and Malia, after winning reelection. Obama's aides had researched the advantages, if any, of dropping Biden from the ticket and swapping in Hillary Clinton. The results showed no substantive gain from a switch, but the quiet scrutiny wounded Biden. Such strategizing underscored the inherent limits of friendship in a high-powered political setting. *(Official White House Photo/Chuck Kennedy)*

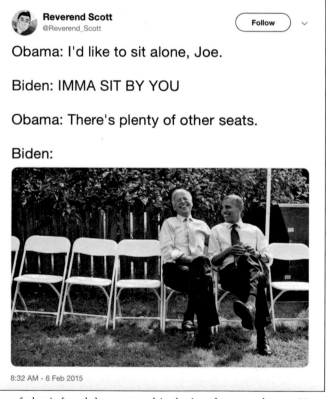

A greater sense of play infused the partnership during the second term. Here, Barack and Joe jog side by side along the West Colonnade in February 2014 in a video promoting Michelle Obama's Let's Move! campaign. Humorous memes shared on the internet highlighted the pair's comfort with each other and reflected their public images: Joe outgoing, Barack reserved. *(Official White House Photo/Pete Souza/Twitter meme by @Reverend_Scott)*

Obama hugs Biden after delivering a eulogy at Beau Biden's funeral in June 2015. The illness and death of Biden's eldest son revealed the deep compassion Obama felt for his anguished vice president. When Beau's battle with brain cancer imposed financial hardship on the Bidens, Obama offered his own funds to help out, though in the end no assistance was needed. *(Courtesy Barack Obama Presidential Library/Pete Souza)*

After Beau's death, Joe Biden faced a tough decision: Could he overcome his grief to mount a serious campaign for president in 2016? Obama discouraged Joe from running, believing that he would have a hard time beating the Clinton machine for the nomination and that Clinton offered a greater chance of preserving the Obama legacy. Again, politics and ego intruded on the friendship. Here, on October 21, 2015, Obama and Biden look over the vice president's announcement in the Oval Office before Joe tells the nation he has run out of time to launch an effective campaign. *(Courtesy Barack Obama Presidential Library/Pete Souza)*

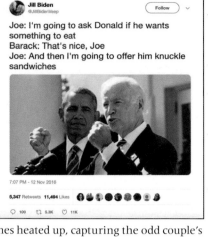

As their second term wound down, the memes heated up, capturing the odd couple's personalities: Barack, cool and rational; Joe, feisty and full of heart. Before Donald Trump's surprise win in the 2016 election, the Obama-Biden memes had a nostalgic tone, ruing the end of an era of president–vice president affection. After the election, the images turned combative in the face of a Trump presidency. *(Official White House Photo/Pete Souza/Twitter meme by Dillon Stevenson, @TheDiLLon1)*

Days before their departure from the White House, Obama awards Biden the Medal of Freedom in a moving ceremony in front of Joe's family and friends. For months White House staffers had worked in secret to fulfill Obama's wish to surprise Joe with the honor. Speaking at the ceremony, an overwhelmed Biden paid tribute to the intellect and strength of his friend Barack. "Mr. President," he concluded, "you know as long as there's breath in me, I'll be there for you, my whole family will be, and I know—I know it is reciprocal." *(Courtesy Barack Obama Presidential Library/Chuck Kennedy)*

Obama and Biden stirred nationwide nostalgia for the Obama era—and for the bromance—when they grabbed lunch at Dog Tag Bakery in Washington in July 2018. As private citizens, they tried to refrain from criticizing the new president. But after a white supremacist march in Charlottesville, Virginia, in August 2017, Biden publicly condemned Trump for emboldening racists. On Barack's birthday, a few days after their lunch together, Joe posted this selfie, taken outside the bakery. *(Courtesy Joe Biden)*

confirmed just how delicate it was for black high-ranking administration officials to speak candidly about race. Barely a month into the Obama presidency, in February, Holder addressed hundreds of Department of Justice employees to mark Black History Month.

"Though this nation has proudly thought of itself as an ethnic melting pot," Holder told the crowd, "in things racial we have always been and continue to be, in too many ways, essentially a nation of cowards."

His point was that if the country wanted to move forward, to achieve true progress, Americans needed to have frank conversations about the many racial issues that still fester unresolved. "We, average Americans, simply do not talk enough with each other about race. It is an issue we have never been at ease with and given our nation's history this is in some ways understandable."

Unlike Obama's words on Gates's arrest, Holder's language on American racial cowardice was no stumble—these were words the attorney general fully intended to use. Conservatives lashed out at him. The *Washington Examiner* cried, "Quite simply, Holder has insulted all Americans, regardless of age or ethnicity." The paper said Holder's comments were "morally bankrupt, demonstrably untrue and compelling proof of his own outlandish hubris."

On his radio program, Rush Limbaugh called Holder's comments "inexcusable." Jonah Goldberg said on the *National Review* website that Holder's opinions were both "hackneyed and reprehensible."

Seeking to quiet the outrage, President Obama distanced himself from Holder's phrasing. "I think it's fair to say that if I had been advising my attorney general, we would have used different language," he told the *New York Times*.

Again playing the long game, Obama placed America's racial pressures within the context of its larger history and progress. "I'm not somebody who believes that constantly talking about race somehow solves racial tensions," he said. "I think what solves racial tensions is fixing the economy, putting people to work, making sure that people have health care, ensuring that every kid is learning out there. I think if we do that, then we'll probably have more fruitful conversations."

With a certain prescience, Obama had noted back in February, "We're oftentimes uncomfortable with talking about race until there's some sort of racial flare-up or conflict." Now, several months later, deep into the Gates controversy, the president discovered how uncomfortable it was to discuss race at all in America—particularly for himself.

Racial reticence was not the promise Obama had dangled in front of Americans during the presidential campaign. The writer Ta-Nehisi Coates remembered that in response to the furor over the Reverend Jeremiah Wright, Obama had asserted that racial truths needed to be addressed. "Race is an issue that I believe this nation cannot afford to ignore right now," candidate Obama had declared in his masterful race speech in March 2008. "And yet, since taking office," Coates lamented in *The Atlantic* some three years after the Gates incident, "Obama has virtually ignored race."

It was a shame, Coates wrote, because "Obama is not simply America's first black president—he is the first president who could credibly teach a black-studies class." He was schooled in black life and culture by his own experience and by his deep reading of great black writers. Obama probed race in his two books. Yet, "with just a few notable exceptions," Coates wrote, the president "strenuously avoided talk of race.... Whatever the political intelligence of this calculus, it has broad and deep consequences. The most obvious result is that it prevents Obama from directly addressing America's racial history, or saying anything meaningful about present issues tinged by race."

Silenced by America's lurking—and often overt—virulence on race, Obama chose to take a quieter path in leadership on the issue. He was not a fire-and-brimstone president—not on any issue. He cloaked his passion in intellect and reason, and relied on thoughtful persuasion. On the combustible tinderbox that was race in America, he led by example and spoke through symbolism.

His pronouncements and actions—and mere presence—as president of the United States served as both the reality of racial progress and symbols of the nation's future. His actions spoke to the moment—he managed the day-to-day affairs of the most powerful nation on earth. He had reached the pinnacle, and his donning of the commander in chief's jacket was a stentorian cry on race without his having to utter a word. He was the living example of the long game he chose to play for America and for the black population. His position was evident for all to see, and so, too, was his color.

As Ta-Nehisi Coates understood, "The irony of Barack Obama is this: he has become the most successful black politician in American history by avoiding the radioactive racial issues of yesteryear, by being 'clean' (as Joe Biden once labeled him)—and yet his indelible blackness irradiates everything he touches."

While President Obama shied away from outspoken leadership on race, he had another, subtle and clever way of expressing his hopes for black-white relations in America. Just by its existence and daily workings, his partnership with Joe Biden served as a badge of racial harmony. He and Joe needed to say nothing, draw no attention to the racial aspect of their unique collaboration; it spoke for itself.

Here was a black president and white vice president—the first arrangement of its kind in American history. If the demands of their jobs caused momentary tensions between them, nevertheless every day the men demonstrated their respect, trust, and fondness for each other. Through their relationship, Barack and Joe led by example, without either man drawing attention to their obvious racial trailblazing. To the end of the Obama administration, this was a story told in its imagery.

When Joe unexpectedly sat down for a nonalcoholic Buckler beer in the Rose Garden in the early evening of July 30, 2009, the Obama-Biden relationship took on potent symbolism. "More important than what was being said was what was being seen," observed Georgetown University sociologist Michael Eric Dyson, looking back at that moment almost a decade later.

Biden's presence sent a clear message to Gates and Crowley—and to the nation—that if a black president and a white vice president could lead the nation, then a black professor and a white cop could overcome their differences. Barack and Joe's relationship was a guiding force. It was, in Dyson's view, "an ideal projection of racial possibility through the skin and the relationship of two men at the top of the political echelon."

Barack and Joe's appearance together in that setting, Dyson added, "spoke volumes to people in so many important symbolic ways." The public heard none of the conversation around the table but saw the four men—two black, two white—interacting. The role of Obama and Biden at that moment, as a black-white team, was instructive. "Their union, with its symbolic power," Dyson said, "radiated such strength and unity that people could see for themselves what was going on."

Joe was indispensable, particularly to a black president given to taciturnity on race. Joe, because of his long career as a proponent of civil rights, was able to give voice to issues of injustice and discrimination that Obama preferred to sidestep.

"Biden had black resonances in a way, ironically enough, that he brought to bear to the benefit of Barack Obama, the black man," Dyson observed. Biden, who worked for years alongside blacks, had a special closeness to African Americans, in Dyson's view, and an empathy for the plight of blacks.

Noting that Obama's upbringing in Hawaii and Indonesia left him in some ways deficient in certain parts of black life and culture, Dyson argued that Biden "was more intimately familiar with some rituals of American blackness than Obama was." According to Dyson, some black people "believed Biden had the racial 'it' factor. Similar to Bill Clinton, he knew the secret handshakes of blackness and was able to joust with blacks in familiar and in humorous fashion."

Biden's racial bona fides were so deeply established, Dyson said, that "in one sense, for a while, the perception was that the blackest man in the White House was the white guy."

Around the Beer Summit picnic table, Biden was a symbol of white amity toward blacks. His presence helped defuse tensions between the cop and the professor and at the same time projected the promise of racial harmony that he and Barack represented and that Obama wanted America to see.

"Gates and Crowley were there, pitted as black against white," Dyson explained. Obama was determined to underscore his commitment to "the ideal of overcoming racial conflict by showing that we can work together, so he brings along exhibit A, Joe Biden."

The racial import of Barack and Joe's relationship stretched far beyond that small gathering in the Rose Garden. Its symbolism played out in the years ahead in photos and memes as it matured into a durable friendship. They were overt in their affections, but Barack and Joe were silent about the racial promise they personified. They let us absorb for ourselves the profound significance of their relationship.

"Of all the political experiments that Obama is given credit for, that relationship was one of the most powerful," Dyson said. "It reimagined the possibility that people from different spectrums of life could come together. It showed that the yin and yang of race, especially of blackness and whiteness, could potentially produce so much that was of worth and value. People saw in this relationship their hopes and aspirations for what they wanted America to be."

The friendship was radical. It epitomized the revolution of Obama's presidency. In practice and in symbolism, Barack and Joe reversed more than two hundred years of American black-white interaction. "They were a two-man wrecking crew against the vicious belief that black and white must forever be divided, that black and white must forever be separate and hierarchical, one superior to the other," Dyson argued. "Their very relationship flipped the script. Black was on top, white was subordinate."

# ELEVEN

# Brothers in Arms

General Stanley McChrystal was on a collision course with Vice President Joe Biden. For months, the two men had staked out their ground over competing visions for how to proceed with America's long war in Afghanistan, which had begun during the previous administration. The latest skirmish had erupted on October 1, 2009, when the general spoke to an audience of military specialists at the International Institute for Strategic Studies in London. At the podium, McChrystal, the top commander of about one hundred thousand NATO coalition forces in Afghanistan, including sixty-eight thousand US troops, looked the part of the lean military man. He wore a crisp army uniform bedecked with badges and decorations spread in a colorful mosaic on his chest, and his four stars marched in step atop each shoulder.

For several months, the Obama administration had been engaged in a wide-ranging review of its Afghanistan strategy in light of deteriorating conditions in the country. As part of the analysis, the president had requested an on-the-ground perspective from McChrystal, who had assumed his command in June. In a sixty-six-page classified report, delivered in late August, the general had laid out a plan that implied an expensive, extended commitment: he wanted to improve local security forces, bolster the Afghan government, promote economic development, and knock back the Taliban insurgency. For his full-bore counterinsurgency operation to succeed, McChrystal argued, the United States needed to commit to a significant increase in US troops.

His strategic goals sharply clashed with Biden's. The vice president, a key White House foreign policy adviser, argued for a less costly, scaled-back mission with a clear end point focused more on taking out local Taliban terrorists and al-Qaeda in Pakistan than on nation building in Afghanistan. He and McChrystal butted heads most stubbornly on the question of beefing up the US military presence—and neither appeared willing to budge. "The only senior official who consistently opposed sending more troops to Afghanistan was Joe Biden," observed Ben Rhodes, Obama's deputy national security advisor.

Top-ranking military officers normally kept themselves off the battle-field of public opinion. But McChrystal believed the Afghan mission was so vital and so complicated, and he was so passionate about it, that he didn't seem to care about the repercussions of speaking out. Barely two weeks before his appearance in London, Bob Woodward of the *Washington Post* had leaked McChrystal's top-secret assessment with explosive repercussions, and everyone knew the general's position. Now McChrystal intended to be frank about what his experience told him was the best way forward in Afghanistan, even if his viewpoint was at odds with that of his civilian masters in Washington.

In front of his audience in London, the general built his case, delivering a smart, thorough overview of conditions on the ground in Afghanistan. The situation, he warned, was "serious" and, "in some ways, deteriorating." But he noted "tremendous" progress in certain aspects of nation building, citing "construction of roads, clean water, access to healthcare, children in school, access to education for females."

Among the rising dangers, he acknowledged, were an increase in violence and a growth in the insurgency. "We need to reverse the current trends, and time does matter," he declared. That reference to time was a rebuke of those wishing to limit the duration of America's role in the nation. If America pared back its presence, McChrystal contended, Afghanistan would fall into chaos. With an implied slap at Biden for urging a more limited mission, he said that some had recommended that "we use a plan called 'Chaosistan,' and that we let Afghanistan become a Somalia-like haven of chaos and that we just manage it from outside."

Instead, he counseled, "we need patience, discipline, resolve, and time."

Onstage, McChrystal projected a self-effacing charm. Author and journalist Evan Thomas, who had spent time with him in Afghanistan, found in him "an appealing earnestness and openness (he doesn't hesitate to tick off his flaws: 'I'm impatient, I shoot from the hip, I ride my staff too hard...'), but one senses a certain wiliness as well." During his visit in Kabul, Thomas got the measure of the man whom he called "a purebred warrior." McChrystal, the son of a two-star general, had graduated from West Point in 1976. "He eats one meal a day," Thomas observed, "works out obsessively every morning at 5, and is so free of body fat that he looks gaunt."

A powerful military voice, McChrystal gained his authority not only from his position as head of the NATO forces in Afghanistan but from his legendary status as former commander of the Joint Special Operations Command. In the framing of Ben Rhodes, "McChrystal had a mythical reputation in the military. He helped to build America's Special Operations capability in Iraq and Afghanistan—the elite troops who kicked down doors, captured or killed terrorists, and mapped insurgencies like doctors tracing the spread of cancer within a patient's body."

During the question-and-answer period after the speech, McChrystal was asked if a scaled-back mission that targeted terrorists in Afghanistan and Pakistan could succeed. "The short, glib answer is no," he replied. "A strategy that does not leave Afghanistan in a stable position is probably a short-sighted strategy."

Though Biden was never mentioned, McChrystal's target was clear. The *New York Times* began its coverage of the London appearance by zeroing in on the conflict between the two men: "The top American commander in Afghanistan, Gen. Stanley A. McChrystal, used a speech here on Thursday to reject calls for the war effort to be scaled down from defeating the Taliban insurgency to a narrower focus on hunting down Al Qaeda, an option suggested by Vice President Joseph R. Biden Jr."

In Washington, the White House was livid over McChrystal's insubordination. While the president hadn't yet come to a decision on strategy, McChrystal's stating his opposition publicly to a possible option was inappropriate. The general's message to Obama was clear. As journalist Jonathan Alter put it: "If the president sided with Biden, the commanding general *couldn't support it*?"

McChrystal later asserted that he had meant no disrespect. Writing in his 2013 memoir, *My Share of the Task*, he explained, "Although Vice President Biden was not mentioned in the question, and I was not thinking of him in my answer, my response was reported as a rebuttal of other policy options for Afghanistan and as criticism of the vice president's views. It wasn't intended as such, but I could have said it better."

Defense Secretary Robert Gates had no doubt about the person McChrystal had in mind when he gave his reply. "Stan's speech was innocuous enough," Gates recalled in his 2013 memoir, "but in response to a question afterward, he dismissed out of hand the option Biden was supporting."

In February, at the start of his administration, President Obama had authorized an additional seventeen thousand troops for Afghanistan, and in March he approved another four thousand troops to serve as trainers of Afghan forces, bringing the total number to sixty-eight thousand. From the outset, Biden had contended that a broader commitment to the country did not reflect America's national interest. He had traveled to Afghanistan and Pakistan on a fact-finding mission, at President-Elect Obama's request, before the inauguration. As a senator, Biden had already made numerous trips to the region, and he knew the issues and players. He came back from his latest visit deeply pessimistic about prospects in Afghanistan. What he discovered there helped shape his outlook for how the United States should wage the war.

"Just let me take two minutes here," Biden said at a National Security Council meeting in March as Obama neared his first decision on Afghanistan policy. "I only have a couple of things to say." He then spoke for more than twenty minutes.

He reminded his listeners of the historical pitfalls of foreign intervention in Afghanistan; he noted that American success was not in sight even with the number of troops already on the ground; he argued that committing more troops was irresponsible amid the worsening conditions and, with an unreliable Afghan government, it would result in more casualties, cause a political backlash, and further sink public sentiment toward the war. By sending in reinforcements, he said, "we're just prolonging failure."

Nonetheless, at that early stage, Obama agreed to increase troop levels. But the last thing he wanted was for the mission to drag on and become his Vietnam. Though Biden held little sway over the early decision on troops, his arguments on limiting America's role in Afghanistan had settled into the president's thinking. In announcing the troop decision in March, the president signaled his impatience with open-ended, full-scale nation building.

Afterward, Obama and Secretary of State Hillary Clinton spoke to the *New York Times* to underscore that Biden's views were not only embraced but incorporated into policy considerations. While their support of the vice president was intended to quiet media talk of conflict within the White House, it also was a measure of Obama's growing appreciation for Biden as an adviser and partner. The *Times* piece highlighted the vice president's hand in narrowing the Afghan mission. "Officials involved in the deliberations said Biden had been influential in Obama's development of a new approach to Afghanistan," the paper wrote, "arguing for a relatively limited increase of military, diplomatic and economic involvement."

Months later, despite the increase in troops, progress in the war was elusive: the Taliban was resurgent, the Afghan government under President Hamid Karzai was corrupt and ineffectual, and the American public was increasingly disenchanted with the war. In August, Afghanistan held a presidential election, and Karzai was reelected amid suspicions of ballot stuffing and widespread electoral fraud. Also in August, forty-seven US troops were killed in action, making it the deadliest month of the eight-year-long war.

In his second Afghanistan strategy review, undertaken in the fall, Obama wanted wide-ranging discussion and full debate. Biden stuck to his proposals and also assumed his role, at Obama's behest, as chief provocateur to challenge participants and ensure that all points were fully addressed.

The Biden style was on full display in one meeting when the vice president raised an issue of abiding concern to Obama: the steep financial cost of Afghanistan and whether the dollars were well spent.

"Can I just clarify a factual point?" Biden put to the advisers in the Situation Room, interrupting the discussion. "How much will we spend this year on Afghanistan?"

When someone said $65 billion, Biden asked, "And how much will we spend on Pakistan?"

That amount, $2.25 billion, was sharply lower.

"Well, by my calculations that's a thirty-to-one ratio in favor of Afghanistan," Biden observed. "So I have a question. Al Qaeda is almost all in Pakistan, and Pakistan has nuclear weapons. And yet for every dollar we're spending in Pakistan, we're spending thirty dollars in Afghanistan. Does that make strategic sense?"

No one had an answer. By confronting the room in dramatic fashion, Biden forced the advisers to deepen their analysis. With McChrystal and the military petitioning for more troops and more funding, Biden believed it was his duty to raise his voice, not only for himself but for the president, to provoke the fullest debate possible.

Biden's performances in the Situation Room quickly won over Julie Smith, who served as his deputy national security advisor in 2012 and 2013. Before joining his staff, Smith had heard tales of Biden's lack of verbal discipline and his sometimes-unconventional foreign policy ideas. But once on the job, she saw a vice president far different from the public billing.

"What I found when I went into the Situation Room is that Biden got very serious. He was kind of uncharacteristically quiet and deferential," Smith recalled. Biden appreciated Obama's style of leadership and conformed to it. Biden's overwhelming, attention-attracting personality vanished during the moments most important to Obama. "In the Situation Room," Smith observed, "Biden was not larger than life, he did not take the oxygen out of the room, it was not all about him."

If Joe was still gregarious Joe in public, he tamed his instincts in the no-nonsense setting of the Situation Room. As Smith saw it, "That was maybe one of the reasons that this relationship, both from a professional and a personal perspective, unfolded in such a positive manner."

Before the fall strategy review began, Biden had called David Axelrod into his office, worried about McChrystal's drumbeating for an expansion of the Afghan operation. In the assessment he'd submitted to the president, the general had laid out a dire outlook for Afghanistan if America didn't send still more troops and commit more resources. In his reporting on the top-secret report, Bob Woodward noted the repeated usage of language uncommon in a general's playbook: the words *defeat* and *failure* appeared again and again.

At one point, McChrystal declared that if operations didn't change the way he suggested, "we run the risk of strategic defeat." In calling for more troops, the general issued a warning: "The status quo will lead to failure." In other words, success equaled a substantial new commitment of troops; though the number was not specified, it was commonly understood to be at least forty thousand.

"The president has asked me to play the bad cop on this," Biden told Axelrod, "and I am ready to do it." The president's aide agreed, noting that he "shared Biden's concern," and added that as a presidential candidate, Obama "had campaigned against nation building and open-ended engagements."

Woodward's reporting on McChrystal's report, a bombshell scoop that was splashed across the front page of the *Washington Post* on September 21, threw a shadow over the deliberations on strategy. A guessing game ensued over who gave Woodward the document, and the weight of speculation landed on someone associated with the Pentagon and probably linked to McChrystal. It was never definitively determined who released the material. "The word-on-the-streets rumor was that it was not McChrystal's team but NATO headquarters," said Georgetown law professor Rosa Brooks, then a counselor to Under Secretary of Defense for Policy Michèle Flournoy. Defense Secretary Gates had his own idea. Writing in his memoir, *Duty*, he revealed, "After I left office, I was chagrined to hear from an insider I trust that McChrystal's staff had leaked the assessment out of impatience with both the Pentagon and the White House." But Gates refused to believe McChrystal himself was behind it. "I'd be very surprised if Stan knew about it."

By throwing McChrystal's perspective into the national spotlight, those responsible hoped to pressure the president to reject Biden's entreaties and go with the McChrystal plan, which most top military officials favored. "The president has been taken hostage, thanks to the leaker," wrote journalist Marc Ambinder in *The Atlantic*. "The colloquial term for this in Washington is, and you'll pardon me, that the president was ratfucked."

Obama was particularly riled that the implied trust among participants to keep this careful, deliberative process private had been broken. "What was supposed to have been a secret review was now a public debate," Axelrod observed.

After the assessment hit the newspapers and cable television, Obama called in Gates and the chairman of the Joint Chiefs of Staff, Michael Mullen, and lit into them. Were they simply careless in allowing the report's leak? Or did they lack respect for him as commander in chief? "Neither is justifiable," he scolded them. Calibrating the president's exasperation, Axelrod recalled: "Even the slow-to-boil Obama was furious."

*Newsweek*'s Evan Thomas was with McChrystal at the coalition force headquarters in Kabul the week after the *Post* published the leaked report. The general told Thomas he was "taken aback" by the flap over his assessment. A military friend described McChrystal's disposition: "It's sort of like, 'Why is this happening to me now?'"

One evening Thomas joined McChrystal for his one meal of the day. Over salmon salad, chicken, and strawberry shortcake, Thomas wrote, the general appeared "clearly troubled." He was "'a bit bothered,' as he put it," by rumors back home suggesting "he might resign over his differences with those unnamed other experts in Washington." But as a soldier and commander at heart, McChrystal rejected the speculation. "It is my responsibility, my duty—my *sacred* duty," McChrystal told Thomas, to deliver the plain truth to his civilian leaders, "but then to carry out their orders. He would not resign, he said, even if they rejected his advice."

However loud the uproar, the White House was not going to be ratfucked into a decision. Summoning his advisers on national security,

Obama redoubled his determination to get a clear perspective on options for Afghanistan. "The goals need to be realistic and narrowly tailored to serve our national interest," he told his team, "and they need to be achievable."

In this tense setting, which included both White House advisers and Pentagon brass, Biden ramped up his role as the president's agitator in chief: he questioned—and challenged—the assumptions the military brought to the table. "The president would not be stampeded," Jules Witcover observed in his biography of Biden. Instead, Obama encouraged "continuing discussion in which Biden played devil's advocate regarding the proposals of the military leadership."

In going after Biden, McChrystal chose the wrong opponent at the wrong time. By now Joe's charms had worked on the president. Joe had grown on Obama, just as he had on almost everyone who got to know him. Coming on board late in the presidential campaign, Biden hadn't had the candidate's automatic trust, unlike others in the inner circle who had been with Obama through his days in Illinois politics and the US Senate. Biden had to earn it, and his puppy-dog loyalty and friendliness—along with his occasional bite, if honesty demanded it— had worked its magic.

Ben Rhodes, Obama's deputy national security advisor and speechwriter, had watched the relationship evolve. "At sixty-six," Rhodes said of Biden, "he was two decades older than Obama, and also embraced a more old-fashioned brand of politics—he'd walk the hallways of the West Wing, stopping to talk to people, gripping your forearm and holding on to it while he spoke." The Biden style won over the president. "Obama liked that Biden had an instinct for this brand of politics," Rhodes observed, "and came to love him with the almost protective sense of devotion to an older family member."

On the president's behalf, Biden drew on his political skills to smooth the way for Obama initiatives. After taking up his post in the West Wing, Joe kept his locker in the Senate gym, showing up there to

jawbone former colleagues on pending legislation. With a battle loom-
ing over the stimulus bill, the White House had asked Biden to target
six Republican senators crucial to the vote. The vice president worked
them, visiting and calling with the skill of persuasion developed over
long years serving in the chamber. In the end, he won the votes of
three of the six, which, Biden's chief of staff Ron Klain said, "wound
up being the difference."

From his rough early start as a gaffe-meister, Biden had shaped
himself into a conscientious, well-informed partner to the president.
Inside the White House, Biden was emerging as the heart to Obama's
brain; in private and in public, Biden's raw feelings about crucial issues
complemented Obama's cool intellect. Even Joe's exuberance at the
signing ceremony for Obama's health-care reform legislation—his
whispering to the president over an open mic, "This is a big fucking
deal!"—quickly became inconsequential and morphed into an example of Biden passion. Shortly afterward, White House press secretary
Josh Earnest agreed publicly with Joe's exclamation, declaring on
Twitter, "And yes Mr. Vice President, you're right."

Dismissing Biden's verbal stumbles, the president's close friend
and senior adviser Valerie Jarrett observed, "We all have to have our
words clarified at times. That's part of what makes the vice president
so endearing. Everyone says, 'Oh my gosh. I could have said that.' And
the press tends to overblow it. We wouldn't change him one bit."

On foreign policy, however, Biden was criticized by some for faulty
judgments through the years—and, to these detractors, his latest pronouncements on Afghanistan fit the pattern. Thomas Ricks, a veteran
journalist who covered the military for the *Wall Street Journal* and the
*Washington Post*, offered a short commentary on a *Foreign Policy* blog
under the headline "Just How Wrong Can Joe Biden Be?" He charged
that Biden didn't "know what he is talking about" on the subject of
McChrystal's strategy of counterinsurgency. The aim was to protect the
population and beat back the Taliban to build support for the Afghan

government—and in Ricks's view, it was not as massive and expensive an operation as Biden had suggested. "Word on the street is that [Biden] has been dozing during the briefings," Ricks wrote. "Request to NSC: Will someone over there have the VP and his posse get a brief on counterinsurgency from the Special Operators on the Joint Staff before he shoots off his mouth again?"

Others pointed out times when Biden's foreign policy choices were misguided: they noted that, as a senator, he voted against the Persian Gulf war of 1991, which drove Saddam Hussein out of Kuwait, and voted in favor of the 2003 Iraq invasion, and opposed the largely successful troop surge in Iraq in 2007. In another blog post, Ricks asked, "When was the last time Biden was right about anything?"

Biden countered by drawing attention to his better foreign policy calls. "From nuclear arms control to ending ethnic cleansing in the Balkans to confronting the threat of terrorism," his communications director, Jay Carney, contended, "the vice president has not only been right on many of the toughest questions of US foreign policy over the past thirty years, he has been consistently ahead of the curve."

By coincidence, the day after McChrystal's speech in London, Obama was aboard Air Force One flying to Copenhagen to personally lobby the International Olympic Committee to bring the Summer Games to Chicago in 2016. In an unprecedented appeal, Obama was to become the first president to address the committee in person on behalf of an American city's bid, believing his direct appeal could lift Chicago past other contenders, such as Rio de Janeiro.

While in the air, the president vented over McChrystal's London performance. "We got to stop this," he told an aide. "This is not helping."

So, in a hastily arranged meeting, as the *Washington Post* reported, McChrystal "was whisked to Denmark at Obama's request." As Obama sat on the tarmac at the Copenhagen airport during his rushed five-hour visit, the general bounded up the stairs of Air Force One and into the cabin. The men had met only once before, when McChrystal had assumed command of the Afghanistan mission in June.

McChrystal's one-paragraph account in his memoir depicted the get-together as genial. "In both our initial greeting with spouses and our one-on-one meeting, the president was focused but friendly and supportive," McChrystal wrote. "I don't remember either of us raising anything about the speech."

During their twenty-five-minute conversation, Woodward reported in his book *Obama's Wars*, "neither [Obama nor McChrystal] dwelt on the speech, but both acknowledged that it wouldn't happen again." McChrystal reiterated his support of his own assessment of the war but bowed to Obama's authority. "Mr. President," he told the commander in chief, "you describe the mission and we'll do whatever we need to carry it out."

The president's aides used the standard reveal-nothing word— "productive"—for describing tough private meetings and "went out of their way to say how fond Obama is of the man he chose to lead the war." Afterward Obama told his aides, "I like him. I think he's a good man." In its coverage, the *Post* said the White House "refused to say whether Obama scolded McChrystal."

On the flight home from Copenhagen, Obama learned that his personal petition to the International Olympic Committee had fallen short. Chicago was voted out of the running for the 2016 Olympics on the first round, coming in fourth out of four cities bidding for the honor. The president looked stunned, as did his staff, as they watched CNN aboard Air Force One while traveling over the Cabot Strait between Newfoundland and Nova Scotia. Back home, Obama leaned on a sports metaphor to describe his own Olympic effort in pitching Chicago. "One of the things that I think is most valuable about sports," he said in the Rose Garden, "is that you can play a great game and still not win."

In late November, Obama came to his Afghanistan strategy decision after three months of intensive deliberations. Meeting with the entire national security team in the Oval Office, Obama passed out a six-page document outlining his orders. He then explained, "There's going to be a hard-and-fast thirty-thousand-troop surge." Though he was providing McChrystal with additional resources to aid the building of an Afghan security force and to improve local governance, Obama was redefining the mission. "This is neither counterinsurgency nor nation building," he directed. "The costs are prohibitive." But, he conceded, it "has many elements of a counterinsurgency strategy."

Stressing that this was not an open-ended exercise, the president ordered that in a year there would be an assessment to gauge how the operation was proceeding, and then about seven months after that, in July 2011, a drawdown of the US forces would begin. "We're going to begin to thin out," he said.

Biden's wish to take the war to the terrorists in Pakistan also got a boost in the president's orders. Two days later, speaking at the United States Military Academy at West Point, New York, Obama laid out his strategy before four thousand cadets. The troop increase was intended to aid stepped-up efforts to take down al-Qaeda. "Our overarching goal remains the same," the president said, "to disrupt, dismantle, and defeat al-Qaeda in Afghanistan and Pakistan, and to prevent its capacity to threaten America and our allies in the future."

The president's strategy was a carefully calibrated compromise recognizing the needs on the ground but also the imperative to head off an interminable commitment. Both Biden and McChrystal got something they wanted. The new initiative should have been the end of their standoff.

But it wasn't.

About seven months later, in June 2010, General McChrystal was asleep in his room at the NATO coalition forces headquarters in Kabul, Afghanistan, when his chief of staff, Colonel Charlie Flynn, woke him at two in the morning: "Sir, we have a problem."

It wasn't incoming fire. It wasn't a dreaded roadside bomb injuring or killing troops. This fusillade posed no physical risk to the general or his men. Rather, it was a journalistic salvo packed with enough explosives to blow up a career.

McChrystal, who kept to a strict regimen of no more than four hours of sleep, had his slumber cut even shorter on this night. Flynn, speaking into the dark, said, "The *Rolling Stone* article is out, and it's really bad."

Later, writing in his memoir, the general demonstrated a certain naivete about the dangers of the press, italicizing his initial thought: *"How in the world could that story have been a problem?"*

For at least a month, McChrystal had allowed a *Rolling Stone* writer, Michael Hastings, to spend time with him and his staff in Kabul and elsewhere in the hope of providing Americans with a transparent view of the Afghanistan mission. Hastings roamed among McChrystal and his command team as they managed a difficult war. With Hastings, the men were themselves: high-spirited, macho, profane, and determined to carry out their mission as they saw fit. Among some inside and outside of journalism Hastings had the reputation of a "troublemaker," as *New York Times* writer Mark Leibovich put it in his book *This Town*.

In large part, the article was an assessment of the success—or in Hastings's eyes, the failure—of the counterinsurgency operations led by McChrystal and his staff. In Hastings's telling, McChrystal's men— British, American, Afghan—were a "handpicked collection of killers, spies, geniuses, patriots, political operators and outright maniacs.... They pride themselves on their can-do attitude and their disdain for authority."

Hastings reminded readers that in selling his demands, McChrystal had gotten "a crash course in Beltway politics—a battle that pitted him against experienced Washington insiders like Vice President Biden, who argued that a prolonged counterinsurgency campaign in Afghanistan would plunge America into a military quagmire without weakening international terrorist networks." The reporter noted that in June Afghanistan had become America's longest war in history, surpassing Vietnam, and he hinted at Biden's prescience.

"The president finds himself stuck in something even more insane than a quagmire," Hastings wrote, "a quagmire he knowingly walked into, even though it's precisely the kind of gigantic, mind-numbing, multigenerational nation-building project he explicitly said he didn't want."

Hastings's negative critique of the war was hardly the worst bombshell in the article. Loose-tongued around the reporter, McChrystal and his team had plunged themselves up to their necks in a mire of their own making; apparently the men had not forgotten—or forgiven—their masters in Washington for opposing their wishes, even though, as the *Rolling Stone* journalist put it, "in the end...McChrystal got almost exactly what he wanted."

In tone and perspective, the *Rolling Stone* piece was as blunt and direct as McChrystal himself. Recounting the general's battle with Washington, Hastings wrote that McChrystal "prides himself on being sharper and ballsier than anyone else, but his brashness comes with a price." The writer noted that in the one year that McChrystal had been in charge of the war, "he has managed to piss off almost everyone with a stake in the conflict."

Describing the general's meeting with Obama aboard Air Force One in Copenhagen, Hastings said McChrystal got "a smackdown from the president," adding: "The message to McChrystal seemed clear: *Shut the fuck up, and keep a lower profile.*" In tough language, Hastings called out McChrystal for "trying to bully Obama" to get his way on the troops. "It was Obama versus the Pentagon," Hastings wrote, "and the Pentagon was determined to kick the president's ass."

The most damning material in the article was the disrespect that McChrystal and his staff showed Obama, Biden, and others on the president's team. An adviser to McChrystal is quoted as describing the general's first meeting with Obama as a "ten-minute photo op." The face-to-face came after the president named McChrystal commander in Afghanistan. "Obama clearly didn't know anything about him, who he was," the adviser told Hastings. "Here's the guy who's going to run his fucking war, but he didn't seem very engaged."

In one scene Hastings captured, McChrystal and his team seemed to rejoice in taking down Biden. The general was with his staff in Paris, a city he openly disdained for its froufrou style, to deliver a speech meant to rally fading NATO support for the war. Preparing for his talk at France's military academy, École Militaire, McChrystal had Biden on his mind. It was as though Biden and his nagging questions on the counterinsurgency haunted the general.

As McChrystal checked over the text of his speech, he asked his staff whether he should expect a question about Biden during the Q and A afterward. If he got one, he wondered, how should he respond? "I never know what's going to pop out until I'm up there," he said, "that's the problem."

McChrystal and his men then acted out what might happen if someone in the audience brought up Biden. Re-creating the scene, Hastings wrote: "Unable to help themselves, [McChrystal] and his staff imagine the general dismissing the vice president with a good one-liner.

"'Are you asking about Vice President Biden?' McChrystal says with a laugh. 'Who's that?'

"'Biden?' suggests a top adviser. 'Did you say: Bite Me?'"

By venting their unfiltered passion, McChrystal and his staff had wandered into territory largely associated with Joe Biden. As Leibovich put it in his book *This Town*, the general's "staff (and by implication, McChrystal himself) had clearly spoken out of school, or 'off-message'—or candidly. Gaffe!" What was lost in the ensuing uproar was whether McChrystal's viewpoint on the war was even worth hearing. "The substance and merit of the remarks were beside the point," Leibovich observed. "Because McChrystal was playing the wrong game. He made a dumb PR move."

In the wee hours of that night in June as McChrystal read the *Rolling Stone* article—headlined "The Runaway General"—he had a sinking feeling of disbelief. "For a number of minutes," he recalled, "I felt as though I'd likely awaken from what seemed like a surreal dream, but the situation was real."

After reading the piece in its entirety, McChrystal knew it was he who had fucked up—and he'd have to face the consequences. He felt Hastings had thrown a harsh light on aspects of himself and his international team. But if viewed through the perspective of military camaraderie, the picture would not have looked nearly as negative. "Regardless of how I judged the story for fairness or accuracy, [the] responsibility was mine," McChrystal acknowledged. "And its ultimate effect was immediately clear to me."

Phones were ringing in Washington. The chairman of the Joint Chiefs of Staff, Michael Mullen, called Defense Secretary Gates to say that a *Rolling Stone* article was coming out "about McChrystal that was potentially very damaging." "As I read it," the defense secretary recalled, "I wondered what in the world Stan had been thinking to give this reporter such access." Gates zeroed in on a calamitous sin in the piece, something that, along with its other offenses, was going to ignite like "dynamite" at the White House. "Most egregiously," Gates assessed, "the article portrayed the general mocking the vice president."

When Gates's phone rang again, it was McChrystal calling to apologize. The defense secretary was already deeply concerned about the impact of the article on the war. "For once I couldn't contain my anger," Gates recounted. He laid into the runaway general: "What the fuck were you thinking?"

In his conversation with Gates, McChrystal didn't claim that the article misquoted him or his staff or that it "was distorted in any way."

Gates listened as "the four-star general replied essentially as he had been taught as a cadet at West Point—'No excuses, sir.'"

Joe Biden was aboard Air Force Two flying back to Washington from an event in Illinois when he got an urgent call from McChrystal. The vice president listened while the general apologized for the contents of an article Biden hadn't read—and didn't even know existed. Biden then phoned the president, who hadn't heard about it either. Obama enlisted Press Secretary Robert Gibbs to round up copies and make sure White House aides got them.

When Obama got the article, according to Jonathan Alter, the "disgusted president didn't read much beyond the first paragraph." He didn't have to read far: the opening anecdote was the scene in Paris climaxing with "'Biden?...Did you say: 'Bite Me?'"

In Alter's estimation, McChrystal—despite his esteemed leadership qualities and Obama's fondness for him—had been in a fragile position since his aggressive push against the White House in the autumn and his attacks on Biden, including his October speech in London. "The *Rolling Stone* interview might have rolled off his back had it not been for the insubordination drama of late 2009," Alter argued.

If the White House earlier had pointed fingers at several members of the military brass for their pressure tactics, condemnation now fell fully on the commander in Afghanistan. "It was McChrystal who was to blame for setting a terrible example by disrespecting civilian authority and the chain of command," Alter concluded.

Later that night, Defense Secretary Gates fielded two phone calls from National Security Advisor James L. Jones to inform him that "the White House was getting very 'spun up' about the article." To Gates, that description was "a classic understatement."

After placing his phone calls, including one to his wife, and brainstorming over crisis management with his staff, McChrystal began a lonely journey, first by taking a run around the inside of the headquarters compound by himself in the dark. Usually, after his brief night's sleep, he ran seven miles each morning; his workout on this morning began even earlier than usual.

Later in the day, the general—thirty-four years in uniform—prepared for a flight back to Washington, summoned by the president. "Anticipation built over his fateful White House meeting," Leibovich wrote. "This Town loves a deathwatch."

While McChrystal was in the air, an expected storm erupted on the ground in Washington. The White House and the Pentagon were suddenly engaged in fresh battle over the actions of the super-disciplined yet incautious four-star general. Obama and his vice president, in particular, already leaned toward dismissing McChrystal, while Gates and others in the military hoped to secure a reprieve. In a statement, the defense secretary acknowledged the job-threatening stumble the article posed and suggested that the general, having apologized to everyone he'd dishonored, had taken the necessary contrite steps.

The White House, however, signaled it was in no mood for mercy. At his press briefing, Press Secretary Robert Gibbs pointed repeatedly to the private meeting planned for the president and the general the following day. Reporters peppered Gibbs with questions: What was Obama's view on the general's insubordination? Did the president have confidence in his Afghanistan commander? Why hadn't the two men talked on the phone yet? What was the fate of McChrystal's job? Gibbs's standard reply was, "We'll have more to say after that meeting."

As reporters pressed further about the president's possible firing of McChrystal, Gibbs at first refused to acknowledged it but then admitted the option was on the table.

"Were you with the president when he reacted in any way to this story?" a reporter asked. "And if so, how would you describe it? Was he surprised? Was he angry?"

"I was—I gave him the article last night." After a few ums and ahs, Gibbs offered: "And he was angry."

"How so?"

"Angry," Gibbs reiterated. "You would know it if you saw it."

A ripple of nervous laughter carried through the room.

Hoping to save McChrystal's job, Defense Secretary Gates met with Obama at about the same time as the press briefing. Gates suspected that Vice President Biden and others, still harboring resentment toward McChrystal because of his bullheadedness over troop levels, saw an opening to take down a vulnerable opponent and were rushing in.

Biden had phoned Gates before his meeting with the president and, in Gates's view, spoke "rather defensively" about his conversation with Obama about the *Rolling Stone* piece. Biden insisted, "I didn't rile him up last night, I just asked him if he'd seen the article." Gates wasn't buying it. "To this day," Gates wrote in his memoir, "I believe [McChrystal] was given the bum's rush by Biden, White House staff, and [the national security staff]."

As the president's closest adviser—and a figure subjected to vulgar ridicule in the article—Biden was in a frontline position to promote his own view. The president also was sensitive to the indignity that McChrystal and his staff had inflicted on the vice president. Describing the competing voices petitioning Obama, writer George Packer noted that the president had "Biden snarling in his ear."

When Gates went in for his private meeting with the president, Obama's first words were, "I'm leaning toward relieving McChrystal." Among his motivations, apparently, was the affront to Biden. Characterizing Biden's reaction to the article the previous night, Obama told Gates, "Joe is over the top about this." Thinking back to Biden's tepid description of his conversation with the president, Gates wrote in his memoir, "So much for Biden's credibility."

That night, on the patio outside the Oval Office, Obama asked his speechwriter and deputy national security advisor Ben Rhodes to prepare two speeches to cover the possible outcomes of the president's meeting with McChrystal: yea or nay on the general's future. "He didn't tell me what his decision would be," Rhodes wrote later in his book *The World as It Is*, "but he tipped his hand when he spent a lot more time giving guidance for a decision to get rid of McChrystal." By this point, in Rhodes's view, "he seemed more sad than angry. 'Stan's a good guy,' he said."

The next morning McChrystal landed at Andrews Air Force Base, showered, pulled on his green uniform, and at 8:30 a.m. went to meet with Gates and the chairman of the Joint Chiefs of Staff, Michael Mullen. A little more than an hour later, he sat briefly in private with President Obama, apologizing for his actions but offering no excuses. When he left the Oval Office, McChrystal was no longer the commander in Afghanistan. His career was over.

Gates laid blame on both the general and Biden. The crisis revealed the sharp division between the White House and the military and the damaging role of politics in management of the war. "McChrystal... had handed Biden and his other adversaries at the White House and [national security staff] the opportunity to drive him from command," Gates lamented. "The article simply was the last of several public missteps by the general."

Obama was intent on reining in the White House–Pentagon conflict and focusing on the chief concern: succeeding in Afghanistan by means of the agreed-upon strategy. To head off any further dissension, he named General David Petraeus to assume command in Kabul. As head of United States Central Command, Petraeus was McChrystal's immediate boss and a famous general who was responsible for the successful counterinsurgency strategy in Iraq.

Though the move was effectively a step down for him, he accepted it and was unanimously regarded as the perfect solution to an unruly problem.

After announcing the shift in command during a Rose Garden address, Obama called in his National Security Council, determined to put the turmoil behind him and the nation. He gave strict orders for no one on his staff to celebrate the outcome, exploit it, or appear triumphant. Unity was required. Ben Rhodes noted that the staff Obama had gathered were "the same personalities who had proved so hard to manage during the Afghan review. It was a brief meeting, and he raised his voice, which almost never happened. 'If people can't pull together as a team, then other people are going to go. I mean it.'"

Obama's decision on McChrystal had a dual purpose: to assert civilian control over the military and to defend his vice president. Something else happened during the McChrystal crisis. The general's conduct had resulted in an unintended consequence: Barack and Joe had moved closer to each other. Their bond was strengthened by their mutual defense. Like battlefield comrades under fire, they became, as administration aide Kate Bedingfield put it, "brothers in arms."

Having weathered their fiercest challenge, Barack and Joe now had a special understanding: anyone who attacked one implicitly attacked the other. "The president had the vice president's back," Bedingfield said. "He always had his back, and he knew the vice president always had his. That underpinned the relationship."

With some irony, McChrystal had blown up his career by shooting off his mouth in a battle with Joe Biden, the gaffe maven. In his monologue after the firing, comedian Jay Leno inadvertently showed that in the world of miscues, Biden, it turned out, wore a suit of armor. Indeed, in his duel with McChrystal, Joe was the last man standing.

"General McChrystal was relieved of his duties because of derogatory comments he made about President Obama and other White House staffers," Leno told his *Tonight Show* audience. "In fact, when he heard that, Joe Biden was shocked and said, 'What? You can get fired for saying something stupid? What? When'd they start that? Is that new?'"

# TWELVE

# "HOW CAN THIS HAVE HAPPENED?"

After thirty-six years in the Senate and nearly four years as President Barack Obama's vice president, Joe Biden was an old hand at the Sunday morning political shows. He'd appeared on NBC's *Meet the Press* perhaps as many as forty times.

But this appearance, on the first weekend in May 2012, was crucial. He needed to hit the issues right on point—the economy, national security, China, Afghanistan—and he had to lay out the case for Americans to stick with President Obama in 2012 over the Republican contender, former Massachusetts governor Mitt Romney.

Biden's staff teamed up with Obama's to drill the vice president on the questions he'd likely get from *Meet the Press* moderator David Gregory. His prepping sessions were long and intense, lasting more than twelve hours over several days.

The mission was clear: stay on message.

In six months voters would go to the polls, and President Obama had chosen this weekend for the official launch of his reelection campaign, jetting to back-to-back rallies on Saturday, May 5, in the battleground states of Ohio and Virginia.

In Columbus, he bounded onto the stage at Ohio State University's

Schottenstein Center. "If people ask you what this campaign is about, you tell them it's still about hope," the president declared, looking lanky and youthful in an open-collar shirt, his sleeves rolled up. "Because I still believe, Ohio," he promised in full candidate lilt, "I still believe that we are not as divided as our politics suggest." And he gave the same riff he'd been serving up since he emerged on the stage of the Democratic National Convention in 2004. "I still believe that we have more in common than the pundits tell us, that we're not Democrats or Republicans but Americans first and foremost."

The Ohio race looked tight. Obama had won the state in 2008 by a 4.6 percent margin over Republican opponent Senator John McCain, but now, a half year before the next vote, polls put the president and Romney in a dead heat. The US economy was fragile, still recovering from the financial disaster Obama had inherited from the previous administration, and the national unemployment rate hovered above 8 percent.

The campaign needed to emphasize the president's successes. One strong talking point: Obama's massive bailout of Chrysler and General Motors had revived America's battered carmakers, as the president reminded his Ohio supporters: "Today our auto industry is back on top of the world." Pivoting to foreign policy, the president touted his drawdown of US troops in Iraq. "For the first time in nine years," he boasted, "there are no Americans fighting in Iraq."

The Schottenstein crowd was exuberant, but it didn't fill the twenty-thousand-seat arena, as the *Toledo Blade* told its readers: "There were a lot of empty seats." In the unforgiving campaign ahead, the Obama team had to storm across the landscape with battlefield precision. The president's wary aides were in agreement: there was no room for error.

After Obama's rallies on Saturday, Biden's *Meet the Press* appearance on Sunday was choreographed as the second punch of the weekend launch. In his pre-show promo, host David Gregory strolled onto NBC's glitzy set, pumped up over his high-profile guest.

"This morning," he announced, clasping his hands together, "an exclusive interview with Vice President Joe Biden. We'll talk about jobs and the economy, the politics of national security, and how the vice president sizes up Mitt Romney. It's a big weekend for the Obama campaign."

When he took his seat on the set at NBC's Washington studio, Biden exuded the image of the president's lieutenant in a crisp charcoal suit, white shirt, and blue-striped tie. After the obligatory pleasantries, Gregory challenged Biden on the state of the economy: slow job growth and a high unemployment rate. The vice president fended off the attack, comporting himself with charm and intelligence and noting the dismal state of the economy when Obama came into office: four million jobs had been lost over several months before the new administration took over. Contrary to Gregory's assertion, Biden said, there was no stagnation: there had been a steady growth in jobs for the past twenty-six straight months.

Without warning, the host then sucker punched Biden by raising a sensitive topic that had already been resolved. "Let me talk about the campaign for the presidency," Gregory began. "Should I assume by virtue of the fact that you're here today that you're a lock for the ticket?"

It was an impudent question, and Gregory answered it by the way he framed it, indicating that the proof was self-evident: Biden *was* there, sitting in front of him, representing the ticket as vice president.

But there was historical precedent for the question. From the early days of the republic, presidents had switched out sitting vice presidents for their reelection bids when it suited their interests. President Thomas Jefferson, never keen on his vice president, Aaron Burr, dropped him as his running mate in the election of 1804, the same year Burr killed Alexander Hamilton in a duel. Before the nineteenth century was out, several more vice presidents had found themselves spurned. In the twentieth century, Franklin Delano Roosevelt, who was elected four times to the presidency, had three vice presidents.

Gregory's questioning of Biden's place on the ticket touched on an inescapable fact of political partnerships—sometimes loyalty only went so far. President Obama had not prevented his aides from quietly assessing the impact of dumping Biden in favor of Hillary Clinton. Obama adviser David Axelrod had privately argued against any change. "Swapping Clinton for Biden would have been seen as weak and disloyal," he wrote in his memoir.

The quiet discussions had burst into public conversation as far back as October 2010, when Bob Woodward appeared on CNN's *John King, USA* to pitch his new book, *Obama's Wars*. Concluding the interview, King asked Woodward to speculate on the possibility of the campaign dropping Biden. "A lot of people think if the president's weak in 2012 he'll have to do a switch there and run with Clinton as his running mate," King said. "In all these conversations when you're doing serious research, [are] things like that coming up?"

Woodward, regarded by many as the best-sourced journalist in Washington, said bluntly, "It's on the table. And some of Hillary Clinton's advisers see it as a real possibility in 2012. President Obama needs some of the women, Latinos, retirees that she did so well with during the 2008 primaries. And so they switch jobs. And [it's] not out of the question."

The White House moved quickly to discredit the idea. The following morning Press Secretary Robert Gibbs showed up on CNN's morning show. "No one in the White House is discussing this as a possibility," he asserted.

But the burbling of the notion didn't go away. It persisted, off and on, into the 2012 campaign. A couple weeks after Biden's appearance on *Meet the Press*, conservative columnist William Kristol wrote a mean-spirited piece in the *Weekly Standard* calling on Obama to rid himself of Biden. "We sincerely suggest to President Obama: Dump Joe Biden. We're sure the thought has occurred to the president." Kristol pointed to a recent Fox News poll showing Obama's favorable rating at

52 percent and Biden's at 41 percent. "In other words," Kristol argued, "Biden will clearly be a drag on Obama's fortunes this fall." He then laid out the case for Clinton: her nearly eighteen million votes in the 2008 Democratic primaries, her 65 percent favorable rating in a *Washington Post* poll not long ago, her pull on the white working-class and middle-class voters Obama needed.

Kristol moved right on to logistics. "Wouldn't a Biden-Clinton switch be messy and embarrassing and chaotic?" he posed. "Not really. There aren't many Biden loyalists around, after all, to cause much of a fuss." And think of the benefits of Biden on the sidelines but still working for the Obama-Clinton ticket. "Biden could still be useful as a surrogate campaigner in third-tier media markets that might be grateful for a visit from a celebrity," Kristol snidely remarked, "even one without much of a future."

The White House stuck with Biden. The results of its polling and focus groups showed that a swap provided no added advantage to the ticket, and the idea was set aside. Joe survived. But his pain and confusion did not lie far below the surface. That Obama stood aside while his aides strategized on Biden's future gave Joe plenty of reason to question the president's commitment to him.

During his *Meet the Press* appearance, Biden didn't respond immediately to Gregory's prying about whether his place on the ticket was secure and instead tilted his head down and laughed. The host persisted with a chuckle: "No question about it?"

When he looked up, Biden was grinning: "There's no—there is no question about it." His tone was jovial but his mind was racing. He chose humor to express his disdain for Gregory's inquiry; he gave a light wave of his hands, as though flicking away the rudeness, and with a big smile and a glint in his eye, he joked: "There's no way out. I mean, they've already printed Obama-Biden."

Sensing Biden's vulnerability, Gregory plowed on. "Has it annoyed you," he probed, "that there's been all of this buzz about, 'Well, if the president would put in Secretary Clinton, you know, he'd be a shoo-in for reelection, if he would just make that switch'?"

Biden resisted Gregory's taunt and demonstrated his value to the ticket. With a deftness born of years in the public spotlight, he deflected the conversation away from himself and shaped his answer into a defense of President Obama. But his mind was still racing, and he tripped over his wording.

"The thing that annoys me about it is the implication that somehow President Clinton is weak and he needs some kind of help," Biden said—and immediately realized his mistake. "I mean—"

But Gregory beat him to it. "President Obama," the host corrected.

When Biden was young and still plagued by a stutter, his mother told him there was nothing wrong with him, his mind just moved too fast for his tongue. "Joey, you're so handsome," his mother insisted. "Joey, you're such a good athlete. Joey, you've got such a high IQ. You've got so much to say, honey, that your brain gets ahead of you."

You could see Biden, even at age seventy, working to tame himself, concentrating on getting his words out right and sometimes repeating a syllable several times while he steadied himself. Though he had worked massively to overcome his galloping mind, it still lay in wait, ready to trip him up in tense situations.

Unfazed, Joe kept talking, as if nothing had crossed him up. He explained that any discussion of switching vice-presidential candidates annoyed him because it wrongly suggested that the president was weak.

Now came a trademark example of Biden loyalty. That anyone would argue that Hillary Clinton should replace Joe Biden, the vice president contended, was merely an attempt to say that President Obama needed a boost in the current campaign—and that was ridiculous, in Biden's view. Joe turned the slap against himself into an endorsement of the president. In some broken language, Joe spoke of the president's strength and his consistent character.

"I think—look, we got the strongest can—We got the best candidate, man. And he—this guy has a backbone like a ramrod. This—I think we're just—I think we have clearly the best candidate."

By most standards, the exchange between Biden and Gregory would have been considered an extraordinary moment of political television. But the media largely overlooked it. Instead, reporters swarmed over what the vice president declared moments later.

Joe still hadn't entirely regained his footing when Gregory plunged into a sensitive matter that hung unresolved over the administration. "You know," the host began, "the president has said that his views on gay marriage, on same-sex marriage, have evolved. But he's opposed to it. You're opposed to it. Have your views…evolved?"

Without hesitation, Biden said he had indeed evolved on the issue—faster and further than the president. Several weeks earlier the vice president had admitted in a private meeting in Los Angeles with thirty advocates for gay and lesbian rights that his view differed from Obama's, and he'd told the group that he had to keep his opinion to himself. But now, on national television, he decided to speak from the heart.

"Look," Biden began. "I just think—that—the good news is"—he set his elbows on the table and interlaced his fingers, almost prayerlike. To Joe, the question wasn't complicated. Gay marriage, he said, came down to "a simple proposition: Who do you love?" He repeated it for emphasis: "Who do you love? And will you be loyal to the person you love?" He explained that most people believed that was what all marriages were about, "whether they're marriages of lesbians or gay men or heterosexuals."

Drawing the vice president out, Gregory asked, "Is that what you believe now?"

"That's what I believe," Biden answered.

Recognizing that Biden had just voiced a controversial split with

President Obama, Gregory pushed onward to the key question: "And you're comfortable with same-sex marriage now?"

Trying to step around the trap, Biden stressed he was only speaking for himself personally, not for the White House.

"I—I—look, I am vice president of the United States of America. The president sets the policy," he clarified. He kept talking, elaborating on his view: "I am absolutely comfortable with the fact that men marrying men, women marrying women, and heterosexual men and women marrying another"—he slowed down now to make his point perfectly clear—"are entitled to the same exact rights, all the civil rights, all the civil liberties. And quite frankly, I don't see much of a distinction beyond that."

The Obama team's carefully planned campaign kickoff suddenly fell into disarray: the vice president had announced, on live TV, that he favored same-sex marriage while the president, as everyone knew, lagged behind him. The Biden bomb ripped through the Obama team, and immediately his aides—always on edge over Joe—raced to handle the fallout. "We were completely shocked—the president, myself... others in the White House—when we got the transcript of the Biden interview," remembered David Plouffe, Obama's 2008 campaign manager, who was now a senior adviser to the president.

What made Biden so appealing—that on the public stage he was more heart than sense—also made him infuriating. In his impulsive and sometimes reckless moments, the polished senior politician was not much different from the impulsive schoolboy he once was, running around Scranton or Wilmington. Despite his stutter, young Joey was a leader and risk-taker, the kind of kid who wouldn't turn down a dare.

Back in Scranton, at age eight or nine, Joey and a friend were watching a dump truck at work on a construction site when the friend dared Joey to run under the giant vehicle as it moved slowly back and forth across the dirt. "Thing was," wrote Richard Ben Cramer in *What*

*It Takes*, his 1992 book on presidential politics, the friend *"never*—NO CHANCE—thought the kid would *do* it...but Joey did it. The dump truck was loaded to the gills and backing up—not too fast—and Joey was small...and he ran under the truck from the side, between the front and back wheels...then let the front axle pass over him. If it *touched* him, he was finished—marmalade—but Joey was quick. The front wheels missed him clean." In his portrait of Biden's abortive run for the presidency in 1988, Cramer saw the child in the adult: "Joe Biden had balls. Lots of times, more balls than sense."

Young, irrepressible Joey was as much a part of the Obama White House as the grown-up politician he later became, and it was precisely Joe's audacity that the reflective president needed at his side. Unintentionally, Biden had nudged the president to have some courage on same-sex marriage and confront the issue publicly before he wanted to do so.

After his unequivocal declaration on *Meet the Press* that same-sex couples were entitled to the same civil rights as anyone, Biden pushed even further to illustrate his point. He told David Gregory about that private meeting he had had with gay advocates in Los Angeles. During the meeting's question-and-answer period, Biden recounted, one of the men wanted to know: "Let me ask you, how do you feel about us?"

In reply, Biden had singled out a gay couple at the meeting. He had visited the two men in their home and met their two adopted children, and when he had walked into the house, the kids, ages seven and five, had handed him flowers. The vice president repeated for the national television audience what he had said to those two men at the private meeting: "I wish every American could see the look of love those kids had in their eyes for you guys. And they wouldn't have any doubt about what this is about."

Obama's aide David Plouffe was enraged by Biden's performance. "WHAT THE FUCK?" he cried, reading over the *Meet the Press* transcript. "HOW CAN THIS HAVE HAPPENED?" Plouffe had long been uncertain about the political repercussions of the president's declaring any change in his views on gay marriage and had persuaded Obama to keep quiet on the issue. The president, ever sensitive to political expediency, had accepted his adviser's caution.

Obama's journey on the issue had been long and contradictory. Back in Chicago in 1996, when he ran for an Illinois state senate seat, he told a gay newspaper in a questionnaire that he favored legalizing same-sex marriage. But in 2004 as a US Senate candidate he pulled back on his support, saying marriage was something just for a man and a woman. The politics of the issue on the national stage could be crushing. In 2008, on the presidential campaign trail, he took an official position against a change in marriage rights, though he let it be known among his confidants that his views were evolving.

By 2011—now in the White House—he had come around: he privately told his advisers he approved of gay marriage. But for public circulation, his aides wanted only to promote the line that he was "evolving." To some of his progressive followers, Obama's reticence reflected a lack of political courage. In his book *The Persistence of the Color Line*, Harvard law professor Randall Kennedy expressed his dismay at Obama's hesitation to speak out forcefully on a range of issues, from racial injustice to gay rights. "He has liberal instincts and will effectuate progressive reforms," Kennedy wrote, "but only if he can do so without getting uncomfortably close to what he perceives to be too high a political price."

Kennedy chided the president for moving slowly on same-sex marriage. "It seems rather obvious that the evolution of his stated position is contingent upon the evolution of public opinion," he wrote. "As the public more fully accepts same-sex marriage, so too will Obama."

As president, Obama demonstrated his sympathy for the rights of the gay community. He led and won the repeal of the Clinton-era "Don't Ask, Don't Tell" policy, which denied openly gay Americans the right to serve in the military. Obama also ended the Justice Department's legal defense of the 1996 Defense of Marriage Act, which defined marriage as a union of a man and a woman and allowed states to refuse to recognize same-sex marriages attained in other states; the Supreme Court would rule the law unconstitutional in 2013.

Though Obama's views on gay marriage had changed, as had public opinion, Plouffe and other advisers wanted to be sure that if he were to come clean, the politics of such an announcement would tip Obama's way. They conducted internal polling and gathered focus groups, but the results were inconclusive: in Plouffe's eyes, a direct Obama statement favoring gay marriage was still too risky ahead of the 2012 general election.

Obama, however, chafed at his own lack of authenticity on gay marriage. His wife Michelle and his longtime friend and adviser Valerie Jarrett told him to disregard the politics and simply declare publicly what he felt. David Axelrod, the chief strategist for both Obama presidential campaigns, and Dan Pfeiffer, a senior presidential adviser, counseled the president that voters responded better to a candidate who delivered his own unvarnished truth.

Others also urged the president on. Ken Mehlman, the former chairman of the Republican National Committee, encouraged Obama to be himself. At a private lunch at the White House, Mehlman, who had come out as gay in 2010, advised the president that showing boldness and strong leadership was often more important than where one actually stood on the issues, and gay marriage presented an opportunity for Obama to assert his leadership.

Before Biden went on *Meet the Press*, the White House had been considering ways for Obama to speak his mind. Aides had drawn up an elaborate strategy allowing the president to seize on gay marriage as a major civil rights issue. If Obama presented his change of heart in the right light, the politics could favor him.

A blueprint for his announcement had come together slowly, hindered by many laborious meetings, delays, and revisions. In the end, the game plan had the president launching his reelection campaign the first week in May, followed by an appearance at an LGBT event in New York on May 14. Then the aides' careful staging would bring Obama to ABC's daytime talk show *The View* to reveal his change of heart. "I was just maniacal about order and planning," Plouffe explained. He recognized that a historic moment lay before the president. "I wanted it to be the president's moment."

But the choreography Plouffe and others had designed was lost as soon as Biden started yapping on *Meet the Press*; the vice president was one of the few people Obama had privately told of his new feelings on same-sex marriage, but his aides had not informed Joe of the public rollout. In the car leaving the *Meet the Press* studio, Shailagh Murray, now the vice president's communications director, told Biden, "I think you may have just gotten in front of the president on gay marriage."

The public reaction was swift and overwhelming. Cable news channels chattered incessantly about Biden's remarks, and newspaper headlines highlighted the president's predicament. The Associated Press declared, "Obama's Vague Gay Marriage Stance Under Scrutiny." The *Boston Herald* warned, "Veep's Marriage 'Gaffe' an Issue for Prez." The gay marriage question, which had had a long, slow burn within the administration, was suddenly white-hot, and pressure mounted on Obama to make his own feelings known. The next few days unfolded in a blur of praise for Biden outside the White House and daggers at the vice president inside the West Wing.

Gay-rights supporters hurried to Biden's side. "I'm grateful that the vice president of the United States is now publicly supporting marriage equality and I hope very soon the president and the rest of our leaders, Republicans and Democrats in Congress, will fall in line with the vice president," declared Chad Griffin, a member of the Obama campaign's national finance committee.

Inside the White House, Obama's aides bad-mouthed Biden to each other and, anonymously, to the press. The vice president had spoiled their well-wrought plans; they planted the notion that Biden's personal ambitions for the White House in 2016 may have blinded him to his responsibilities to the current administration.

Doing damage control for the president, the advisers stressed that there was no division on policy within the White House, that Biden was just speaking off the cuff, and in any case his remarks were not unlike what President Obama had said in the past. David Axelrod went so far as to say that Biden's view was "entirely consistent with the president's position, which is that couples who are married, whether they're gay or heterosexual couples, are entitled to the very same rights and the very same liberties."

While Obama's aides railed about Biden, Obama, for his part, was more annoyed at the appearance of White House chaos than at Biden's comment, for he knew his sentiments were in concert with Joe's.

The vice president, who had hit the road for two days of campaigning after his *Meet the Press* interview, felt the heat from the White House. The toxic whispering painted him as selfish, wanting to steal the spotlight on a hot-button issue, and duplicitous, that he had intended all along to push Obama to publicly admit his change of heart.

The attacks surprised—and stung—Joe. If anything, he felt, he was the finest team player within the White House. "I don't understand why everyone's so mad at me," he confided to an aide. "I didn't go out volunteering a position, but when asked a question...I had to respond to it."

Obama realized that the reaction of his excitable West Wing aides was inevitable, but he had no intention of leaping on Joe himself. The president wanted to hear from his buddy, an apology perhaps, but while Joe was traveling over the next two days, no apology came from the distraught vice president.

\*     \*     \*

By Monday, the White House was losing control of the issue. Obama's advisers watched aghast as Education Secretary Arne Duncan appeared on MSNBC's *Morning Joe* political talk show. The segment, which was set up to honor Teacher Appreciation Week, kicked off with a video of former NBA star Shaquille O'Neal in cap and gown receiving his doctorate degree in education from Barry University in Florida on Saturday.

When the conversation turned to the controversy over same-sex marriage, the show took a playful approach to the president's predicament. Cohost Joe Scarborough explained to Duncan that MSNBC political analyst and author Mark Halperin had a plan to question all administration officials on the issue.

"We're going to start this," Scarborough said, "try it on you first."

Halperin took over: "Just a little icebreaker, Mr. Secretary. We're going to go through the whole cabinet. Do you believe that same-sex men and women should be able to get legally married in the United States?"

Cohost Mika Brzezinski groaned off-screen: "Oh come on! You're going to start there?"

Without hesitation, Duncan replied, "Yes, I do."

"Have you ever said that publicly before?" Halperin asked.

Duncan, typically straightforward, answered, "I don't know if I've ever been asked publicly."

Someone off-screen said, "OK, we made news."

For the interview, Duncan sat in a studio in Washington, taking the questions through an earpiece. His staff was standing by listening to his answers but couldn't hear the questions. The words *gay marriage* never came out of the education secretary's mouth. Afterward, Duncan recalled, his staff walked out with him and said, "Oh, that interview went really well."

No one, including Duncan, knew that he had stepped into a minefield: the education secretary had completely missed the escalating

Biden controversy. He hadn't watched the Sunday talk shows the day before and hadn't seen any of the coverage about Joe's statements, and his staff had no idea that gay marriage had played any part in Duncan's interview.

The gay marriage question took Duncan by surprise, and reflecting on it later he was pleased at the way he answered it. Like Biden, he'd spoken from the heart and answered honestly. "I did it without thinking," he said. "I was actually very relieved that I just told the truth." He didn't want to sound like a Washington politician who equivocated or dodged an issue. "That's not who I wanted to be," he said.

But soon enough he realized his role in the rising storm. Now both Biden and Duncan inadvertently had pressured the president on gay marriage. "It may have caused short-term pain," Duncan observed. "But I knew where the president's heart was on this. You know, he hadn't said it publicly, but I knew down deep exactly what he thought. Frankly I think the vice president and I actually accelerated getting him to where his heart was."

Duncan feared that the president might ask him to resign, and he was prepared to accept the consequences of his comments. But Obama never mentioned anything about it. "I got one call from the White House," Duncan acknowledged, though he declined to say who the caller was. "I'm so glad you spoke from the heart," this person told Duncan. "I'm glad you told the truth." Duncan knew he'd added to the administration's stress and that some insiders were angry at him. "I give the White House immense credit," he said, "because they could have easily thrown me under the bus."

For his part, Biden was delighted by the education secretary's *Morning Joe* admission. Later the two men laughed over it as Biden confided to Duncan, "I'm glad you were the bastard who had my back on this."

After Duncan's television appearance, some Democratic members of Congress urged the president to follow the lead of the vice president and education secretary. But the president and his aides had not yet sorted out what steps to take.

Later in the day, Press Secretary Jay Carney walked into the White House briefing room, flipped open his thick white binder on the podium, and said, "I have no announcements to make at the top, so I'll go straight to questions." He then bobbed and weaved in reply to inquiries about President Obama's position on gay marriage.

A reporter wondered: Have Arne Duncan today and Vice President Biden yesterday boxed in the president?

"I have no update on the president's personal views," Carney managed. Duncan's comments, he added, were his own "personal opinion."

How would the president respond if asked to give his personal opinion?

"I think the president is the right person to describe his own personal views."

To a barrage of questions on the president's personal view, Carney kept to his script, repeating again and again: "I don't have an update for you."

Do the president and vice president disagree on same-sex marriage?

"No, I don't think that's what the vice president said yesterday."

Where does the president stand on the ban on gay marriages just enacted in North Carolina, the latest of thirty states to deny the marriage right to gay couples?

"The president has long opposed divisive and discriminatory efforts to deny rights and benefits to same-sex couples."

One reporter summed up the lack of clarity in Carney's comments, saying that on the one hand, the president opposed bans on gay marriage, but on the other, he didn't yet support gay marriage. No wonder, the reporter concluded, there was so much confusion.

By Tuesday, the president's staff realized his silence was untenable: something had to be done. Watching his press secretary parry the assaults of reporters, Obama cringed in sympathy: "I've got to put Jay out of his misery."

*     *     *

On Tuesday, Robin Roberts, anchor of ABC's *Good Morning America*, got a call from the White House informing her the president wanted to tape a one-on-one interview with her the following day. But Roberts was left guessing about what exactly the president had to say. "No guidelines," she said, "no real indication of what he wanted to discuss."

On Wednesday morning before the Roberts interview, Biden—back from two days on the road—caught the president for a quick moment alone after the daily intelligence briefing. He was aware that Obama was troubled that his vice president had been incommunicado since the *Meet the Press* interview. Joe apologized for causing a stir; he told the president he never thought his remarks would prove such a headache for him. "The act of contrition was all the president needed to hear to put him back on Biden's side," explained Mark Halperin and John Heilemann in their book *Double Down*.

Joe complained about his rough treatment from the president's aides, and Barack urged Joe to pay no attention to the digs and to ignore the newspaper and television coverage. The president seemed to have gotten past the noise. He told Joe that his remarks were of little consequence to them personally. In Halperin and Heilemann's telling, Barack wanted to protect the relationship: he wanted Joe to know that no one was going to divide them, that they were "in this thing together, and that can never go astray."

In his memoir, Joe described his *Meet the Press* remarks as "a 'Biden gaffe' that sent the White House and 2012 campaign staff into paroxysms." But, he said, it "didn't cause any real disturbance" between him and Barack. When they discussed it, Joe reported, the president "joked I had sent everybody into an uproar and said the campaign did have some work to do, but he didn't take me to task for speaking my mind about an issue I cared about deeply."

\*     \*     \*

Before the president's television interview, Obama and Roberts settled into facing leather chairs in the Cabinet Room and were all laughs and smiles. The setting, however, evoked grandeur: gold curtains at the white French doors, a bust of Benjamin Franklin presiding from a corner. Obama, looking presidential in a crisp blue suit, had an American flag over his shoulder, and a view out a window showed the peaceful White House grounds.

Obama chose to speak to Robin Roberts because he could trust her. She and the Obama family were friends; the president and the well-respected African American journalist had a strong rapport, a mutual love of sports, and a history of comfortable interviews.

As the tape rolled, Roberts asked the question of the moment: "Mr. President, are you still opposed to same-sex marriage?"

His answer was so striking—coming from a sitting president—that ABC News broke into the network's Wednesday afternoon programming with a special report, anchored by George Stephanopoulos and Diane Sawyer. Sawyer announced, "Big breaking news from the White House. This is a historic political and cultural moment in this country, and the issue: gay marriage."

The anchors then cut to Robin Roberts stationed after the interview in front of the White House; she provided a little background on the week to introduce the president's public change of heart. Then Obama came on the screen and spoke in a calm reflective tone, quite in contrast to the hysteria of the past three days:

> I have to tell you, as I've said, I've—I've been going through an evolution on this issue. I've always been adamant that gay and lesbian Americans should be treated fairly and equally....I've stood on the side of broader equality for the LGBT community. And I had hesitated on gay marriage—in part, because I thought

civil unions would be sufficient....But I have to tell you that over the course of several years, as I talk to friends and family and neighbors. When I think about members of my own staff who are incredibly committed, in monogamous relationships—same-sex relationships—who are raising kids together. When I think about those soldiers or airmen or Marines or sailors who are out there fighting on my behalf and yet feel constrained... because they're not able to commit themselves in a marriage. At a certain point, I've just concluded that, for me personally, it is important for me to go ahead and affirm that I think same-sex couples should be able to get married.

The president's assent on gay marriage was promptly sucked into the journalistic maw—reported, debated, discussed in print, online, and on television. NBC broke into its regular programming, running its competitor's scoop. CNN also rushed onto the air with its "Breaking News" logo accompanied by a sizzling sound and breathless Wolf Blitzer crying out, "Truly historic and potentially watershed moment....With the election less than six months away, the political implications are enormous."

ABC replayed its exclusive on *World News Tonight* and again the next day on *Good Morning America*. *GMA* aired a clip of Roberts and the president strolling along the White House colonnade, birds chirping loudly in the background.

Roberts asked about Biden's remarks the previous Sunday: "Did he jump the gun a little here?"

As he had been all along, Obama seemed unperturbed, noting that he'd already decided to announce his position before the election. He lightly chastised his vice president in a way that revealed what he understood about Joe. Certainly the vice president was impetuous, but, the president knew, Joe cared deeply about the way Americans were treated.

Barack said of his friend, "He probably got out a little bit over his skis—out of generosity of spirit."

Republicans scoffed at the president's reversal, saying it was only a political ploy that would drive Republicans to the polls to vote against him in November. By contrast, the president reaped glowing newspaper editorials. A *New York Times* encomium began, "It has always taken strong national leadership to expand equal rights in this country, and it has long been obvious that marriage rights are no exception. President Obama offered some of that leadership on Wednesday." The *Kansas City Star* noted the historic moment: "For the first time, the millions of gay and lesbian Americans who want nothing less than the full privileges of citizenship can claim the president of the United States as an ally."

Plouffe's consternation over the political risk to the president now seemed unfounded. In his ingenuous way, Biden had nudged the president to fall in line with the mood of the country, as indicated in a poll taken that week. Gallup found that 50 percent of Americans said they supported legal rights for gays wishing to marry; 65 percent of Democrats and 57 percent of independents agreed, while 22 percent of Republicans were of like mind.

As president, Obama now owned the issue; if Biden had stepped into the limelight, the vice president now receded into the background. All attention focused on the president and his view on the matter. By speaking up and igniting the furor, Biden had thrown a sharper spotlight on this civil rights need of gays—and the accolades for the administration's position were now Obama's.

Robin Roberts had asked the president during her interview, "So you're not upset with anybody?"

Acknowledging the bumps along the way, Obama said he would have preferred to have had it all happen a little more smoothly.

"But," he added, "all's well that ends well."

# THIRTEEN

# "As Good as Friends Get"

Joe Biden had his son Beau on his mind. It was August 23, 2013. He was playing things light in front of a friendly crowd in his old hometown of Scranton, Pennsylvania, ever the faithful vice president. He had flown in from Wilmington, Delaware, to join President Obama to promote the administration's efforts to cut college costs for students.

Both men looked casual in blue shirts and dark blazers, no ties. But something weighed on Joe, as much as he tried to seem buoyant. When he addressed the crowd, he turned first to the latest health scare that his son was staring down.

Less than two weeks earlier, Beau—the eldest of Biden's three children—had been enjoying a family vacation in Indiana when he began to feel weak and disoriented. The event was the latest in a series of strange, unexplained episodes that caused the forty-four-year-old at times to fear he was losing not only his physical health but his mind. Tanned and fit, he often took long, vigorous runs, but sometimes he was troubled by dizziness and loss of balance—and he heard things. While running, he had moments when he was sure a jet with its roaring engines was bearing down right over his head and he'd stop and duck on the side of the road, but there was nothing in the sky.

Beau was the much-loved two-term attorney general of Delaware, a charming family man who'd interrupted his first term to deploy to Iraq in 2008 with his National Guard unit. He was expected to seek a third term as attorney general, with whispers that he had his future sights on a run for Congress or even the presidency.

The nation got a glimpse of his charm and good looks when he introduced his father, the vice-presidential candidate, at the 2008 Democratic National Convention: "Good evening, I'm Beau Biden, and Joe Biden is my dad."

As a politician—and in manner—Beau was starkly different from his father. He was calm, disciplined, cerebral, and cautious when speaking publicly. Nora Caplan-Bricker, writing in the *National Journal*, observed, "The types of words that people use to describe Beau Biden— 'careful,' 'deliberate'—suggest a marked contrast to his famously garrulous father."

Like Joe's friend Barack Obama, Beau controlled his emotions. Delaware supreme court justice William T. Quillen knew both father and son well. With Beau, he explained, "there's less theater."

But drama had a way of finding Beau. It came to him at the age of three in the car crash that killed his mother and baby sister just weeks after his father had been elected to his first term in the US Senate. The world first met Beau in the images from his father's swearing-in at the hospital; Beau had his leg in traction while Hunter sat on his brother's bed for the ceremony in the hospital chapel.

Decades later, in 2010, Beau woke up one morning paralyzed on one side of his body and unable to speak. The symptoms, which pointed to a stroke, disappeared after a few hours at a hospital. Catching sight of his dad, Beau called out to him and showed him a miracle: his leg and arm moved just fine.

Crises illuminated the extraordinary bond of the Biden family. After the tragic car crash in 1972, Joe's sister Valerie—who had managed his first Senate campaign—moved into his home at age twenty-seven to help with his sons. The family's closeness was instinctual. Obama's senior adviser David Axelrod caught a glimpse of it at Joe's final interview as possible running mate in the 2008 campaign. Before settling down for his chat, Joe first gave Beau a kiss and told him that he'd come over to see the grandchildren once he was finished. The genuine affection among the Bidens made a deep impression on Axelrod. When reporting back to Barack the candidate, Axelrod remembered, "The first thing I said to Sen. Obama was, 'There's something really special about that family.' It was just palpable, and really disarming and sweet."

Beau's sudden health emergency in 2010 tightened the bond between the president and vice president. Barack and Joe shared a fierce devotion to their families, and Barack felt Joe's palpable adoration of his children. When Joe returned to the White House after Beau's brush with paralysis, Barack raced to comfort him. The president by then regarded Joe as family.

Witnessing their greeting, Axelrod said the two men were unabashed in expressing their affection. "I was sitting in my office, which was right next to the Oval Office," Axelrod recalled, "and I saw the president kind of sprint down the hall because he had heard that Biden was back. I ran into the hall to see where he was running." Axelrod found the president down at the end of the hall near the vice president's office. "And I saw them in an embrace."

Obama's sprint and hug were reflexes that told Joe a lot about the president. Normally Barack stifled his emotions, or at least was superhuman in keeping the lid on them: it was a survival skill for a mixed-race kid with an absent father and later for a rising political newcomer. But Joe knew that sometimes Barack's heart spilled over, crushing the self-discipline. As Joe was fond of saying: "People say this guy Obama is lacking in emotion—don't buy it."

Though Beau seemed fine after his stroke scare, uncertainty

hovered over the family and everyone close to them, including the president. One of Obama's defining virtues was his rigorous preparation for every meeting; he always read his brief and arrived ready for deep engagement in the topic at hand. At one meeting, however, Axelrod recalled that Obama was unusually distracted. "He simply wasn't attending," Axelrod said. "He was looking out the window. People were talking." But Obama's mind was elsewhere. "Finally, he said, 'I don't know how Joe is going to go on if something happens to Beau.'"

Three years later, Obama's concern became reality. After his weakness and disorientation while on vacation, Beau wound up at Northwestern Memorial Hospital in Chicago. Scans turned up a brain tumor. From Chicago, Beau went home to Wilmington, then consulted with doctors at Thomas Jefferson University Hospital in Philadelphia. More tests and more scans led neurologists to outline several possible diagnoses, ranging from a benign growth to potentially curable lymphoma to a dreaded, fast-growing tumor known as a glioblastoma.

Within days, Beau and his wife, his brother and sister and their spouses, and Joe and Jill boarded Air Force Two for the University of Texas MD Anderson Cancer Center, one of the top cancer treatment centers in the world. Doctors there leaned toward a diagnosis of glioblastoma and prepared to operate. The Bidens were sequestered in a large room with the Secret Service and a secure phone line.

On Monday, August 19, neurosurgeon Raymond Sawaya performed what was known as an awake craniotomy. Throughout most of it, Beau was conscious and responding to prompts, a procedure that helped the doctor avoid cutting into certain areas of the brain, which could result in serious cognitive damage.

More than seven hours after Beau was rolled to the operating room, Dr. Sawaya came to see the Bidens. The good news was that the doctor had removed a tumor a little larger than a golf ball and Beau had suffered no complications. The only reminder would be a scar on the left side of his head. There would be no damage to his speech, mental abilities, or motor skills from the surgery.

But there was some bad news, too. The doctor had been unable to get all of the tumor, and it was in fact a glioblastoma: stage IV. Joe was at the back of the room near the corner when the doctor dropped this bomb. Staring downward, Joe recalled, he felt like he had been knocked to the ground. "I was glad no one in the family was looking at me," he said. "I reached for my rosary and asked God to give me the strength to handle this."

Knowing him too well, Beau was worried about his dad. He knew Joe was tough, but he also knew his heart was huge; he'd already suffered through devastation and darkness over his wife Neilia and infant daughter. As Beau was being rolled into surgery, he had taken the doctor's hand and implored him, "Doc, promise you're going to take care of Pop."

The doctor made a promise right back: "You're going to be around to take care of your dad, Beau."

Tough news came the next day. Genetic tests on the tumor revealed that Beau did not have a mutation needed to slow its growth; rather, he had two mutations likely to accelerate it. An aggressive treatment plan was laid out. Though a patient in Beau's condition typically was given twelve to fourteen months of life, Joe clung to the slimmest of hopes: after treatment, some 2 percent emerged in remission without any remaining tumor. Joe thought, "Why not Beau?"

Of similar spirit, Beau had no intention of giving up, and the family rallied around him. He opted for the most aggressive treatment possible: he took three times the standard dose of chemotherapy and participated in a trial of an experimental drug aimed at enhancing the effectiveness of the chemo. He also took a still-unapproved drug targeted at taming the mutation that made his tumor so virulent.

On Wednesday, August 21, the family's private trauma became public, though the seriousness of Beau's condition remained strictly within a small circle. In a statement, the vice president revealed only that Beau had undergone a "successful procedure" in Texas. "He is in great shape," the statement said, "and is going to be discharged tomorrow and heading home to Delaware."

On Thursday, Air Force Two took Beau and the family home, touching down in the afternoon at New Castle Airport just outside of Wilmington. Around 4 p.m. a small motorcade of SUVs pulled up at the vice president's home in Greenville, Delaware, the passengers hidden behind dark tinted windows.

Earlier that day Beau had tweeted a photo of himself with his wife and parents all smiles at the hospital, everyone dressed casually, as if about to head off for lunch at a favorite restaurant; there was no sign he had just had brain surgery. Standing with an arm around his mother and wife, Beau is pictured from the left side; the right side of his head, where the incision was made, isn't shown. In his tweet Beau issued an upbeat message: "On our way home! Can't wait to get back. Thank you, Houston."

The next day, Friday, August 23, Joe was in Scranton, with Obama at his side, speaking to about twenty-five hundred people inside the student union at Lackawanna College. Joe thrived on the love of his supporters, and in Scranton there was plenty of love.

"I just want you all to know, since so many of you have asked me about my son," Biden began, "things are—it's not only good to be here, but things are good at home in Delaware. My son Beau is fine." The student union erupted into cheers and applause.

Joe was not inclined to convey the true state of Beau's condition to the public or to almost anyone. Beau wanted his circumstances and his treatments kept private. Over the weekend Barack had called Joe to check in and offer support. But it wasn't until they met up in person in Scranton that Joe laid out the nature of the Bidens' heartache. "Barack was the first person outside my family to know about Beau's illness," Joe remembered.

The vice president felt, in part, he had to inform the president because, whatever his personal trauma, Joe still had major initiatives he'd undertaken for Obama. As Joe put it, "I wanted to reassure him that he could count on me, that I wouldn't let anything fall through the cracks."

Joe also had a self-sustaining motive: he had been told by one of Beau's doctors to maintain hope and, most important, keep focused on a purpose in daily life. On his return to Washington, Joe told his chief of staff, Steve Ricchetti, about Beau's battle, without going into the darkest details. And he insisted on a day-to-day plan of attack for himself.

"I wanted to do anything I could to help the VP through this," Ricchetti recalled. "He said to me, he had lived through enormous tragedy and sadness in his life before, and the only way to get through it was to be busy."

Biden insisted that Ricchetti keep him focused, keep his schedule full, keep him working. Biden owed it to Beau and to himself to show that he could still work while dealing with his son's illness. It was an essential part of Joe and Beau's support for each other through hard times: just keep going.

Barack and Joe's joint appearance in Scranton was especially poignant for both of them because Joe had chosen to fill the president in on Beau's health crisis. With his usual restraint, Barack didn't pry, and in any case Joe didn't want to overwhelm the president with too much detail.

Conscious of Joe's fragile state, the president sent a message of affection to his vice president through his remarks in the student union. Taking the microphone, Barack addressed the crowd, but he also was speaking directly to Joe. "I love Scranton," he said, "because if it weren't for Scranton, I wouldn't have Joe Biden."

After a burst of applause, the president continued: "And today is a special day for Joe and me because five years ago today, on August 23, 2008, I announced in Springfield, Illinois, my home state, that Joe Biden was going to be my running mate."

The crowd applauded again.

"And it was the best decision that I ever made, politically, because I love this guy. And he's got heart, and he cares about people.... And so I just want all of you to know that I am lucky to have Joe—not just as a running mate, but more importantly, as a friend. And we love his family.... Thank you, Joe, for saying yes five years ago."

After the event, Joe flew back to Wilmington to be with Beau.

Beau was away from his job for three weeks and did not attend public events for a few months. Before the end of 2013, his intensive treatments brought signs of hope, prompting him to tell his local newspaper in November that he felt great: "The docs have given me a clean bill of health."

By April 2014, however, Beau's unpredictable path had taken a distressing turn: his speech had begun to falter, and he was starting to worry that his mental sharpness might weaken. Doctors were uncertain what was causing the aphasia, but they put their patient on yet another new drug.

Joe fretted that Beau would need to step down as attorney general, putting his family at risk because he was the sole breadwinner. During one of his private lunches with Barack, Joe revealed his latest worry.

"What are you going to do?" Barack asked.

"Well, he doesn't have much money. But we're okay," Joe explained. Among senators, Joe ranked low in personal wealth, but he was prepared to come up with funds to help his son. "Jill and I can take out a second mortgage on our house in Wilmington if we have to. We'll be fine."

Joe noticed a wave of emotion cross Barack's face. During their weekly lunches, the two men discussed impossible crises confronting the nation and the world: economic catastrophe, war, mass shootings. In an instant, all the world's woes melted away. Now it was personal.

Barack got up, walked around the mahogany table, and laid his hands on Joe's shoulders. The private dining room was a sanctuary for the two men, adorned with photos of Barack's daughters and a pair of red boxing gloves signed by Muhammad Ali, set off in a glass case.

Barack told Joe that he'd made some money selling his books and he wanted to dissuade his friend from taking out a second mortgage. "Don't do that," Barack said with surprising force from behind Joe, his fingers still gripping his buddy's shoulders. "I'll give you the money. I have it. You can pay me back whenever."

Joe's longtime friend and adviser Ted Kaufman had seen the way Joe stirred people to act on his behalf, just by being Joe. "It's what I say about Joe being a friend," Kaufman observed. "I mean, he is such a friend that people—I'm talking about good friends, family and friends—you really want to do things for him."

Obama was no exception. It was painful for Barack to see Joe go through this anguish, paternal, medical, and now financial. Barack was searching for ways to help. Kaufman recalled, "You could just see how hurt Obama was."

The Bidens never availed themselves of Obama's generosity. For Joe, Barack's financial offer had meaning far beyond its stated intent. Obama's education secretary, Arne Duncan, observed that, while the offer was real, its true significance lay in its symbolism. "It wasn't about the money," Duncan said. "It was about the closeness, and shared pain and anguish, the concern and compassion, and—I'll say it—the love. This love was deeply, deeply moving and deeply meaningful to the vice president at a time of obviously unimaginable heartache."

Their affection for each was all the sweeter because they had overcome their profound differences. "They're polar opposites," explained Julie Smith, Biden's deputy national security advisor in 2012 and 2013. "Obama is the classic introvert and Biden is the classic extrovert." She recalled watching the two of them respond to crowds over long days of greetings, meetings, and speeches. During the NATO summit in Chicago in 2012, Obama was obviously worn down, even frustrated and impatient with all the hobnobbing. "I could see his energy level drain-ing from him," Smith said. "A few more eye rolls, you know. Just kind of slumped over, like, 'This is ridiculous.'"

Almost everyone seemed to react that way, except Joe Biden. Trav-eling with Biden on other occasions, Smith marveled at how two men so opposite became so close. "As the day goes on, Biden gets more and more energized with each meeting, each handshake, the crowds, the dinners, the lights." If Obama needed time to separate and recharge, Biden reenergized himself by shaking more hands and plunging into more crowds. Barack and Joe were two very different social creatures, Smith observed, and in personality, there was a vast distance between them. But as friends they crossed that gulf.

In August, Beau was stoic in the face of his next battle: His strength was weakening and his right arm and leg were becoming numb. When the doctor suggested another drug, a quite potent one likely to cause severe side effects, Beau didn't flinch.

He kept working as Delaware's attorney general through the end of his term in January 2015. The following month, the Bidens con-fronted grim news: the tumor had flared anew and was spreading rap-idly through Beau's brain. "The news could not have been worse," Joe wrote in his memoir. "This was the moment we had been dreading from the day Dr. Sawaya removed the original tumor."

Beau's treatment and cancer had left him gaunt, and his skin had lost some color. But he wanted to fight on and agreed to subject himself to an untested, newly designed immunotherapy treatment that posed huge risks. It involved surgery to remove some of Beau's cancer cells to create a special virus to be injected into the tumor; the process was intended to allow Beau's own immune system to fight his cancer.

Though the strategy held out a sliver of success, Joe nonetheless felt his hopes draining away. At the vice president's residence on the grounds of the Naval Observatory, he had listened on a conference call with the doctors, Beau, and his son Hunter as the details were laid out. Afterward, fearing he'd break down in front of his wife Jill, he slipped away into their bedroom and found comfort in his rosary and prayer.

In early March, the vice president was scheduled to represent the White House at a summit in Guatemala with the presidents of Guatemala, Honduras, and El Salvador, capping months of administration efforts to bolster those countries' ineffectual governments, tackle gang violence, and bring down their murder rates, among the highest in the world. Joe was torn: Cancel the trip and stay with Beau, or carry out his White House duty?

Joe knew if he called Barack and told him he just couldn't take on the task right then, the president would tell him to be with Beau as long as he wished. Joe feared that Beau would be disappointed in him if he canceled because his father had failed to execute his responsibility to the country.

With another president, Joe realized, he might have stepped away from his job for a while. But something tugged at him to serve Obama, no matter what. "I felt an obligation to Barack, who was my friend," Joe concluded. "The president had put his trust and faith in me. He was counting on me." So, with Beau filling his thoughts, Joe jetted to Guatemala.

On his return to Washington, Joe had trouble sleeping. Just as he had railed at the heavens after Neilia's car crash in 1972, Joe challenged God to explain why Beau had to suffer. "I was tired and worried and a little bit angry at the Fates," he recalled. "Why was this happening to my son? He just didn't deserve this."

In late March, Joe and Beau and the family flew back out to MD Anderson Cancer Center in Houston for the surgery. Throughout the family's struggle, Joe marveled at his son Hunter, who stood strong as a pillar of brotherly support for Beau. Hunter interpreted the doctors' complicated cancer-treatment talk for the family and spoke for Beau when his brother couldn't talk. After the surgery, which Beau weathered well, doctors set April 2 as the day to inject the live virus into the tumor.

Back in Washington before the procedure, Joe met with Barack for their weekly lunch. By now he was in the habit of filling the president in on many details of Beau's treatment, and he fought to restrain his emotion in the telling. In the formal setting of the private dining room, the conversation on this Wednesday, April 1, was personal, devoted almost exclusively to Beau.

Joe outlined the medical strategy in cold, clinical language in the hope that this type of detachment would snuff the welling of tears. But his performance didn't fool the president, whose own eyes moistened. "He is not a demonstrative man, in public or in private, and I felt bad," Joe recalled. "I found myself trying to console him."

Finally, Barack said simply, "Life is so difficult to discern."

The conversation turned to the injection planned for the next day in Houston. Joe had already decided to go there that night to be with Beau when he woke up the next morning for his procedure, but he told Barack he was debating what to do.

"Joe, you've got to go down tonight," the president urged.

A few hours later Joe was on Air Force Two on his way to Houston. While he knew all along he had to go, the president's encouragement was consoling. As Joe recalled later, "It meant something to me to hear it from Barack."

After the injection of the virus, Joe and Beau and the family rode a seesaw of hope and disappointment. At first the live virus attacked the tumor; its growth slowed and there were signs that the virus, using Beau's own immune system, was killing some cancer cells. This cutting-edge experiment, which hadn't performed this well in any of its previous applications on other patients, encouraged everyone.

But after Beau returned home to Wilmington, he didn't get out of bed for two days and didn't want to eat. He became lethargic and unresponsive.

Two days later he was whisked off to Thomas Jefferson University Hospital in Philadelphia and admitted under an alias to protect his privacy. He was so weak that he was unable to keep his eyes open and communicated only by a limp thumbs-up or a soft "Yes."

Joe sneaked in and out repeatedly to see his son while maintaining his vice-presidential schedule to ward off possible revelations to the public. He accompanied Secretary of State John Kerry at a State Department lunch for visiting prime minister Shinzo Abe of Japan, joining in a sake toast and noting his happiness at seeing Kerry's wife, Teresa Heinz Kerry, who hadn't ventured into public much since suffering a seizure nearly two years earlier.

Several days later, Joe flexed his credentials among the African American community when he took to the stage at the Cobo Center in Detroit on May 3. Speaking to more than seven thousand people, he delivered the keynote address at the NAACP's sixtieth annual Fight for Freedom Fund Dinner at a time of much black unease.

Just a couple of weeks earlier, a twenty-five-year-old black man named Freddie Gray had fallen into a coma under suspicious circumstances while being transported by Baltimore police after his arrest in a poverty-stricken neighborhood known for drug dealing and violence. Gray's death a week later sparked violent protests in Baltimore. "We need to see each other beyond race, creed or color," Biden told the huge crowd. "We as a country need to do a lot of soul-searching."

Around this time, Joe played his role as grandpa for Beau's ten-year-old daughter Natalie, whose school class came to the vice president's Naval Observatory residence for pizza after a field trip to the White House. Joe put on a happy face for the kids, but he was riding through dark days. While his son struggled through good and bad periods, Joe clung to the hope that the wonders of cutting-edge medicine would save his boy.

During these hard times, President Obama made a point in his public appearances to send messages of comfort and friendship to his suffering pal. Without saying a word about Beau, Barack let Joe know he was thinking of him.

Lighthearted, humorous asides about Joe were slipped into the president's remarks, for instance, when Obama hosted NASCAR Sprint Cup champion Kevin Harvick outdoors beneath the columns of the South Portico of the White House. Parked nearby, in sporty contrast to the federal architecture, was Harvick's red-and-white number four Budweiser Chevrolet. Standing beside Harvick and his crew—all dressed like the president in business suits, not their usual matching red-and-white, Budweiser-adorned, flame-retardant racing duds— Obama praised the team for melding into a championship force. Harvick had assembled a new team at the start of the season, Obama reminded the crowd, and the driver and the crew were quick to meld.

They "seemed to figure out each other in a hurry—sort of like when Joe Biden joined my team," Obama said, pausing with a smile as the crowd laughed. He then trumpeted the NASCAR crew's teamwork and his own dynamic with his vice president in a single breath: "So they had instant chemistry. And as Kevin can tell you, when you have a trusted partner shouting world-class advice into your ear at every turn, you can't lose."

In late April Obama sent humorous love-grams to Joe from the podium at the White House Correspondents' Association dinner. The annual press–White House gathering came amid controversy over an Indiana law, signed by Governor Mike Pence, that allowed companies to invoke religious reasons for denying service to gays. In his comedic commentary at the dinner, Obama mocked the law while managing to joke about his special relationship with Joe.

"You know what, let me set the record straight," the tuxedoed Barack began. "I tease Joe sometimes, but he has been at my side for seven years now. I *love* that man." The room gave Joe, in his absence, a round of applause. And Obama continued on to his punch line: "He's not just a great vice president, he is a great friend. We've gotten so close, in some places in Indiana, they won't serve us pizza anymore." There were a few whistles, heads flew back in laughter, and the room warmed to applause for both the takedown of the law and Barack's edgy riff in appreciation of Joe.

Obama, who had stayed away from the journalists' Gridiron Club dinner in his first year, joked about his presidency having eased into its fourth quarter. "The fact is, I feel more loose and relaxed than ever," he told the crowd. And the reason for his laid-back vibe led right to his White House partner, whose well-known penchant for hands-on affection would later become controversial as he prepared to enter the 2020 presidential race. "Those Joe Biden shoulder massages," Obama told the room to a wave of laughter, "they're like magic."

Over the next few weeks, Joe kept acting like the upbeat father, but he felt helpless. He showed up at Beau's bedside as much as he could, psyching himself up before entering his room. Beau was now at Walter Reed National Military Medical Center in Bethesda, Maryland, just outside Washington. "Smile, I'd say to myself. Smile. Smile. Smile," Joe coached himself.

On some days, Beau showed small gains, but overall he wasn't really improving. Each step forward was complicated by a tumble backward. Toward the end of May, Joe had to reckon with reality: though teasing hope, the treatments were not going to save Beau.

Soon after Memorial Day, with his entire brood surrounding him, Joe watched as his son's heart stopped beating. Joe inscribed the moment in his diary: "May 30. 7:51 p.m. It happened. My God, my boy. My beautiful boy."

Beau's death reaffirmed the nation's love of Joe. This father crushed by the loss of his son was swept up in a massive outpouring of sympathy. *Boston Herald* columnist Joe Battenfeld reminded his fellow conservatives: "Make fun of Joe Biden all you want—and we have— but no one can question his heart." The nation fell into group mourning, as *Politico*'s chief Washington correspondent Edward-Isaac Dovere put it at the time: "He's Uncle Joe. And his son's death has resonated like a death in the American family."

It also sealed the bond between Barack and Joe. In the time of Joe's greatest need, Barack had lent a shoulder and an ear. "I never said this publicly," Education Secretary Arne Duncan observed, "but when Beau was going through hell, obviously, and ultimately died, the president was just an unbelievable personal support to the vice president, and it was my sense that that brought them much closer." In his conversations with Duncan, Joe revealed that "he was just unbelievably moved and appreciative and grateful for the president's personal support."

The day after Beau died, the president canceled a White House reception already on his calendar and instead spent time with Joe, Jill, and the family at the Naval Observatory residence. In his statement on Beau's death, Barack echoed the sentiments of many Americans who regarded Joe as one of their own family members.

"The Bidens have more family than they know," Obama said. "In the Delaware they love. In the Senate Joe reveres. Across this country that he has served for more than forty years. And they have a family right here in the White House, where hundreds of hearts ache tonight...for the entire Biden clan."

Barack said he was grieving for his friend Beau and his family. "And," he added, "Joe and Jill Biden are as good as friends get."

The White House posted a remembrance of Beau on Medium.com that included his thoughts on conscience, and family, and duty; it was illustrated with strikingly handsome photos of Beau and his family and Beau and his father. Joe sparkled when pictured with his son. Striding alongside him or simply gazing at him, Joe had joy in his eye.

As attention turned to planning the funeral, the usual reflexive tensions between the president's and vice president's staffs melted away. Respect for Beau and sympathy for Joe and his family sent White House staffers flying into action with an instinct for teamwork and cooperation. Some aides, like Liz Allen, had worked for both Obama and Biden. Allen had served as Biden's deputy director of communications before moving over to the Obama team in the same capacity.

"Five years in the Biden family, you're in the Biden family," she said. "So when Beau died, a bunch of us who no longer worked for the vice president were in touch with the vice president's staff, saying, 'If you need us, we're here.'" And their assistance was welcomed.

Allen wound up in charge of managing the press for the week of the funeral. She remembered telling her bosses she had to leave the Obama operation for a week to help on the Biden side: "I gotta leave, I gotta do the Beau funeral," she told them. "And they were like, 'Of course.' It wasn't even a question. It was, 'Whatever they need.'" So she and some other Biden alums raced to help out. "We all just decamped to Delaware."

President Obama offered to deliver the main eulogy, and when Joe accepted, Barack began writing it himself. His was a formidable task; his words had to capture Beau for his family and the nation and radiate the compassion that sustained his friendship with Joe.

Ever since his own tragedy in 1972, Joe knew how to talk to the grieving, a sympathy he showed a few years before Beau died in remarks to military families who had lost a loved one. He recalled the unbearable pain he'd felt after he got the dreaded phone call about the accident. Hard as it was to go on, Joe was now able to give the mourning military families words of hope—words that would have served him well in his own fresh bout of grief over Beau. "There will come a day," he insisted, "I promise you—and you parents as well—when the thought of your son or daughter, or your husband or wife, brings a smile to your lips before it brings a tear to your eye. It will happen."

On the morning of the funeral, Saturday, June 6, Liz Allen was walking around outside St. Anthony of Padua Roman Catholic Church in

Wilmington, Delaware, when an email came in from Cody Keenan, President Obama's director of speechwriting. Keenan, who had helped Obama touch up his eulogy, sent the final version to staffers for an early look.

For Allen, it had been a week of emotional laceration, with the rawest grief no doubt still to come at the Mass in a few hours. Walking around the grounds, Allen read the Obama eulogy. "His words did perfect justice to Beau and Joe Biden. No one else but Obama could have done it," she said. "I fully broke down in front of the church."

Cable news was at the church early, too. CNN was live at 10 a.m., a half hour before the scheduled start of the Mass, and the conversation quickly turned to Barack and Joe's friendship. On the broadcast, presidential historian Douglas Brinkley noted that Joe usually brightened Barack's day with a laugh, and now it was Barack's time to lift his grieving friend. "President Obama loves Joe Biden," Brinkley observed. "It's not a word we often talk about in the political sphere, the love, but there is a huge amount of love."

Joe and his family arrived at about 10:40 a.m. and assembled solemnly beside the hearse carrying Beau's flag-draped coffin. With the corners of his lips turned down, Joe glanced up toward the sky through his dark aviator sunglasses just before the hearse door swung open. He grimly looked on as the honor guard hoisted the coffin out. As if unable to witness it, Joe bowed his head briefly while holding the hand of Beau's ten-year-old daughter, Natalie. His other arm around Beau's widow, Hallie, Joe turned and kissed her on the head.

As the coffin was carried toward the church entrance, Joe raised a hand and placed it on his heart. Bagpipes wailed in mourning. Dazed, Joe moved into the church behind the coffin, clutching Jill's hand.

After prayers and soaring hymns, General Ray Odierno stepped up to the podium for the first eulogy. Two days after Beau died, the general, who was the top commander in Iraq during Beau's deployment, had called Joe to ask if he could attend the funeral. He profoundly admired the younger Biden and even expected him one day to lead the country. Now Odierno stood before the mourners in uniform, a tough, burly, no-nonsense look, his head shaved, his chest full of decorations and awards, and a row of four stars dotting each shoulder. As he spoke, he revealed a soft, compassionate core.

"As I look for the perfect words to say today," Odierno said, "I actually think back to 2012, when you, sir, Vice President Biden, addressed the surviving family members of our military forces who gave the ultimate sacrifice. You spoke about a day that would come when the thought of their son or daughter or their husband or wife or brother and sister would bring a smile to their lips before it brought a tear to their eye." Then, naming each family member, the general promised: "That day will come." Then, in honor of Beau's lifetime of service, General Odierno awarded him a posthumous Legion of Merit.

President Obama then moved slowly toward the podium in a dark suit and gray tie. He looked drawn; his eyes were small. Before uttering a word, while adjusting his notes in front of him, Barack tightened his bottom lip as if gathering his strength. He began by addressing each Biden family member individually, and as he ended with Jill and then Joe—the final name on his list—he caught himself, his lip quivering almost imperceptibly.

"We are here to grieve with you," he said, "but more importantly, we are here because we love you."

Obama spoke of the cruelty of life and of God's fate, the way it came down upon both Beau and Joe long ago and now again. "To suffer such faceless, seemingly random cruelty can harden the softest hearts or shrink the sturdiest," Obama offered. "It can make one mean or bitter or full of self-pity."

But both father and son, similar in so many ways but each original in his own way, lifted themselves up and asked God to grant them broad shoulders to bear not only their "own burdens but the burdens of others. Shoulders broad enough to shield those who need shelter the most." Again, seeing the boy in the father, Barack added, "Like his father, Beau did not have a mean bone in his body. The cruelty he endured in his life didn't make him hard; it made him compassionate."

Barack wanted Joe to know that Beau's goodness was also Joe's. Beau had learned from his dad how to get up after being knocked down, had learned that public service was a noble pursuit, that he was no better than anyone else, that everyone mattered. "It's no secret," Barack said, his eye falling on Joe, "that a lot of what made Beau the way he was, was just how much he loved and admired his dad."

The president praised Beau for demanding to earn his own way and refusing the privilege that might have been his because of his father. He told the story of Beau in his twenties getting pulled over for speeding outside of Scranton. "The officer recognized the name on the license, and because he was a fan of Joe's work with law enforcement, he wanted to let Beau off with a warning," Obama said. "But Beau made him write that ticket. Beau didn't trade on his name."

After the September 11, 2001, terrorist attacks, Beau felt an obligation to do something for his country, so he joined the National Guard and deployed to Iraq. When he was shipping out of Dover, Barack noted, "there was a lot of press that wanted to interview him. Beau refused. He was just another soldier."

In delicate detail Obama portrayed the deep, instinctual love that Beau and his father shared for each other. He reminded mourners that early in his career, Joe had raced home on Amtrak each night from Washington to Wilmington to kiss his young sons before bedtime.

"As Joe himself confessed to me," Barack said, "he did not just do this because the kids needed him. He did it because he needed those kids." Beau understood his father's pain and sorrow, and it glued father and son together in empathy that extended beyond themselves to others less fortunate. "That very young boy made a very grown-up decision," Barack explained. "He would live a life of meaning. He would live a life for others."

At times, Barack seemed to fight off tears. Now and then he stopped and took a breath. He kept a tissue in his pocket, and under the weightiness of the moment he dabbed it at his lips or touched it to his nose. He told Beau's children there weren't words big enough to express how much their father loved them. And, with pride, he assured them, "But I will tell you what. Michelle and I and Sasha and Malia, we've become part of the Biden clan, we're honorary members now. And the Biden family rule applies: we're always here for you. We always will be." To a rumble of laughter, he added, "My word as a Biden."

Looking again at his vice president, Barack said, "To Joe and Jill: just like everybody else here, Michelle and I thank God you are in our lives." His lips tightened as he fought back emotion, and creases framed his mouth. "Taking this ride with you is one of the great pleasures of our lives. Joe, you are my brother."

Inside the packed church, in front of live television cameras, Barack spoke to Joe as intimately as if they were alone. "I'm grateful every day," he told him, "that you've got such a big heart and a big soul and those broad shoulders. I couldn't admire you more."

Looking spent, the president then stepped away from the podium and, with his back to the audience, stopped and nodded in respect toward the altar. Before taking his seat, Barack walked along the front row of the church toward Joe, who got to his feet, and the two men locked in a full-body hug, the president's eyes closed as they held each other. Barack consoled Joe with several pats low on his back. Before breaking from the embrace each man, first Joe, then Barack, kissed the other on the cheek.

The affection was not lost on the nation. It wasn't just the friendship but its public display that shattered White House history. Presidents and vice presidents didn't behave this way; they were never this close.

While President Jimmy Carter and Vice President Walter Mondale helped set the model for the modern vice presidency and had a deep respect for each other, their partnership stopped far short of the friendship of Barack and Joe. Likewise for President Bill Clinton and his vice president, Al Gore. Sometimes they worked closely together, and Gore took on major tasks, but they never became each other's emotional rock.

At the other extreme, President Richard Nixon had only contempt for his vice president, Spiro Agnew. Nixon, his counsel and adviser John Ehrlichman said, believed that Agnew's perfidy protected the president from assassination. "No assassin in his right mind would kill me," Nixon often joked. "They know if they did that they would wind up with Agnew!"

Barack and Joe were of a different order entirely from previous White House pairings. Hugging and kissing, it just wasn't done. Sizing up the affinity between this president and vice president, adviser David Axelrod put it simply: "It was a very, very good relationship, and rare—unprecedented."

Hard-bitten political observers were struck by the break with tradition. MSNBC's Chris Matthews ended his show, *Hardball*, on the Monday after the funeral with a commentary on what he called "the revelation" at St. Anthony of Padua on Saturday. It came, Matthews said, in Barack's eulogy. He noted Obama's "remarkable profession of love for his vice president" and pointed out, "If you think this is normal in American politics these days, let me break it to you—'love' is not the word you hear, isn't the bond you notice."

He went on: "Attention needs to be paid to the close relationship we saw in that little Italian church on Saturday. People need to realize what was revealed up there on that altar, when a president of the United States not only admitted an affection for his vice president but celebrated it for all to witness."

Matthews admitted to being a romantic about politics; he professed his love of stories about the Kennedys and Franklin Roosevelt and Winston Churchill. He said he had found much to admire in Obama's earlier speeches. But what transpired between the president and vice president at the church went beyond what Matthews had ever imagined about the romantic nature of politics. "Nothing...was as human as this weekend," he asserted, "and I say, good for them. Good for them that they don't mind us knowing that two people who work together day after day through successful missions and mistakes and, yes, gaffes, have found in their work and struggle at the top, the most sublime of human emotions."

That public moment of unguarded emotion helped shape the legacy of the Obama-Biden relationship. "Long after the last partisan battle has been fought over Obamacare, long after Barack Obama has settled into a comfortable post-presidency, and long after the last joke has been made about some Joe Biden verbal misstep," wrote George E. Condon Jr., the White House correspondent for *National Journal*, "people will remember the moment when the always-in-control president struggled to control his emotions. They will remember the moment when president and vice president embraced in front of the altar and exchanged heartfelt kisses on the cheek."

This authenticity carried the men into history. "In an age when so many political moments are scripted," Condon continued, "this was real. In a country whose presidents and vice presidents have rarely been close, this was genuine closeness. In an administration that prides itself on being hip, this was decidedly old-fashioned love."

It was Joe Biden—his heartbreak and his nature—who had brought out this moment. Over the years Joe, by the force of his personality, had loosened up the cool and circumspect Barack. So many times, Joe had thrown an arm over Barack's shoulder, massaged him, or close-talked him, or razzed him, and lifted him by his incorrigible high spirits.

If Barack seemed disheartened after a grim meeting on an intractable problem, Joe picked up on his pain. At these times, Joe hung back in the Oval Office after everyone had gone. "Remember, Mr. President," he'd tell him, "the country can never be more hopeful than its president." He told Obama, "You gotta go out there and *be* 'Hope.'"

Joe's tutelage in passion and undaunted self-expression helped unlock a warmth in Barack that may not have been fully realized in public until he got Bidened, and because of this union of two strong men, a generous hug and kiss in front of the entire world became a mere reflex, an instinct. Whatever their differences, they hardly mattered anymore. They were both better for having mastered their friendship. If Biden taught Obama to loosen his tie, give a hug instead of a handshake, throw the speech out the window, Obama showed Biden the path to discipline, to crossing every t and dotting every i. "That bled into the office of the vice president," said Julie Smith, Biden's deputy national security advisor.

As Barack and Joe became ever closer, Smith couldn't help wondering at the miracle. "It was oil and water, but oil and water that somehow did come together eventually through the years," she said. "It could have gone the other way. They could have ended up really angry at each other."

Breaking with two centuries of presidential history, Barack and Joe found a way through the thicket of high office and politics to form a lasting bond. "This was not a president and a vice president," former education secretary Arne Duncan explained. "This was two men, two people with a deep friendship who at a time of greatest need knew that someone had their back. That transcends politics and position. It's way way way bigger and much simpler, much more basic and human."

# FOURTEEN

# Joe, Searching for Words

Joe expected just a small get-together: Barack, Michelle, Jill, and a few senior staffers raising a glass to their shared journey over the past eight years. On the White House schedule the event was billed as a toast from the Obamas to the Bidens. Joe assumed it was the president's elegant way of saying thank you to the vice president and his staff for their hard work over two grueling terms.

But when Joe glimpsed the crowd assembled in the White House State Dining Room on January 12, 2017, he knew something was up. The place was packed with the vice president's family and friends, people stretching back over the four decades Joe had served the nation. There were rows and rows of them seated in front of a podium bearing the seal of the president of the United States. This was no intimate send-off. But what it was, Joe had no inkling.

Thanks to a months-long top-secret operation masterminded by a commando team of White House aides, the vice president had been kept in the dark about the real purpose of the gathering.

Now, moments before he entered, he stood peeking out at the crowd. The podium suggested there was going to be a speech. Joe saw the media had congregated, with television cameras: that would not have been the case for a private White House toast.

"So why is there a podium?" a confused vice president asked his aide. "I thought this was just a thing to recognize my staff. What's going on out there?"

The staffer had kept the secret so long, she wasn't about to let it go now at the last minute. So she lied, right to the vice president's face, and immediately felt guilty: she'd never lied to him before. "Oh, it's just a nice moment for the Obamas to recognize you and your family and staff," she told him.

By all appearances, the mission was a success. President Obama himself had conceived the idea, put it in motion, and insisted upon total secrecy and flawless execution. White House aides, knowing this was a delicate task, relied on meticulous subterfuge.

"To have the impact that he wanted, Obama felt it needed to be a surprise," said presidential staffer Liz Allen. "But it's very hard to keep a surprise in the White House."

Only a handful of privileged insiders were let in on the planning. "The loop was incredibly small," remembered Kate Bedingfield, Biden's communications director. "I mean, we did an undercover trip to Iraq with the VP, and that had a wider circle of knowledge beforehand."

Working in complete clandestine mode, the team resorted to extraordinary measures. Uncomfortable as it was, staffers were knowingly disrespectful to the vice president: they misled him, tricked him, held back information, and, yes, lied to him. They had no choice.

"This just wasn't done," Allen said. "But we knew that it was so important to Obama to give this moment to Biden. People moved mountains to make this all work logistically because it was about Obama and Biden and the relationship, which everyone had such reverence for."

Now the moment had arrived. The vice president was in the wings; the room was filled with his friends and family, all in ignorance of what was in store for him. The White House commandos finally were able to take a breath. The secret had held. The vice president had been utterly fooled. Just before stepping into the State Dining Room, Joe Biden, still mystified, worried to his staffer, "Nobody's told me anything about this."

It was eight days before the inauguration of President Donald Trump. For Joe, the past year and a half had been particularly hard: he was still grieving over the loss of his son Beau in May 2015 and was coming to grips with his decision not to run in the 2016 presidential election. In recent weeks, Obama staffers had been busy packing up their offices. Some had already departed; the rest were preparing to turn in their cell phones, computers, and White House badges. With the election shock still fresh, gloom pervaded the West Wing.

In offices and cubbies, boxes had been filled, photos, desk toys, and mementoes packed away to be carted off to new lives. Congratulations over a job well done were tinged by distress over what lay ahead for each of them individually and for the nation as a whole. Bedingfield became emotional at the sight of moving trucks parked on West Executive Avenue. "It felt like the end of the world," she said. "It truly felt like the end of the world."

But before the world ended—before the new president took up his imagined throne in the Oval Office—President Obama had one final important matter of business. In a very public display of affection, Barack wanted to let his vice president know how much he had valued him, respected him, and, without getting too sappy about it, loved him. And he'd found just the way to do it.

Barack had decided to confer the Presidential Medal of Freedom, the nation's highest civilian honor, on his vice president, Joe Biden. In doing so, Barack intended not only to show his personal gratitude for Joe's contribution to his presidency but also to bestow an honor that acknowledged the vice president's long and exemplary service to the nation.

Typically recipients were informed of their selection long before the ceremony. But not in this case. For full effect, Barack wanted to spring it on his buddy just days before he flipped off the lights in the Oval Office and walked out for the last time. At his urging, back in November, an elite group of White House aides had swung into action.

Only gradually did the circle of those in the know widen. The White House calligrapher, for one, had to design the program and the citation under a vow of silence. Once the programs were ready, they had to make their way from the Government Printing Office to the White House for safekeeping without anyone the wiser. "Just to make sure that they did not get into the wrong hands," Liz Allen recalled, "we had them transported to the White House with an escort—which is never done."

In his remarks at the ceremony, President Obama was eager to capture Joe's character in just the right words, so he had a strong hand in shaping the language. But still, his speechwriter was let in on everything a few days before the event to help ensure Barack hit all the notes perfectly.

On the day of the event, staffers raced toward the climax. Since military aides had a ceremonial role in the awarding of the Medal of Freedom, at least two of them had to be on hand. One was charged with reading out the citation, the other with handing the medal to the president before he placed it around the vice president's neck. But military aides at a White House toast would have been sorely out of place, a dead giveaway that something else was up. Staffers tucked them away in a back room out of sight for as long as possible.

Handling the press was always a tricky matter, especially so under these circumstances. Television reporters were invited to cover the event but were told it was only a White House toast. But pushy TV producers demanded to know more. Liz Allen was in a tight spot: she had to make sure the cameras showed up, but she had to convince them without giving away too much. "You're going to want to be live," she teased the producers, keeping the details to herself. "I said, 'Trust me, it will be worth it for you to be live.'"

By now, the goal for the tight-knit planning team was just to get across the finish line. Everyone had done their absolute best, Kate Bedingfield remembered thinking as the big moment approached. "So here we go," she told herself. "Let's not ruin it in the eleventh hour."

Biden's normally laid-back chief of staff, Steve Ricchetti, was a ball of tension. "His whole attitude is very easygoing," Bedingfield explained. But the medal experience from start to finish had been harrowing for him. On the morning of the ceremony, he seemed distracted, short with people. He refused to consult on several matters Bedingfield brought to his attention, saying again and again they'd deal with it later, deal with it later, deal with it later. "I remember distinctly, the morning of the event, he was keyed up in a way that he rarely is."

Ricchetti admitted, "I was petrified."

When Joe entered the room, Barack had him come stand beside him at the podium in front of the State Dining Room's tall fireplace. Two reasonable men, in their trim suits, white shirts, and blue ties, just days from closing out eight years together, days before handing the keys to the White House to Donald Trump. Behind them the marble mantel bore an inscription of words that President John Adams wrote to his wife on taking up residence in the White House in 1800, reading in part: "May none but honest and wise Men ever rule under this roof."

The State Dining Room, a site for events of great dignity and ceremony, was once the private office and library of President Thomas Jefferson. Later President Theodore Roosevelt enlarged it and mounted a moose head over the fireplace. The moose was long gone, and now in its place, just over Barack and Joe's shoulders, hung a portrait of a brooding President Lincoln, chin in hand, peering off into the distance. Overhead was a silver-plated chandelier dating to 1902.

It was here in this room that President John Kennedy entertained forty-nine Nobel laureates, quipping in his prepared remarks to the assemblage, "I think this is the most extraordinary collection of talent, of human knowledge, that has ever been gathered together at the White House, with the possible exception of when Thomas Jefferson dined alone."

With Joe next to him, Barack was gearing up to reveal his secret. "I don't want to embarrass the guy," he began, loose and twinkly, to a burst of laughter.

After Joe's period of deep sadness over Beau's death and his wrenching decision not to run for president in 2016, Joe's friends and family and staff were eager to celebrate him. It was a "welcoming and warm" room, said Kate Bedingfield. "Everybody in his life he loved and cared about."

Barack continued: "I just wanted to get some folks together to pay tribute to somebody who's not only been by my side for the duration of this amazing journey, but somebody who has devoted his entire professional life to service to this country. The best vice president America's ever had, Mr. Joe Biden."

As Barack spoke, Joe fidgeted at his side, gazing toward the heavens as if seeking strength, then mugging to a familiar face in the audience, leaning to his left for a clear view, raising his eyebrows and nodding. Then, suddenly realizing that the president's words had the ring of solemnity, Biden lowered his head like a kid caught goofing off and stared at his shoes in a way that suggested he was at once bracing himself for the spotlight and showing reverence for the speaker.

When Barack finished his brief introduction with the declaration, "the best vice president America's ever had, Mr. Joe Biden," Joe didn't look up. He kept staring at his shoes, rubbing a forefinger across an eyebrow, as the audience shot to its feet: a standing ovation with prolonged cheers and clapping. At last Joe raised his head, gave a wave of appreciation, and nodded, his face a little shrunken, eyes fighting back tears. He turned sheepishly toward the president and mouthed a thank-you.

But things had only just begun.

Everybody in the room was well aware of the affection these two men had for each other, the partnership they'd formed in governing, the warmth they expressed in public—the clasping of hands, the laughing, the hugging. The internet was flooded with memes combining their photos with funny, made-up dialogue showing Barack and Joe as a team, sometimes yukking it up, other times facing down a world of trouble. In that endless stream of jokey images, internet humorists had them calling each other bros.

Now, as the crowd settled down and Biden tried to collect himself, Obama alluded to their friendship as meme fodder. Knowing that today there were going to be declarations of affection, and gratitude, and love, Barack told the room, "This also gives the internet one last chance to talk about our bromance."

Smiling, Joe shuffled over to Barack and clapped him on the shoulder bro-like as the crowd erupted again in laughter. "This has been quite a ride," Barack continued. "It was eight and a half years ago that I chose Joe to be my vice president. There has not been a single moment since that time that I have doubted the wisdom of that decision."

Barack drew out the suspense on the secret a little longer. Before revealing the purpose of the gathering, he reviewed Joe's long career in the Senate, his accomplishments both domestic and international, and his role as an active vice president, playing watchdog on the stimulus program, fighting gun violence, and leading the Cancer Moonshot initiative, which aimed for a cure.

"He . . . made friends with Lady Gaga," Obama said to laughter, "and when the Pope visited, Joe was even kind enough to let me talk to His Holiness, as well."

Barack noted Joe's eagerness to whisper in the ear of the president. "Behind the scenes," he said, "Joe's candid, honest counsel has made me a better president and a better commander in chief. From the

Situation Room, to our weekly lunches, to our huddles after everybody else has cleared out of the room, he's been unafraid to give it to me straight, even if we disagree. In fact, especially when we disagree. And all of this makes him, I believe, the finest vice president we have ever seen."

Working his way through Joe's other contributions to America and to the White House, Barack provoked a burst of laughter when he concluded, "All told, that's a pretty remarkable legacy, an amazing career in public service. It is, as Joe once said, 'a big...deal.'"

In response, Joe smiled, stepped toward the audience, and pointed, as though recalling his outburst over the health-care reform bill caught on an open mic: "This is a big fucking deal." Now, as laughter filled the room at the memory, Joe opened both palms as if to say, *Well, what can I do?*

Seeking to convey Joe the man, Barack highlighted his lovable quirks: his aviator sunglasses, his hours spent on Amtrak, his long stories of advice from nuns in grade school, Senate colleagues, and especially his parents. In a spirit of fun, Barack quoted some favorites everyone had heard innumerable times: "No one's better than you, but you're better than nobody." Recognizing the oft-spoke words, the audience broke into laughter.

Obama went on: "Bravery resides in every heart, and yours is fierce and clear." And an old favorite: "When you get knocked down, Joey, get up." More laughter. "Get up," Barack called out a second time, and there was more laughter, and a round of applause as Joe wiped tears from his eyes with his knuckles.

Turning serious, Barack spoke of Joe's challenges through life: deaths, sorrow, stuttering, and always sticking up for the little guy. "Through trial after trial, he has never once forgotten the values and the moral fiber that made him who he is," Barack reminded his listeners. "That's Joe Biden, a resilient and loyal and humble servant. And a patriot, but most of all a family man."

Barack extolled the strength of Joe's family, especially his wife, Jill, and his kids, and Beau, who, the president reminded everyone, "was watching over us with those broad shoulders and mighty heart."

So many Bidens, filled with so much energy. "There are these Biden kids and grandkids, they're everywhere!" Barack called out to laughter, adding, "They're all good-looking." He spoke of Joe breaking out the squirt gun to play with the grandkids. "This is the kind of family that built this country," he observed. "That's why my family's so proud to call ourselves honorary Bidens."

Drawing on the Irish poet William Butler Yeats, Barack began to quote: "As Yeats put it—" and he stopped amid knowing laughter from the crowd, because no Biden event can escape a few words from an Irish poet. But Barack's options on which Irish poet he could use were limited because, even for a toast, Joe no doubt arrived with a quote from his old favorite, Seamus Heaney.

"I had to quote an Irish poet and Seamus Heaney was taken," Barack explained to more laughter. So it was Yeats whom Barack called upon to express his feelings for Joe, reciting:

*Think where man's glory most begins and ends,*
*And say my glory was I had such friends.*

The family ties of the Obamas and the Bidens went deep: the Obama girls and the Biden grandchildren, Barack reminded everyone, "are close, best friends at school, inviting each other for vacations and sleepovers."

Kids and adults were all intertwined, the president concluded. "Even though our terms are nearly over, one of the greatest gifts of these past eight years is that we're forever bonded as a family."

After this considerable preamble, both a recitation of personal affection and an argument for why his friend deserved the award he was about to confer upon him, Barack got to the point: "So, Joe, for your faith in your fellow Americans, for your love of country, and for your lifetime of service that will endure through the generations, I'd like to ask the military aide to join us onstage."

A uniformed aide walked to the front, his fingers holding two blue ribbons supporting a white star with thirteen gold stars. A second aide carrying a declaration followed him and went to a microphone off to one side.

"For the final time as president," Obama said, "I am pleased to award our nation's highest civilian honor, the Presidential Medal of Freedom."

Overcome, Joe tossed back his head, as if punched in the stomach, his lips mouthing in disbelief, "No!" Startled and needing a moment, he swung around and faced the fireplace, his back to the room, and dug into his pocket for a handkerchief while everyone shot to their feet, whooping and clapping. As the place erupted, Joe hovered at the mantel, his face hidden, wiping his eyes and nose with the handkerchief.

The military aide stood stock-still, staring straight ahead, the award dangling from his fingers, waiting to play his part, as Joe turned around, shaking his head, barely able to look up, blowing air out through his puffed cheeks. He scratched his temple and wiped a tear from his eye with a forefinger, then turned his eyes toward heaven, trying to catch his breath.

He was an emotional mess. He reached into his back pocket again for the handkerchief and wiped his nose and dabbed each eye. Throughout Joe's riot of feelings, Barack watched his friend, studied him, shifting his feet, his own emotion making it impossible for him to stand still.

Biden straightened up, like a child trying to bring himself to attention, again tilting his eyes toward heaven, as Obama continued: "And for the first and only time in my presidency," he said, "I will bestow this medal with an additional level of veneration, an honor my three most recent successors reserved for only three others: Pope John Paul

II"—here, Biden tipped backward a bit as if on weak knees, his eyes blinking and flickering upward, as Barack finished naming the others who had earned an award of similar status—"and President Ronald Reagan, and General Colin Powell."

The color had drained from Joe's face; his lips were curled down as if he were about to burst into tears. "Ladies and gentlemen," the president went on, "I am proud to award the Presidential Medal of Freedom *with distinction* to my brother, Joseph Robinette Biden Jr."

The military aide at the microphone read the declaration: "In a career of public service spanning nearly half a century, Vice President Joseph R. Biden Jr. has left his mark on almost every part of our nation." It described his work on behalf of the economic recovery, the middle class, foreign policy, crime prevention, a cure for cancer, and his support for US troops. "While summoning the strength, faith, and grace to overcome great personal tragedy, this son of Scranton, Claymont, and Wilmington has become one of the most consequential vice presidents in American history, an accolade that nonetheless rests firmly behind his legacy as husband, father, and grandfather. A grateful nation thanks Vice President Joseph R. Biden Jr. for his lifetime of service on behalf of the United States of America."

A silence fell over the room, except for the snapping of camera shutters, as President Obama stepped forward to receive the medal from the military aide, who stood ramrod straight, the ribbons between his fingers.

Obama took a ribbon in each hand and from behind Joe, he draped the white enamel star over the vice president's tie, then secured the medal around his neck. With a smile, Barack patted Joe on the shoulders, and Joe turned slowly and shook his hand, and the two men embraced in a bro hug.

Joe turned to go toward the podium, moving heavily, like a man stunned. As he went, Barack patted him a couple times on the arm and gave him one more encouraging tap on the back. Joe made his way to the microphone to prolonged applause; he wiped his face and seemed about to collapse from emotion.

Joe then stepped around the podium and went out to the first row to kiss his wife Jill and son Hunter and daughter Ashley in a shower of resounding applause. Returning to the microphone, he began to speak, but the crowd was still cheering.

Having stepped to the side, Barack kept a watchful eye on his friend and applauded along with the room. Looking on from the audience was Ted Kaufman, longtime friend and adviser to Biden and fellow Delawarean. "I was tearing up," Kaufman remembered. "It was more than tearing up." He thought of Barack and Joe, in the hot seat of the White House for eight years. Despite the pressures, the high-intensity spotlight, the conflicts, and the politics, their friendship not only took root but blossomed.

"I think just being president and vice president either brings you together or kills you, drives you apart," Kaufman said. He marveled at the strength of their friendship, which survived the sometimes-toxic environment of Washington. He had taken pleasure in watching it evolve to the point that the president had run an elaborate ruse to surprise the vice president with "the highest honor he could possibly give him."

Kaufman felt Biden's joy but also saw Obama beaming with pride. "I didn't know whether to feel better for Joe or feel better for the president," Kaufman said. Barack had conceived this moment; it flowed from him: the magnificence of the award, its surprise, the affection it expressed. Knowing there was more joy in giving than in receiving, Kaufman decided he felt better for the president. "Obama was so pleased. You could just see it in him standing there," Kaufman recalled. "What a great thing to do for somebody you care about."

Humbled by the tenacious applause, Joe tried to wave it down while wiping his eyes and nose with a tissue. Once the room quieted and everyone had settled into their seats, Joe searched the audience for his chief of staff and, when he found him, deadpanned, "Ricchetti, you're fired!"

Steve Ricchetti, whose job was to keep his boss apprised of everything, had withheld from Joe the biggest personal surprise of all in the entire two terms. Yet, with good-natured humor, the boss was loving it. After calling out Ricchetti, Joe the comedian, the raconteur, held the moment for several seconds while the room full of insiders shook with loud guffaws. "For the press," Joe explained, wiping his nose, making sure the joke wasn't lost on anyone, "Ricchetti's my chief of staff."

From his vantage point in the audience, Ricchetti welcomed his star turn as a punch line. "I remember everybody got a good laugh out of that," he said. It was worth it. Most of all the chief of staff, teary himself, felt relieved everything had come off without a hitch.

Never one to go silent, Joe didn't know what to say next. He sighed. "I had, ah..." Searching for words, he paused for five seconds, a seeming eternity, then said, "I had no inkling....I thought we were coming over, Michelle, to—for you, Jill, and Barack and I to—and a couple of the senior staff to...to toast one another. And say what a...what an incredible journey it's been."

Then for twenty minutes, in a free-association monologue, Joe was Joe: emotional, humble, humorous, bracingly sincere. He spoke of his family, his wife, his children, and his devotion to Barack and his love for the man. At times he paused, looked downward, gathered his thoughts, trying to keep on track, and spoke slowly, carefully.

"You know," he observed, "I get a lot of credit I don't deserve—to state the obvious....Because I've always had somebody to lean on." His wife Jill, for one, and many of the people in the room.

He then recalled the 1972 car crash that took his wife and baby daughter. "I leaned on my sons Beau and Hunter," he said. Though just toddlers, they kept him going, kept him racing home each evening from Washington to Delaware, to kiss them good night.

"Then," he said, "Jill came along and she saved our life, she—no man deserves one great love, let alone two."

And now with Beau gone, Joe said, "I continue to lean on Hunter, who continues to, in a bizarre kind of way, raise me."

Moving on to his professional life, he reiterated that the vice presidency really has no power. But under Barack, Joe reminded his listeners, this vice president had had a role unlike any other.

"Mr. President," Biden said, "you have...you have more than kept your commitment to me by saying that you wanted me to...to help govern....Every single thing you've asked me to do, Mr. President, you have trusted me to do."

Joe glanced over at Barack, standing beside him, to emphasize his point. Joe pondered the history. "I don't think, according to the presidential and vice-presidential scholars, that kind of relationship has existed," he said. "I mean, for real. That's all you, Mr. President. It's all you."

And it was true. No presidential team since the beginning of the republic had flourished on a personal and professional level like this one: not Washington and Adams, Adams and Jefferson, Jefferson and Burr, nor the modern matchups of Kennedy and Johnson, Carter and Mondale, George H. W. Bush and Dan Quayle, Clinton and Gore, Bush and Cheney.

Wishing to underscore Barack's inherent decency, Joe couldn't help repeating that the president had insisted on helping the Bidens financially through Beau's illness. After acknowledging that Barack was initially upset that Joe had let the story out, he again painted the scene of their weekly lunch meeting when Barack grabbed him by the shoulders and implored him not to make any unwise financial moves. In Joe's telling this time, Barack had asserted, "I'll give you the money. I'll give you the money."

Beyond Barack's decency, Joe was drawn to his strength of

character. Having watched the president in action, Joe wanted him to know he marveled at his friend's steel backbone.

"I get to give you advice. I get to be the last guy in the room and give you advice on the most difficult decisions anyone has to make in the whole world," Joe said, turning toward the president, addressing him. "But I get to walk out. And you make it all by yourself."

Finishing the thought slowly, waving a finger at the president, uttering each word singly, Joe repeated: "All—by—yourself." Jabbing a finger in the air for emphasis, he asserted, "And I've never, never, never, never, never, never once doubted, on these life-and-death decisions." He never thought Obama's judgment was flawed. "Not once," he said. And if it wasn't clear enough, he declared it again: "Not once."

As Obama had noted earlier, the debates between him and Joe weren't always easy. Now Joe pointed out, "We've disagreed and argued and we've raised our voices at one another. We made a deal we'd be completely open, like brothers with one another. But, Mr. President, I've watched you under intense fire."

Here's where Barack's intellect and coolness astonished Joe. "And I watched that prodigious mind and that heart as big as your head," he said, turning toward the president. "I've watched you—I've watched how you've acted. When you see a woman or man under intense pressure, you get a measure"—and he looked now at the president's wife and children in the audience—"and you know that, Michelle. And your daughters know it as well. This is a remarkable man."

Joe concluded, "And I just hope that the asterisk in history that is attached to my name when they talk about this presidency is that I can say I was *part of*—part of the journey of a remarkable man who did remarkable things for this country."

That brought people to their feet clapping and cheering for Barack, a final send-off to the president, who stood to the side smiling and pointing at Joe to redirect attention back at him.

Amid the ovation, Joe reached into the inside pocket of his jacket and pulled out a piece of paper, the only prepared words he had with him. Of the many words he put before the audience, he wanted to get these right. Looking down at the page, he joked, "You know I can't let a comment go by without quoting an Irish poet." The shtick busted up the room—everyone, it seemed, had been waiting for it.

Before quoting the poet, Joe offered a brief setup. He mused on Barack's character, the special qualities that made him the man he was. He revealed that he and Jill had spoken a lot about Barack, and Joe had gone to Michelle at times for insight on the president, wishing to know about the man who so generously shared his presidency with him.

Over the years, Joe had discovered a core trait of his friend. "Mr. President," he told him in front of the crowd, "there's not one single solitary ounce of entitlement in you, or Michelle, or your beautiful daughters....Not one ounce of entitlement."

Now Joe was ready for his poet: "And Seamus Heaney, one of his poems said—" The room erupted in laughter. Of course, everyone knew, Seamus Heaney had to make an entrance here.

Turning serious, Joe quoted Heaney's words, which aptly described Joe's sense of Barack as a man and president:

*You carried your own burden and very soon*
*your symptoms of creeping privilege disappeared.*

Joe tapped the medal lying on his chest, lifted it. "Mr. President, this honor"—and he gazed at it for a moment—"is...is not only well beyond what I deserve..." Joe paused, his face blurred by gratitude, then continued slowly, deliberately: "But it's a reflection of the extent and generosity of your spirit." Another pause, three seconds. "I don't deserve this."

Joe stared off into the distance for a moment, lost in thought, fingering the medal. "But..." Four more seconds elapsed. "I know it came from the president's heart."

He turned toward Barack, addressing him: "There's a Talmudic saying that says what comes from the heart enters the heart. Mr. President, you have creeped into our heart—you and your whole family—and you occupy it. It's an amazing thing that happened....I never fully expected that you'd occupy the Bidens' heart—all of us."

Emotionally drained, Joe managed: "And Mr. President—" But, unable to go on, he stopped, searching for words. Over the next fifteen seconds all he could get out was, "I, ah..." and then a deep inhale, and another: "I, ah..." until finally he put the words together: "I'm indebted to you. I'm indebted to your friendship. I'm indebted to your family."

Recovering, Joe became the other Joe, the Joe who, when he was down, got up, the humorous Joe who always had a story to tell. And one of his favorites was the one when he and Barack, during one of their weekly private lunches together, suddenly discovered what fate had bestowed upon them.

At these lunches, the men talked about whatever was on their minds. "We talk about family an awful lot," Joe said. "And about six months in, the president looks at me, said 'You know, Joe. You know what surprised me? How we've become such good friends.'"

Laughter swept the room. And Joe, twinkling and grinning, delivered his punch line: "And I said, 'Surprised *you*?'"

Amid still more laughter was a recognition: it was indeed an unlikely friendship, forged against the historical odds, the political odds, and the personal odds.

Now here they were in their final official act together as president and vice president, and though it was tinged by sadness for the two of them and uncertainty for the nation, the predominant emotion throughout the room was joy for what they had had for eight years together.

"Mr. President," the vice president concluded, "you know as long as there's breath in me, I'll be there for you, my whole family will be and I know—" Joe stopped for a breath then said quietly, "I know it is reciprocal."

He thanked Barack, and everyone for showing up. To thunderous applause, Barack and Joe shook hands, embraced, close-talked, even seemed to giggle together. Then, with his arm around Joe, the president called out to the room: "Joe Biden!"

The moment it was over, the ceremony swept across the country in tweets and Facebook posts. It had been carried live by some news networks. The video went viral. At four o'clock that afternoon, comedian Jimmy Kimmel tweeted, "I don't care which side you're on, the tribute @POTUS just paid @JoeBiden was one of the most touching I've ever seen. Watch it."

Each one of us, observing the president and vice president from a distance, saw the relationship through the lens of our own lives. Barack and Joe were a canvas on which we painted our own hopes of friendship. If the president and vice president could love and respect each other, why couldn't all of us? One woman, in a post on the CBS website, confessed to a White House–inspired longing. Wishing she had in her life the affection Barack and Joe had for each other, she wrote, "I want a man who looks at me like Biden looks at Obama."

# Presidents, Politics, and Friends

By early April 2019, a diverse field of nineteen Democrats had leapt into the race for president in 2020.

In the wings, still undeclared, was the best known among them, the top-polling front-runner: Joe Biden. Joe had much to ponder. His long experience and strength among working-class voters and in states that Donald Trump had won put a sheen on a Biden candidacy. But his age, seventy-six, would make him the oldest president in US history at his inauguration, if he were elected. A Democratic Party that was invigorated by youthful newcomers and skewing left posed a challenge for the more traditional, centrist Biden. His track record in presidential campaigns wasn't stellar; his two previous runs had stumbled and quickly lost steam. But that was before he served as an effective vice president for eight years during the transformative presidency of Barack Obama.

As Biden neared an announcement, however, there erupted an explosive controversy that struck at the core of the Biden character. Several women accused the former vice president of rubbing their backs, smelling their hair, kissing their heads, and even rubbing noses with them at public events. The vice president's behavior, the accusers said, was unwanted and made them uncomfortable. Joe, long known for his folksy charm and physical affection with people, was vilified for getting too close. Questions arose about whether Biden was too out of touch in the #MeToo era, which placed strict boundaries on acceptable male behavior. In support of Joe and his effusive nature, several women both inside and outside the Obama administration came forward to praise him for the warmth and comfort he had given them in times of need. Yet even before he jumped into the fray of another presidential campaign, the media and some in his own party began to speculate whether Joe was the right Democrat for 2020.

Former president Obama remained silent amid the uproar, though a source close to him said, "As someone in touch with President Obama, I can tell you that he continues to think the world of Joe Biden, has vouched for his character countless times, and all of that is still operative. Nothing...has changed his views on him."

But whether Obama supported his old buddy for president was another matter. As their terms wound down in 2016 and the men moved on, their relationship inevitably took a different shape. Now they were no longer a working team day to day, brothers in arms protective of each other for the good of their administration and the nation; they were two high-profile politicians considering their own futures. For Obama, that meant preserving and extending his legacy. For Biden, it meant weighing and possibly seeking the next step up: a move into the Oval Office. Not surprisingly, as individuals with separate, self-interested goals, Barack and Joe confronted tensions and disappointments within their relationship during their post–White House years.

The Barack-and-Joe relationship began to take a new shape as far back as the run-up to the 2016 presidential election. Biden had been strategizing on a possible campaign for at least two years. But after his son Beau's death in late May 2015, Joe was plunged into deep mourning and struggled to decide whether to press forward with his presidential bid the following year. A careful reading of this period in Joe's memoir, *Promise Me, Dad*, and other sources, illuminates the delicate interplay between Barack and Joe and the constraints on their friendship as they both planned for a future beyond the Obama White House. While Joe was gracious and openhearted about Barack in his memoir, he also laid out scenes revealing that Obama was unwilling to support him in the 2016 election; indeed, Obama asserted his considerable will to steer Joe away from his life's ambition, the presidency.

In January of 2015, Obama was already trying to dissuade Joe from leaping into the 2016 race, according to the memoir. "He had been subtly weighing in against—for a variety of reasons," Joe wrote. Joe suggested one possible Obama motive. If the media were to begin focusing on a Biden candidacy for 2016, that attention would dim the light on Obama, his policies, and his legacy as his time in the White House wound down, and turn the public's gaze onto Joe. "The minute I announced I was running for the nomination," Joe explained, "Barack and I both knew, coverage in the West Wing would shift from his agenda to my chances."

Obama trusted in political speculation, presented as strategic reasoning, to discourage Biden from pursuing the White House. "The president was convinced I could not beat Hillary, and he worried that a long primary fight would split the party and leave the Democratic nominee vulnerable in the general election," Biden wrote. Obama also believed Hillary had the better chance of defeating a Republican opponent in the battle for the presidency. Obama, it seemed, was most concerned about what a Republican victory would mean for his own place in the history books. His health-care program, among other advances, was at risk. "I got it, and never took issue with him," Biden said. "This was about Barack's legacy, and a significant portion of that legacy had not yet been cast in stone."

In the following months of 2015, Barack was kind and attentive as Joe struggled with Beau's illness and death. Each time the president asked, Joe waffled on a decision about running in 2016. Though he and Barack had been through a lot together, Joe didn't feel comfortable exploring his feelings in detail with him on a subject so close to his heart. "Barack Obama was my friend, but I found myself unable to fully confide in him," Joe acknowledged in his memoir. "This much I knew, I explained to him: I had two choices. I could have a good ten years with my family, laying the foundation of financial security for them and spending more time with them. Or I could have ten years trying to help change the country and the world for the better. 'If the second is within reach,' I told him, 'I think that's how I should spend the rest of my life.'"

As Joe leaned toward running, Obama gently but firmly guided him in the other direction. Some Democrats saw Biden as the party's best standard-bearer, and a Draft Biden movement picked up steam. But Obama tried to tamp down Joe's delight. "The president was urging caution," Biden recalled. "He wanted me to make sure I didn't let this chatter get too loud."

Soon it dawned on Joe that Barack had made up his mind: "I found myself saying, 'Look, Mr. President, I understand if you've made an explicit commitment to Hillary and to Bill Clinton.'"

By early August, Joe had gained his strongest position in the polls in six months. His favorability numbers were higher than those of anyone running in either party, including Clinton. He scored high on trustworthiness, honesty, and empathy, and he thumped Clinton in voter surveys in the swing states of Pennsylvania, Ohio, and Florida. Momentum was building, and the media was speculating heavily about a Biden candidacy. The still-unannounced campaign was generating heat. But Joe hadn't yet pulled himself out of the shadow that Beau's death had cast over his heart and his life: he wasn't sure he had the strength to give the run the commitment it needed.

When Joe told Barack at one of their weekly lunches that he still was on the fence—that he just didn't know if he could muster the energy for a run—"the president was not encouraging," Joe wrote.

Still, the Biden team believed Joe could enter the race and win. In October, while Joe's head was still spinning over what to do, he and his advisers nonetheless plotted out a campaign. Finally, at a meeting in late October, his staff ran through the nitty-gritty of the campaign's rollout. All through the presentation, chief strategist Mike Donilon kept his eye on Joe. Donilon, who had been advising Joe for more than thirty years, was a good friend, sensitive to Joe's needs and moods.

What Donilon detected that night worried him. Joe's jaw was clenched, and Donilon saw unimaginable pain on his face. Joe's wife Jill also was sending out silent messages. Donilon couldn't help seeing the dread in her eyes. Joe caught his strategist looking at him and asked what was up. Donilon, who had believed wholeheartedly in the success of a Biden campaign since they'd started discussions two years earlier, answered simply and definitively:

"I don't think you should do this."

The next day, Joe stood in the Rose Garden with Jill on one side and Barack on the other. Obama had offered the lovely setting, reserved mostly for a president's use, and Joe began his announcement by thanking Barack for "lending me the Rose Garden for a minute." To which Barack quipped, "It's a pretty nice place." The crowd laughed.

This was not a lighthearted moment, though Joe did all he could, as he wrote, "to be upbeat, to keep my shoulders back, to smile." He said he and his family were working through the grieving process, and it took time. "It may very well be that that process, by the time we get through it, closes the window on mounting a realistic campaign for president," he explained. "I've concluded it has closed."

Mike Donilon, sitting with the crowd, watched his friend end his flirtation with the 2016 election. When it was over, Donilon observed, "Joe Biden looked a little less pained, and a little less alive."

Joe didn't want to be standing in the Rose Garden making this announcement. He wanted to run; he wanted more than anything in the world to be president. His son Beau had been sensitive to his father's ambitions and had believed in him as the candidate with the right values for the country. "You've got to run," he'd told his father a few years earlier. "I want you to run." Later, as he struggled with cancer, Beau "tried to make his father promise to run," according to Maureen Dowd of the *New York Times*.

It's impossible to know, of course, what the outcome might have been if Obama had also encouraged Joe's dream and urged him to mount a campaign. Seeking to guard his legacy, Barack instead placed his bet on Hillary Clinton. Perhaps he saw her as his true successor, the one who would confirm his revolutionary stamp on America's political culture: here was the first black president passing the baton to the first woman president. Change had come to America! Joe Biden, after all, despite his many virtues, was just another white guy, one in a long line of American presidents—hardly the symbol of the tectonic change that Obama hoped would mark his place in the history books.

"Biden had known for years that the party would want to follow the first African-American president with the first woman president," Dowd observed. In her harsh assessment, after Joe decided against a run, Obama presented him with the Medal of Freedom as a kind of consolation prize. "They pushed [Joe] aside, giving him the Medal of Freedom to assuage the dis," she wrote.

Joe Biden was all heart. Barack Obama was all brain. In going with Clinton over Biden, Obama went with the brain instead of the heart. The irony of his decision lingers. We all know what happened to Hillary Clinton in November 2016. We also know that Joe was strong in those midwestern states that were her undoing. Instead of carrying his legacy into a Clinton presidency, Obama has had to stare largely in silence as Donald Trump has worked to roll back Obama-era achievements in health care, civil rights, worker and consumer safety, immigration, education, and environmental protection.

\*    \*    \*

Obama's loyalties were often hard to gauge. His commitment to Joe did not appear unconditional, even as Obama often reiterated that making Joe his vice president was the best decision he'd made. The public embarrassment Biden suffered over whether he would remain on the 2012 ticket left bruises enough. But it reflected a pattern of political expediency from the Obama team that put a strain on Barack's relationship with Joe, especially as they went their separate ways after the White House.

As Joe pondered yet another run for president in 2020, Obama again hesitated to embrace his vice president. Hewing to his steadfast political pragmatism, Obama refrained from early endorsements, and as Democratic hopefuls considered or announced their bids for 2020, he met with them. The men and women seeking his blessing typically emerged tight lipped, saying they'd discussed the grind of a presidential campaign and big-picture issues confronting the Democratic Party.

The media characterized Biden as offended by Obama's chats with other potential candidates. After Obama sat down with Beto O'Rourke, the rising Texas politician who nearly defeated Ted Cruz in the 2018 US Senate race, *Vanity Fair* reported that Biden was "upset—not specifically by Obama's conversation with O'Rourke, but by the former president's willingness to talk to other plausible Democratic contenders while Biden is still deciding whether to run himself." Although a Biden spokesperson vehemently rejected that appraisal, Joe had to accept that he was just one of many in Obama's sights for 2020.

When Obama said at an event in Hawaii in January 2019 that there was a need for "new blood" in the ranks of leadership, *The Hill*, a political newspaper in Washington, described it as "a blow to Joe Biden." The paper quoted an unnamed Obama ally describing the deep love the president had for Joe. "But that's different than giving his brand to him," this person told *The Hill*. "He has an incredible soft spot for him...but he won't come out and make Joe his candidate. And I think that hurts Joe."

When Joe finally announced his decision on April 25 to seek the

Democratic nomination in 2020, Barack made his feelings known in a bland statement issued by his spokeswoman, Katie Hill. "President Obama has long said that selecting Joe Biden as his running mate in 2008 was one of the best decisions he ever made," Hill said. "He relied on the Vice President's knowledge, insight and judgment throughout both campaigns and the entire presidency. The two forged a special bond over the last 10 years and remain close today."

With the former president offering only this dribble of support in well-worn language, Biden insisted soon after his announcement that he had asked Obama not to endorse anyone during the primary season. "Whoever wins the nomination should win it on their own merits," Joe asserted.

Obama adviser David Axelrod explained to *Politico* that the former president believed it's best for the Democratic Party and the candidates to duke it out in the primaries so the strongest one will emerge. "The expectation that he would [endorse anyone], I find kind of baffling," Axelrod said. He added that it was not "folklore" that Barack and Joe were "genuinely friends. Unlike almost every other vice president and president, these guys got closer and closer over eight years."

Barack and Joe had come together for a specific purpose: to win an election and govern as president and vice president. Within that context, they succeeded beyond measure in shaping a historic White House partnership. They set new standards for the working relationship between a president and vice president. Barack and Joe relied on each other's strengths, overlooked the other guy's faults, and together addressed America's needs as a formidable duo. Over their eight years, the two men gained enormous respect for each other, shared in joys and sorrows, and created a unique friendship that serves as a model for future presidential teams.

The Barack-and-Joe friendship did something else: it stirred the imagination. It gave Americans hope that the nation could work together harmoniously. Barack and Joe looked beyond color and age and personal quirks to the importance of shared values. As Barack told us all in his electrifying speech in 2004, our differences do not define us but rather make us great. He rejected the divisiveness of the terms *liberal* and *conservative* and asserted that there is no black, white, Latino, and Asian [America]. "There is," he observed, "the *United States of America*." Barack and Joe personified that America.

In many ways, their relationship was a thing of beauty. We couldn't turn our eyes away from it. "Beauty," Harvard professor of aesthetics Elaine Scarry has noted, "causes us to gape and suspend all thought." Essayist Robert Boyers, writing about a friend, "the most beautiful man" he'd ever known, said that his "beauty inspired intensities of admiration and interest." If that is a definition of beauty, then Barack and Joe together were a beautiful sight. Watching the two of them, many people were mesmerized, and many experienced sensations akin to being in the presence of beauty. Barack and Joe moved us the way beauty moves its admirers. "Beauty quickens. It adrenalizes. It makes the heart beat faster," Scarry wrote in her book *On Beauty and Being Just*. "It makes life more vivid."

The extraordinary partnership of Barack and Joe did that—and more. It rose in another way to the level of beauty. Scarry has noted that we marvel at something beautiful because it has a freshness about it, a newness—to our eyes, it is unprecedented. As a president and vice president who worked harmoniously together, had mutual respect, and even loved each other, Barack and Joe were unlike anything America had ever seen. There was a unique and renegade quality to their friendship that delivered it into the realm of beauty. As Scarry has observed, "It is the very way the beautiful thing fills the mind and breaks all frames that gives the 'never before in the history of the world' feeling." With that sense of beauty, Barack and Joe broke all frames and for eight years filled the American mind with wonder, hope, and optimism.

# Acknowledgments

My wife Suzanne, my extraordinary partner, watched innumerable videos of the Obama-Biden era for fact-checking purposes, from Jon Stewart routines to the presentation of the Medal of Freedom. I once caught her reviewing the funeral of Beau Biden. She watched the Biden family procession into the church to the song "Bring Him Home" from *Les Misérables* and later Coldplay's Chris Martin performing "'Til Kingdom Come," muttering to herself, "Poor Joe, poor Joe." She feels the work she does; she felt this book. Like my other books, this one could not have been done without her. It is richer for her touch.

Her contributions were essential. From early conception to outline through writing and submission and publication, she has provided ideas, backup, and meticulous work. With speed and care, she transcribed hours of interviews I conducted with Obama and Biden staffers. Her research skills are unparalleled. I once asked, "Where is the White House putting green in relation to the Oval Office?" Minutes later she had a diagram clearly showing the layout. And that was an easy one.

Her patience in finding and sorting through possible photos for the book was superhuman, and her steady, hour-after-hour preparation of endnotes was hard for me to comprehend. If she weren't here, this book would have no endnotes, and maybe no photos, because I simply couldn't do it. She is also a scrupulous fact-checker and taste-master, forcing me to reconsider overblown notions. That said, any errors, misstatements, or outrageous conclusions are mine alone.

I'd like to thank the academics and Obama and Biden advisers who graciously gave their time for interviews or their assistance. Among them: Douglas Brinkley, Rosa Brooks, Michael Eric Dyson, David Garrow, Geoffrey Greif, Chuck Kennedy, Randall Kennedy, Liz Allen, David Axelrod, Kate Bedingfield, Antony Blinken, Arne Duncan, Ted Kaufman, Bill Russo, Eric Schultz, Julie Smith, and Herbie Ziskend. Others offered insights but wished to remain anonymous.

I'm also indebted to colleagues at the *Washington Post*. Among them: Marty Baron, for setting a standard of excellence; Adam Kushner, for permitting me to take on this project; Tracy Grant, for guiding me in the rules of the road; and other friends and colleagues at the paper who have provided their thoughts and enthusiasm or assistance: Ron Charles, Nora Krug, David Rowell, Juliet Eilperin, Patricia Howard, Carlos Lozada, Margaret Sullivan, and Eddy Palanzo.

I'd also like to thank Paul Whitlatch, my receptive and superlative editor at Hachette, and assistant editor Mollie Weisenfeld, project editor Cisca Schreefel, and copy editor Erin Granville, and the publicity and marketing team of Michelle Aielli, Joanna Pinsker, Michael Barrs, Quinn Fariel, and publisher Mary Ann Naples.

My thanks go to my agent, Dan Lazar of Writers House, for his steadfast support and smart suggestions and insight.

And finally, I can't help smiling every time I think of our two kids, Katie and Ben, not only because of their ready kindness and generosity but because of their professional talents—which they have shared with me for the creation of the book's speaking and promotional material, Katie on social media and video production, and Ben on music composition.

# A Note on Sources

We do not yet have the distance of history to fully assess the Obama presidency and Barack and Joe's friendship. It is all still too fresh, and the accumulation, indexing, and curating of the administration's papers and those of Obama and Biden are yet to come. Oral histories of those close to the White House are still to be recorded, and though a number of memoirs already have hit the shelves, no doubt many more will come. There is still much to tell. Obama and Biden, in their own ways, will have an impact on the 2020 presidential election, and how that plays out still remains to be seen. So any rendering of the Obama years at this point remains largely a journalistic enterprise, as they say, "a rough draft of history."

Yet, in our rich information age, I had the benefit of abundant resources. Videos, blogs, and real-time reporting gave me the opportunity to peer in on history as it was made. A plethora of media outlets in print and online put out an endless stream of coverage of Obama and Biden, and television news programs and the nearly twenty-four-hour chatter on cable channels layered on interpretation, detail, and sometimes silliness. I spent many hours watching and studying the media's coverage and reading transcripts of television chatter, press conferences, and interviews.

Once the friends, close advisers, and staffers of Obama and Biden move further away from their time in the White House, it is hoped they will be more willing to offer their perspectives in the interests of history. I sought interviews with dozens of people who served in the White House and am grateful to those who graciously spent time with me in person and on the phone.

I asked repeatedly for interviews with Barack Obama and Joe Biden, to no avail. I also emailed questions to Obama, at the direction of an aide, but never received replies from the former president. It has seemed curious to me that, despite their busy schedules, Barack and Joe could not find time to discuss their complicated but largely felicitous relationship. I have no doubt that as the years pass and history is allowed to play upon the Obama administration, new truths and interpretations will be unearthed. A writer in my position, so soon after the end of the Obama presidency, can only present the broadest portrait possible from current available information and from insiders willing at this time to offer their reminiscences.

For the chapter on the "Beer Summit" I asked to speak with both Harvard professor Henry Louis Gates Jr. and Cambridge police sergeant James Crowley, neither of whom replied to inquiries. Likewise, General Stanley McChrystal declined to be interviewed for the chapter in which he is featured. I also conducted interviews with others— scholars, political observers and advisers, and journalists—who had either close association to the events in the book or enlightening perspectives.

In addition to the abundant journalism and videos, I delved into many books: Obama and Biden biographies and their own memoirs; accounts of their campaigns; assessments of their policies; memoirs of their staffers, Cabinet members, and military officers; books on male bonding and on friendship; and general histories and biographies that shed light on Barack and Joe and their times.

# Notes

*Introduction*

2 **"friend Joe":** Barack Obama (@BarackObama), "Proud to cheer on Team USA at the Invictus Games today with my friend Joe. You represent the best of our country," Twitter, September 29, 2017, 9:22 p.m., https://twitter.com/BarackObama/status/913952069765271559.

2 **"Your service has":** Joe Biden (@JoeBiden), "Your service has been a great gift to the country, and your friendship and brotherhood are a great gift to me. Happy birthday, @BarackObama," Twitter, August 4, 2017, 9:26 a.m., https://twitter.com/joebiden/status/893478138822479872?lang=en.

2 **"Happy Birthday":** Barack Obama (@BarackObama), "ME: Joe, about half-way through the speech, I'm gonna wish you a happy birth—BIDEN: IT'S MY BIRTHDAY! ME: Joe," Twitter, November 20, 2017, 1:02 p.m., https://twitter.com/BarackObama/status/932685522820042754.

2 **"hugged them":** Helena Andrews-Dyer, "Barack Obama and Joe Biden Grab Lunch in Georgetown, and the Crowd Goes Wild," *Washington Post*, July 30, 2018.

3 **"Hold on…Joe's paying":** Daniela Galarza, "Barack Obama and Joe Biden Met Up for Lunch and It Was Just Like Old Times," *Eater*, July 31, 2018, www.eater.com/2018/7/31/17634184/barack-obama-joe-biden-dog-tag-bakery-vets-dc-lunch.

3 **"Don't you miss":** Millennial Politics (@MillenPolitics), "Barack Obama and Joe Biden got lunch together in DC today. Don't you miss these guys?" Twitter, July 30, 2018, 2:01 p.m., https://twitter.com/millenpolitics/status/1024037190970605568.

3 **"Miss them so":** Sara Pearl (@skenigsberg), "omgg @BarackObama and @JoeBiden just ate lunch together in dc. miss them so much," Twitter, July 30, 2018, 2:04 p.m., https://twitter.com/skenigsberg/status/102400784705361100 09?lang=en.

3 **"We loved this"**: Kate Leaver, *The Friendship Cure: Reconnecting in the Modern World* (New York: Overlook, 2018), 74.

3 **"Barack Obama...100 percent alive"**: Emma Baty, "Barack Obama and Joe Biden Went to Lunch Yesterday and It Was Cuter Than Your Last Date," *Cosmopolitan*, July 31, 2018, www.cosmopolitan.com/entertainment /a22600719/barack-obama-joe-biden-date/.

4 **"The former president"**: Stacey Leasca, "Barack Obama and Joe Biden Went on a Lunch Date and Adorably Ordered the Same Sandwich," *Travel and Leisure*, July 31, 2018, www.travelandleisure.com/travel-news/barack-obama -joe-biden-lunch-date-washington-dc.

4 **"bromance through...and Joe Biden"**: "Barack Obama and Joe Biden's Bromance Through the Years," *New York Daily News*, www.nydailynews.com /news/barack-obama-joe-biden-bromance-years-gallery-1.2877983.

5 **"Obama had the remoteness"**: George Packer, *Our Man: Richard Holbrooke and the End of the American Century* (New York: Knopf, 2019), 464.

5 **"It was clear"**: Joe Biden, *Promise Me, Dad: A Year of Hope, Hardship, and Purpose* (New York: Flatiron, 2017), 70–71.

5 **"The romantic husband"**: Leaver, *The Friendship Cure*, 71.

6 **"gentle subversion...male stoicism"**: Ibid., 73.

7 **"My brother and friend"**: Barack Obama (@barackobama), "My brother and friend @JoeBiden is back on Instagram. Welcome back, Joe," Instagram, September 8, 2018, www.instagram.com/p/BneQYW7nhkb/.

7 **"What a real"**: Edzarco, comment on Obama, "My brother and friend."

*Chapter One*

9 **"God-awful"**: US Congress, Senate, Committee on Foreign Relations, *The Nomination of Dr. Condoleezza Rice to Be Secretary of State: Hearings Before the Committee on Foreign Relations*, 109th Congress, 1st session, January 18 and 19, 2005, www.govinfo.gov/content/pkg/CHRG-109shrg22847/pdf/CHRG-109 shrg22847.pdf, 170.

9 **"a seven-hour ride"**: Ibid., 171.

9 **"It's an incredible thing"**: David Axelrod, *Believer: My Forty Years in Politics* (New York: Penguin, 2015), 167.

10 **"Well, let me now call"**: US Congress, Senate, Committee, *The Nomination of Dr. Condoleezza Rice*, 86.

11 **"I stand here...of America"**: Barack Obama, keynote speech at the Democratic National Convention, Boston, Massachusetts, July 27, 2004, "Obama's 2004 DNC Keynote Speech," YouTube video, posted by CNN on July 27, 2016, www.youtube.com/watch?v=ueMNqdB1QIE.

11 **"I have to tell you"**: *Hardball with Chris Matthews*, aired July 27, 2004, on MSNBC, transcript, www.nbcnews.com/id/5537682/ns/msnbc-about_msnbc _tv/t/hardball-chris-matthews-july-pm/#.Wx_lSnInbx4.

11 **"I realized at that moment"**: David J. Garrow, *Rising Star: The Making of Barack Obama* (New York: William Morrow, 2017), 940.

# Notes

11 **"A superstar is born":** Clarence Page, "Obama's Drama and Our Dreams," *Chicago Tribune*, August 1, 2004, 2.9.

11 **"I just cannot wait":** David Mendell, *Obama: From Promise to Power* (New York: Amistad, 2007), 285.

11 **"Barack Obama's...Biden":** Peter Beinart, "Ask Not," *New Republic*, August 16, 2004, 6.

12 **"Radical fundamentalism...swords":** Joe Biden, speech at the Democratic National Convention, Boston, Massachusetts, July 29, 2004, video, C-SPAN,www.c-span.org/video/?182721-2/democratic-national-convention-day-4-evening.

12 **"On Thursday night":** Beinart, "Ask Not."

13 **"Speaking of butts...Baracking my world":** *Will & Grace*, season 7, episodes 10–11,"Queens for a Day," directed by James Burrows, written by Kirk J. Rudell, featuring Eric McCormack, Debra Messing, Megan Mullally, and Sean Hayes, aired November 25, 2004, on NBC.

13 **"He looked ready":** Robin Givhan, "At the End of the Race, Dressed to Impress," *Washington Post*, November 5, 2004, C.1.

13 **"I think Barack...intellectually":** David Remnick, *The Bridge: The Life and Rise of Barack Obama* (New York: Alfred A. Knopf, 2010), 274.

13 **"As a consequence":** Mendell, *Obama*, 217.

14 **"few people end up":** Barack Obama, *The Audacity of Hope: Thoughts on Reclaiming the American Dream* (New York: Three Rivers, 2006), 104–105.

14 **"I'm so junior":** Jeff Zeleny, "New Man on the Hill: Sen. Obama's First Year in Washington," *Chicago Tribune*, March 20, 2005, 1.

14 **"He had the magic...good senator":** Pete Rouse, "Interview: Pete Rouse," interview by Jim Gilmore, *Frontline*, WGBH, July 11, 2008, www.pbs.org/wgbh/pages/frontline/choice2008/interviews/rouse.html.

15 **"a headline hunter":** Ibid.

15 **"I like Lugar":** Axelrod, *Believer*, 167.

16 **"a living, breathing fragment of history":** Obama, *The Audacity of Hope*, 73.

16 **"Learn the rules...of the Republic":** Ibid., 100.

16 **"He's a good man":** Remnick, *The Bridge*, 402.

16 **"decent guy...and talk":** Axelrod, *Believer*, 167.

16 **"I am announcing":** Jules Witcover, *Joe Biden: A Life of Trial and Redemption* (New York: William Morrow, 2010), 72.

17 **"Boggs!...tired":** Richard Ben Cramer, *What It Takes: The Way to the White House* (New York: Vintage, 1993), 635.

17 **"Every week...their lives for":** Joe Biden, *Promises to Keep: On Life and Politics* (New York: Random House, 2007), 65.

17 **But Biden was no:** Witcover, *Joe Biden*, 73.

18 **"It was Joe...enemy of him":** Cramer, *What It Takes*, 636.

18 **"You know...president":** Ibid., 425.

18 **"a real gentleman":** Witcover, *Joe Biden*, 86.

19 **"Something's gonna...happen":** Cramer, *What It Takes*, 638–639.

19 **"I'd always remember":** Biden, *Promises to Keep*, 77.

20 **"When she hung up…isn't she?":** Ibid., 79.

20 **"I could not speak…merciful God":** Ibid., 80–81.

20 **"sucked inside a black hole":** Ibid., 80.

21 **"jumping in bed":** Jules Witcover, *Joe Biden*, 99.

21 **"I remember his entire focus":** Ibid., 100.

21 **"When I look back":** Biden, *Promises to Keep*, 89.

21 **"He'd end up":** "The Mondale Vice Presidency and Its Legacy," from the symposium *Walter Mondale: Living Legacy*, George Washington University, Washington, DC, October 20, 2015, "Evolution of the Vice Presidency," video, C-SPAN, www.c-span.org/video/?328827-1/walter-mondale-joe-biden-reflections-office-vice-president.

22 **"Senator Biden, do you remember me":** Biden, *Promises to Keep*, 104.

22 **"I will always be a Senate man":** Joe Biden, farewell address to the Senate, Washington, DC, January 15, 2009, video, C-SPAN,www.c-span.org/video/?283385-2/senator-biden-farewell-address.

22 **"It was clear that Obama":** Axelrod, *Believer*, 168.

22 **"we could get a hundred bills":** Richard Wolffe, *Renegade: The Making of a President* (New York: Three Rivers, 2010), 41–42.

22 **"It was his general":** David Axelrod, interview by the author, June 5, 2018.

23 **"Blah, blah, blah":** Axelrod, *Believer,* 168.

23 **"Does he look happy":** Mendell, *Obama*, 308.

23 **"Since it's the day":** US Congress, Senate, Committee, *The Nomination of Dr. Condoleezza Rice*, 86.

24 **"They weren't in sync":** Antony Blinken, interview by the author, May 30, 2018.

24 **"I would not describe":** Axelrod, interview.

24 **"Now, when I…said, you know:** US Congress, Senate, Committee, *The Nomination of Dr. Condoleezza Rice*, 172.

24 **"Shoot. Me. Now."** John Heilemann and Mark Halperin, *Game Change: Obama and the Clintons, McCain and Palin, and the Race of a Lifetime* (New York: HarperPerennial, 2010), 28; *Frontline*, "Dreams of Obama," written and directed by Michael Kirk, reported by Jim Gilmore, aired January 20, 2009, on PBS, transcript, www.pbs.org/wgbh/pages/frontline/dreamsofobama/etc/script.html.

*Chapter Two*

26 **"This young man":** Garrow, *Rising Star*, 951.

26 **"Look hard, honey":** Ibid., 953.

26 **"You need to run":** Ibid., 944.

26 **"bright, beautiful":** Ibid., 229.

26 **"calling":** Ibid., 271.

26 **"resolution of [Obama's] 'black' ":** Ibid., 271.

26 **"already had his sights"**: Ibid., 270.

26 **"I remember very specifically"**: Ibid., 271.

27 **"Barack was like...about that"**: Mendell, *Obama*, 101.

27 **"Ohio, Texas, Massachusetts...sneaky about it"**: Lynn Sweet, "What's Up with Obama Secrecy?," *Chicago Sun-Times*, September 9, 2004, 37.

28 **"We've got to tamp"**: Axelrod, *Believer*, 163.

28 **"I am not running"**: David Mendell, "After Reaching Heights, Obama Lowers His Sights," *Chicago Tribune*, November 4, 2004, sec. 1, 1.

28 **"Lynn, you're dictating...you've done this"**: Scott Fornek, "Obama for President?," *Chicago Sun-Times*, November 4, 2004, 17.

29 **"I don't think we're"**: Mendell, "After Reaching Heights."

29 **"This is all"**: David Mendell, "Heady Week Yields to Hard Work," *Chicago Tribune*, August 2, 2004, 2C1.

30 **"We need to talk"**: Biden, *Promises to Keep*, 358.

30 **"Why invite more pain"**: Ibid.

31 **"I want you...unite the country"**: Ibid., 359.

31 **"emerging as one"**: Joseph Biden, interview by Bob Schieffer, *Face the Nation*, CBS, June 19, 2005, transcript, www.cbsnews.com/htdocs/pdf/face_061905 .pdf, 1.

32 **"a gigantic gap"**: Ibid., 2.

32 **"Why would Secretary Rice"**: Ibid., 3.

32 **"A lot of people...news today, Senator"**: Ibid., 7.

32 **"It makes sense...this makes sense"**: Garrow, *Rising Star*, 983.

33 **"Now we set...Party"**: Axelrod, *Believer*, 175.

33 **"People can believe...of 2006"**: Rouse, "Interview."

33 **"absolutely...I will not"**: Barack Obama, interview by Tim Russert, *Meet the Press*, NBC, January 22, 2006, transcript, www.nbcnews.com/id/10909406/ ns/meet_the_press/t/transcript-january/#.XESzLs9KjUo.

34 **"a political phenomenon"**: Ellis Cose, "Walking the World Stage," *Newsweek*, September 11, 2006, 26.

34 **"The charismatic Obama"**: Lynn Sweet, "What Obama Needs to Reach the Next Level," *Chicago Sun-Times*, September 7, 2006, 41.

34 **"a breath of fresh air"**: Mendell, *Obama*, 244.

35 **"He's a Rorschach test"**: Don Terry, "The Skin Game," *Chicago Tribune*, October 24, 2004, 10.15.

35 **"the perfect mirror"**: Cose, "Walking the World Stage."

35 **"muddled, uninspiring proposals"**: Review of *The Audacity of Hope*, by Barack Obama, *Publishers Weekly*, October 2, 2006, www.publishersweekly .com/978-0-307-23769-9.

35 **"read like outtakes"**: Michiko Kakutani, "Foursquare Politics, with a Dab of Dijon," *New York Times*, October 17, 2006, E.1.

35 **"I don't think Michelle"**: Garrow, *Rising Star*, 1004.

35 **"Seize the day"**: Clarence Page, "Enjoy, Senator, It'll Get Worse," *Chicago Tribune*, October 22, 2006, 2.5.

35 **"With so many people"**: Axelrod, *Believer*, 183.

36 **"How would one…Positive"**: David Remnick, "Testing the Waters," *New Yorker*, November 6, 2006, www.newyorker.com/magazine/2006/11/06 /testing-the-waters.

36 **"It may not be exactly"**: Axelrod, *Believer*, 202.

36 **"Well, I've decided"**: Rouse, "Interview."

36 **"It's a go"**: Axelrod, *Believer*, 204.

37 **"I will be filing"**: "Obama Exploratory Committee," video, 3:36, C-SPAN, January 16, 2007, www.c-span.org/video/?196212-1/obama-exploratory -committee.

37 **"campaigns as an author"**: Ben Wallace-Wells, "Obama's Narrator," *New York Times Magazine*, April 1, 2007, 32.

37 **"We can build…United States"**: Associated Press, "Illinois Sen. Barack Obama's Announcement Speech," *Washington Post*, February 10, 2007, www.washingtonpost.com/wp-dyn/content/article/2007/02/10/AR2007 021000879.html; Barack Obama, presidential candidacy announcement, Springfield, Illinois, February 10, 2007, video, *Washington Post*, www .washingtonpost.com/video/politics/barack-obama-announces-presidential -candidacy/2015/02/10/fd573f98-b154-11e4-bf39-5560f3918d4b_video.html.

38 **five-to-one odds:** "British Bookies Make Hillary Clinton Favorite for 2008," Associated Press, November 3, 2004.

38 **"Are you running…can't, I lose"**: Joe Biden, interview by Tim Russert, *Meet the Press*, NBC, January 7, 2007, transcript, www.nbcnews.com/id/16456248/ ns/meet_the_press/t/mtp-transcript-jan/#.XEXili-ZPUq.

39 **"Biden Tosses Hat"**: Jill Zuckman, "Biden Tosses Hat in Ring, Puts Foot in Mouth," *Chicago Tribune*, February 1, 2007, 1.4.

39 **"Nothing but disaster…a tactic"**: Jason Horowitz, "Biden Unbound: Lays into Clinton, Obama, Edwards," *New York Observer*, February 5, 2007, https: //observer.com/2007/02/biden-unbound-lays-into-clinton-obama-edwards/.

39 **"skeptical…that's a storybook, man"**: Ibid.

40 **"Senator Biden has launched"**: *NBC Nightly News with Brian Williams*, "Sen. Biden Apologizes for Remarks on Obama," reported by David Gregory, aired January 31, 2007, on NBC, transcript, www.nbcnews.com/id/16911044/ns /nbc_nightly_news_with_brian_williams/t/sen-biden-apologizes-remarks -obama/#.XEX748-6PUo.

40 **"Obama today refused…he didn't mean it"**: *ABC World News Tonight*, "Biden's Launch," reported by Jake Tapper, aired January 31, 2007, on ABC.

40 **"In Delaware, the…I'm not joking"**: "Joe Biden 7-11 Gaffe," video, 00:32, C-SPAN, June 17, 2006, www.c-span.org/video/?c4555824/joe-biden -7-11-gaffe.

41 **"How's your daaaay been?"**: Joe Biden, interview by Jon Stewart, *The Daily Show with Jon Stewart*, Comedy Central, January 31, 2007, www .cc.com/video-clips/h6ribr/the-daily-show-with-jon-stewart-joe-biden.

41 **"When you're about to say"**: Biden, interview by Jon Stewart.

41 **"an old way...campaign is over"**: Nicole Guadiano, "Tangled Tongue, but a Civil Record," *News Journal* (Wilmington, DE), November 4, 2007.

42 **"It was a gaffe...what he meant"**: *NBC Nightly News*, "Sen. Biden Apologizes."

42 **"I didn't take...call them inarticulate"**: Ibid.

42 **"any offense"**: Ibid.

42 **"The day the campaign ended"**: Witcover, *Joe Biden*, 376.

43 **An instant poll by SurveyUSA:** "S.C. Gives First Round to Obama," *New York Post*, April 28, 2007; "Here are the Results of SurveyUSA News Poll #12069," SurveyUSA.com, April 26, 2007, www.surveyusa.com/client/Poll ReportEmail.aspx?g=ba1ebc70-a734-4185-8532-2e4a9ba45d96.

43 **"If I had to pick"**: *Larry King Live*, "The First Democratic Presidential Debate," guest John King, aired April 26, 2007, on CNN, transcript, http://transcripts.cnn.com/TRANSCRIPTS/0704/26/lkl.01.html.

43 **"Biden did a brilliant job"**: "Press Release—Debate Reviews: Biden Earns High Marks," news release, April 30, 2007, American Presidency Project, University of California, Santa Barbara, www.presidency.ucsb.edu/documents/press-release-debate-reviews-biden-earns-high-marks.

43 **"They mostly didn't see...better debaters"**: Axelrod, interview.

44 **Democrats voted in massive numbers:** Janell Ross, "Why Does Iowa Get to Vote First," *The Fix* (blog), *Washington Post*, February 1, 2016, www.wash ingtonpost.com/news/the-fix/wp/2016/02/01/making-sense-of-the -iowa-caucuses/?utm_term=.5b5fb654fd20; "Iowa Caucus Results: Election 2008," *New York Times*, December 16, 2016, www.nytimes.com/elections/2008 /primaries/results/states/IA.html.

44 **"In the language of American"**: Gary Younge, "'Skinny Kid with a Funny Name' Reshapes US Politics," *Guardian* (US edition), January 4, 2008, www .theguardian.com/world/2008/jan/04/uselections2008.usa4.

44 **"For Barack Obama"**: *CNN LIVE Event/Special*, "Obama, Huckabee Win in Iowa," hosted by Anderson Cooper, aired January 3, 2008, on CNN, transcript, http://transcripts.cnn.com/TRANSCRIPTS/0801/03/se.02.html.

45 **"So I called Barack"**: "Biden on the Biden Story," *Observer*, January 31, 2007, https://observer.com/2007/01/biden-on-the-biden-story/.

45 **"I think Obama's reaction"**: Axelrod, interview.

45 **"Barack Obama...context"**: "Biden on the Biden Story," *Observer*.

46 **"Obama didn't go...in his heart"**: Axelrod, interview.

*Chapter Three*

47 **"It was one of those...existential threat"**: Brian Abrams, *Obama: An Oral History 2009–2017* (New York: Little A, 2018), 30.

47 **"I have never"**: Caroline Kennedy, "A President like My Father," *New York Times*, January 27, 2008.

47 **"all things being equal"**: Abrams, *Obama: An Oral History*, 29.

# Notes

48 **"We want to…to roost"**: *Good Morning America*, "Rev. Jeremiah Wright," hosted by Chris Cuomo, reported by Brian Ross, aired March 13, 2008, on ABC.

49 **"No, I wouldn't call him radical…particularly controversial"**: Ibid.

49 **"By then, we were en route"**: Abrams, *Obama: An Oral History*, 30.

50 **"What is undeniable…because it's real"**: Barack Obama, interview by Anderson Cooper, *Anderson Cooper 360°*, CNN, March 14, 2008, transcript, http://transcripts.cnn.com/TRANSCRIPTS/0803/14/acd.01.html.

50 **"I want to do a speech"**: Axelrod, *Believer*, 272.

50 **"I'm going to give you"**: Abrams, *Obama: An Oral History*, 31.

51 **"He emailed me"**: Ibid., 32.

51 **A CBS poll**: "CBS Poll: Pastor's Remarks Hurt Obama," CBS, March 18, 2008, www.cbsnews.com/news/cbs-poll-pastors-remarks-hurt-obama/.

51 **A Gallup poll**: "Clinton Overtakes Obama Nationally for First Time in over a Month in Tracking Poll," Associated Press, March 19, 2008.

52 **"I'll give this speech"**: Axelrod, *Believer*, 274.

52 **"Barack Obama had some explaining"**: T. Denean Sharpley-Whiting, "Chloroform Morning Joe!," in *The Speech: Race and Obama's "A More Perfect Union,"* ed. T. Denean Sharpley-Whiting (New York: Bloomsbury, 2009), 1.

52 **"I can no more disown…must achieve tomorrow"**: Barack Obama, "A More Perfect Union," speech, Philadelphia, Pennsylvania, March 18, 2008, National Constitution Center Presents, https://constitutioncenter.org/amoreperfectunion.

53 **"I don't know"**: Abrams, *Obama: An Oral History*, 33–34.

53 **"the speech was a breakthrough…fact of our country"**: *Good Morning America*, "Senator Obama's Speech," aired March 19, 2008, on ABC.

54 **"Instead of completely cutting"**: "Obama's Grand Slam: Was Speech Enough to Calm Concerns over His Link to His Hate-Spewing Pastor?," editorial, *Augusta (GA) Chronicle*, March 19, 2008.

54 **"undercurrent to his…they were adults"**: *The Daily Show with Jon Stewart*, "Barack's Wright Response," hosted by Jon Stewart, aired March 18, 2008, on Comedy Central, www.cc.com/video-clips/4hgl61/the-daily-show-with-jon-stewart-barack-s-wright-response.

54 **"If his religion"**: Theodore H. White, *The Making of the President 1960* (New York: Atheneum, 1961), 116.

55 **"Those moments give"**: Abrams, *Obama: An Oral History*, 34.

55 **"I think you and Bill"**: Ryan Lizza, "Biden's Brief," *New Yorker*, October 20, 2008, 48.

55 **"one of the most important…in our country"**: Nedra Pickler, "Obama Tries to Halt Damage from Pastor's Comments, Encourages Us to Break 'Racial Stalemate,'" Associated Press, March 19, 2008.

56 **"Did you hear…admiration"**: Blinken, interview.

56 **"The arc of"**: Martin Luther King Jr., "Address at the Conclusion of the Selma to Montgomery March," Montgomery, Alabama, March 25, 1965, Martin Luther King Jr. Research and Education Institute, Stanford University, https

://kinginstitute.stanford.edu/king-papers/documents/address-conclusion
-selma-montgomery-march.

56 **"I wanted to get":** Christina Jedra, "Wilmington Names Pool After Joe
Biden, Former Lifeguard," *News Journal* (Wilmington, DE), June 26, 2017,
www.delawareonline.com/story/news/local/2017/06/26/wilmington
-names-pool-after-joe-biden-former-lifeguard/408917001/.

57 **"I actually got pulled…exchange students":** Witcover, *Joe Biden*, 30.

57 **"No, I don't…at most gas stations":** Jedra, "Wilmington Names Pool."

57 **"It was a real awakening":** Witcover, *Joe Biden*, 30–31.

57 **"Every day…cuts a day":** Biden, *Promises to Keep*, 44.

57 **"The city was in turmoil":** Witcover, *Joe Biden*, 53.

58 **"decided he needed":** Ibid., 54.

58 **"What made you run…Good, good, good":** Biden, "Farewell Address."

58 **"Senator Biden was for civil rights":** Guadiano, "Tangled Tongue."

58 **"Having watched the arc":** Blinken, interview.

*Chapter Four*

59 **"You know, I'm thinking":** Axelrod, *Believer*, 281.

59 **"People agree":** Heilemann and Halperin, *Game Change*, 336.

59 **Obama's aides sensed:** Ibid., 338.

60 **"No," he said:** Nicole Guadiano, "Election Night Brings Redemption for Biden
on National Stage," *News Journal* (Wilmington, DE), November 5, 2008.

60 **"If you win…you'd like best":** Lizza, "Biden's Brief," 48.

60 **"Barack's focus":** Wolffe, *Renegade*, 216.

61 **"I am more concerned":** David Plouffe, *The Audacity to Win: The Inside Story
and Lessons of Barack Obama's Historic Victory* (New York: Viking, 2009), 284.

61 **"when he took his seat":** Ben Wallace-Wells, "Destiny's Child," *Rolling Stone*,
February 22, 2007, 48–57.

62 **In a speech before the Chicago Council on Foreign Relations:** Peter
Slevin, "Obama Calls on Bush to Admit Iraq Errors," *Washington Post*, November 23, 2005.

62 **"Joe Biden doesn't just meet you":** Mark Bowden, "The Salesman," *The
Atlantic*, August 30, 2010.

62 **"The space was":** Ibid.

63 **"Some have concluded…genuinely nice one":** David Brooks, "In Praise of
Joe Biden," *New York Times*, January 15, 2006.

64 **"very team oriented":** Garrow, *Rising Star*, 367.

64 **"He was still a leader":** Witcover, *Joe Biden*, 24.

64 **"At some point":** Wolffe, *Renegade*, 106.

64 **"As he put it":** Nicole Guadiano, "Post-caucus Biden Just Runs Out of Steam,"
*News Journal* (Wilmington, DE), January 6, 2008.

65 **"That's how they were":** Arne Duncan, interview by the author, March 29,
2018.

65 **"If I picked her":** Plouffe, *The Audacity to Win*, 287.

65 **"We all remember"**: Anne E. Kornblut, "Clinton Sorry for Remark About RFK Assassination," *Washington Post*, May 24, 2008, A.1.

66 **"agents insisted"**: Axelrod, *Believer*, 282.

66 **Biden and Obama's two advisers gathered**: Plouffe, *The Audacity to Win*, 290.

66 **"nearly twenty-minute soliloquy…edgewise"**: Ibid.

66 **"two-hour monologue"**: Axelrod, *Believer*, 298.

66 **"In our interview…making sense"**: Ibid., 297.

66 **"The last thing…number two"**: Plouffe, *The Audacity to Win*, 290–291.

67 **"I wanted to make sure"**: Lizza, "Biden's Brief."

67 **"would be a good soldier"**: Plouffe, *The Audacity to Win*, 291.

67 **"One of the reasons"**: Ted Kaufman, interview by the author, April 12, 2018.

67 **"He was genuinely impressive"**: Axelrod, *Believer*, 297.

67 **"This is a jump ball"**: Plouffe, *The Audacity to Win*, 293.

68 **"It'll be like…in the corral"**: Ibid.

68 **"No way"**: Ibid., 294.

68 **"While he would readily accept"**: Ibid., 291.

68 **"spirited and pragmatic"**: Monica Langley, "Democrats Begin Their Final Assault," *Wall Street Journal*, August 25, 2008, A.1.

69 **"All these years"**: Lizza, "Biden's Brief."

69 **published in 1995…royalties in 2007**: Garrow, *Rising Star*, 943, 1044.

69 **"Will this job…a confidant"**: Jonathan Alter, "Biden's Unified Theory of Biden," *Newsweek*, October 13, 2008, 46.

69 **"You have a great interest"**: Lizza, "Biden's Brief."

70 **"In the first fifty-two years"**: Witcover, *Joe Biden*, 396.

70 **"Gentlemen, I feel"**: William Maclay, *Journal of William Maclay*, ed. Edgar S. Maclay (New York: Appleton, 1890), 3, https://archive.org/stream/journalwilliamm01maclgoog#page/n24/mode/2up/search/Gentlemen%2C+I+feel.

70 **"My country has"**: John Adams to Abigail Adams, December 19, 1793, Adams Family Papers: An Electronic Archive, Massachusetts Historical Society, www.masshist.org/digitaladams/archive/doc?id=L17931219ja&bc=%2Fdigitaladams%2Farchive%2Fbrowse%2Fletters_1789_1796.php.

71 **"Yet the country survived"**: Joel K. Goldstein, *The White House Vice Presidency: The Path to Significance, Mondale to Biden* (Lawrence: University Press of Kansas, 2016), 19.

71 **"more work in it"**: Ibid., 20.

71 **"much of anything"**: Ibid.

71 **"worth a bucket"**: Patrick Cox, "John Nance Garner on the Vice Presidency: In Search of the Proverbial Bucket," Center for American History, University of Texas at Austin, www.cah.utexas.edu/documents/news/garner.pdf.

72 **"If you give me a week"**: Don Gonyea, "How JFK Fathered the Modern Presidential Campaign," *Weekend Edition Saturday*, NPR, November 16, 2013, www.npr.org/2013/11/16/245550528/jfk-wrote-the-book-on-modern-presidential-campaigns.

72 **"LBJ's simple presence":** Benjamin C. Bradlee, *Conversations with Kennedy* (New York: W. W. Norton, 1975), 194.

72 "With the best will": Arthur M. Schlesinger Jr., *Robert Kennedy and His Times* (Boston: Houghton Mifflin, 1978), 621.

72 **"Every time I":** Doris Kearns Goodwin, *Lyndon Johnson and the American Dream* (New York: St. Martin's, 1991), 164.

72 **"For the Vice President":** Schlesinger, *Robert Kennedy*, 621.

73 **Richard Nixon's second-in-command, Spiro Agnew:** For more information, see the Rachel Maddow podcast *Bag Man*, www.msnbc.com/bagman.

73 **"Barack, look":** Lizza, "Biden's Brief."

73 **"That person…want to do":** Ibid.

74 **"We knew Biden":** Witcover, *Joe Biden*, 409.

74 **"by his nature":** Duncan, interview.

74 **"I *know* you'll…Absolutely":** Heilemann and Halperin, *Game Change*, 341.

*Chapter Five*

75 **"the look of him":** *This Week*, "Roundtable," hosted by Jake Tapper, aired August 10, 2008, on ABC.

76 **"The ability of people":** Dennis Oda, "Obama Comes Home," *Honolulu Star-Bulletin*, August 9, 2008.

77 **"We call on Russia":** Condoleezza Rice, "Russia Move into Georgia," statement, US Department of State, August 8, 2008, https://2001-2009.state.gov /secretary/rm/2008/08/108083.htm.

77 **"Russia should act":** Congressional Documents and Publications, "Biden Issues Statement on Recent Outbreak of Violence in Georgia," news release, August 7, 2008.

77 **"get the facts":** Agence France-Presse, "US Senator Biden to Visit Georgia for Crisis Talks," August 16, 2008.

78 **"send a clear message":** "Senator Biden's Statement on Georgia," *New York Times*, August 18, 2008, www.nytimes.com/2008/08/18/us/politics/18text -biden.html.

78 **"fortuitously well-timed…his going":** Monica Langley, "Democrats Begin Their Final Assault," *Wall Street Journal*, August 25, 2008.

78 **"While other potential":** John M. Broder, "As Running Mate, Biden Offers Foreign Policy Heft but an Insider Image," *New York Times*, August 18, 2008.

78 **"He would bring to any administration":** Ibid.

78 **"I'm not the one…funny":** Langley, "Democrats Begin."

79 **"We must help Georgia":** Barack Obama, speech at VFW national convention, Orlando, Florida, August 19, 2008, Vote Smart, https://votesmart .org/public-statement/371839/remarks-of-senator-barack-obama-at-the-vfw -national-convention#.XM-g6S-ZPR0.

79 **"Obama set off a buzz":** *CBS Evening News*, "Barack Obama to Announce His Running Mate Saturday," reported by Dean Reynolds, aired August 19, 2008, on CBS.

79 **"It's a very personal decision"**: Jeff Zeleny and Jim Rutenberg, "In 'Very Personal Decision,' Aides Say Obama Chose a Partner in Leadership," *New York Times*, August 24, 2008, A18.

79 **"My guess is"**: Wolffe, *Renegade*, 217.

79 **"I've decided"**: Plouffe, *The Audacity to Win*, 294.

79 **"were hungry for assurances"**: Biden, *Promises to Keep*, 88.

80 **"hole in your heart…father to my children"**: Julie Bosman, "Obama Calls for More Responsibility from Black Fathers," *New York Times*, June 16, 2008.

80 **"a myth to me"**: Barack Obama, *Dreams from My Father: A Story of Race and Inheritance* (New York: Broadway Paperbacks, 2004), 5.

80 **"There was still this quite raw"**: David Maraniss, *Barack Obama: The Story* (New York: Simon & Schuster, 2012), 494.

81 **"One of the reasons"**: Ibid.

81 **"very, very quiet"**: Garrow, *Rising Star*, 88.

81 **"I was…prone"**: Obama, *Dreams from My Father*, 3.

81 **"I had grown"**: Ibid., 4.

81 **"He would bring up"**: Garrow, *Rising Star*, 89.

82 **"I talked like Morse Code"**: Biden, *Promises to Keep*, 3.

82 **"Other kids looked at me"**: Ibid., 3–4.

82 **"I was young"**: Ibid., 4.

82 **"By the time he got to the top"**: Cramer, *What It Takes*, 252.

83 **"If I'm in the room"**: *60 Minutes*, "Obama Explains His Choice, Reacts to Palin," reported by Steven Kroft, aired August 31, 2008, on CBS.

83 **"He's on that BlackBerry…root canal"**: Sandra Sobieraj Westfall, "Barack Obama Reveals How He Popped the Question to Joe Biden," *People*, August 25, 2008.

84 **"Even for Joe"**: Plouffe, *The Audacity to Win*, 296.

84 **"Let's do us all a favor"**: Ibid.

84 **"Hey, I have something"**: Westfall, "Barack Obama Reveals."

84 **"Barack has chosen"**: Adam Nagourney and Jeff Zeleny, "Obama Chooses Biden as Running Mate," *The Caucus* (blog), *New York Times*, August 23, 2008, https://thecaucus.blogs.nytimes.com/2008/08/23/obama-chooses-biden -as-running-mate/#more-5962.

85 **"As a child…United States of America, Joe Biden!"**: Barack Obama, announcement of vice-presidential pick, Springfield, Illinois, August 23, 2008, "Sen. Obama Introduces VP Pick Joe Biden," video, C-SPAN, www .youtube.com/watch?v=lqpIe1bC6tA.

86 **"I'm not sure"**: *Meet the Press*, "Obama Chooses His Running Mate," hosted by Tom Brokaw, aired August 24, 2008, on NBC, transcript, www.nbcnews .com/id/26377338/print/1/displaymode/1098/.

87 **"Obama and Biden looked great"**: Plouffe, *The Audacity to Win*, 298.

87 **"ninety-five percent…if you get up, you can make it"**: Joe Biden, acceptance of vice-presidential nomination, Springfield, Illinois, August 23, 2008,

"Democratic VP Candidate Sen. Joe Biden," video, C-SPAN, www.youtube .com/watch?v=r56zQu00fiE.

88 **"I don't worry about it":** Westfall, "Barack Obama Reveals."

89 **"Guess...much better now":** Avi Zenilman, "Biden's Helmet," *Politico*, August 24, 2008, www.politico.com/story/2008/08/bidens-helmet-012760.

89 **"Let me tell you":** Roxanne Roberts, "The Very Senior Senator," *Washington Post*, March 10, 1993.

89 **"YO, JOE...raise eyebrows on the campaign":** Jotham Sederstrom and Celeste Katz, "Joe Biden's Lack of a Wedding Band Could Fuel Talk," *New York Daily News*, August 23, 2008, www.nydailynews.com/news/politics /joe-biden-lack-wedding-band-fuel-talk-article-1.314062.

89 **"a little like a shotgun wedding":** Bowden, "The Salesman."

90 **"Biden's persona":** Dan Balz, "Choice of Biden Fits the Reality If Not the Starry-Eyed Message," *Washington Post*, August 24, 2008, A10.

90 **"It was hard to tell...We'll see":** John M. Broder, "On Obama-Biden Chemistry, Clues Are Scarce," *The Caucus* (blog), *New York Times*, August 23, 2008, https://thecaucus.blogs.nytimes.com/2008/08/23/on-obama-biden-chemistry -clues-are-scarce/.

## *Chapter Six*

91 **"I guess the best way":** Axelrod, *Believer*, 304.

91 **"Who's Sarah Palin?":** Ibid., 305; Heilemann and Halperin, *Game Change*, 351.

91 **a decided jump in the polls:** United Press International, "Poll: Obama Leads McCain by Eight," August 30, 2008.

92 **"Hey, coach":** Shailagh Murray, "Democratic Candidates Begin Touring Rust Belt," *Washington Post*, August 30, 2008.

92 **"I'm loaded":** Jeff Zeleny, "On the Trail, Adjusting to Life as a Couple," *New York Times*, September 1, 2008.

92 **"posing for pictures":** Shailagh Murray, "Biden, Obama: A Comfortable Fit on the Campaign Trail," *Washington Post*, September 1, 2008.

92 **"You are gorgeous...gorgeous, too":** Ibid.

93 **"He's just this cheerful":** Ibid.

93 **"have just really hit it off...chemistry":** Ibid.

93 **"In a new CBS poll":** *Late Show with David Letterman*, "Obama-Biden Nicknames," hosted by David Letterman, aired on August 25, 2008, on CBS, www. youtube.com/watch?v=SX5JWLzZoQU.

94 **"Hillary Clinton's as qualified":** *CNN Election Center*, "Democrats Worry About Poll Numbers," reported by Jim Acosta, aired September 14, 2008, on CNN, transcript, www.cnn.com/TRANSCRIPTS/0809/14/ec.01.html.

94 **"Sometimes Joe Biden":** Susan Estrich, "Say It Ain't So, Joe," *Tribune* (Elkin, NC), Creators Syndicate, September 11, 2008.

94 **"She's easily qualified"**: *CNN Election Center*, "Democrats Worry."

95 A *Washington Post*/**ABC News poll showed**: Bonnie Erbe, "Barack Obama's Problem with White Female Voters," CBS News, September 9, 2008, www.cbsnews.com/news/barack-obamas-problem-with-white-female-voters/.

95 **"Chuck, stand up...buddy"**: "A 'Stand Up' Slipup," September 9, 2008, video, "Top Ten Joe Biden Gaffes," *Time*, content.time.com/time/specials/packages/article/0,28804,1895156_1894977_1841630,00.html.

95 **"When the stock market"**: *CBS Evening News with Katie Couric*, "Behind the Scenes with Joe Biden," reported by Katie Couric, aired September 22, 2008, on CBS.

96 **"a human verbal wrecking crew"**: John M. Broder, "Hanging On to Biden's Every Word," *New York Times*, September 12, 2008, A18.

96 **bailout of American International Group**: "AIG's $85 Billion Government Bailout," *DealBook* (blog), *New York Times*, September 17, 2008, https://dealbook.nytimes.com/2008/09/17/aigs-85-billion-government-bailout/.

96 **Biden Gaffe Clock**: Broder, "Hanging On."

96 **poll found that voters favored Obama**: Dan Balz, "Post Poll Shows Challenge for McCain," *Voices* (blog), *Washington Post*, September 24, 2008, http://voices.washingtonpost.com/44/2008/09/post-poll-shows-challenge-for.html.

96 **"I am very proud"**: The *Today Show* clip appears in the transcript for *Countdown with Keith Olbermann*, aired September 23, 2008, on MSNBC.

96 **"Mark my words"**: Mike Memoli, "Biden Turns Another Page in His Open Book," *National Journal*, October 20, 2008; Sarah Palin interview setup video, *Anderson Cooper 360°*, aired October 21, 2008, on CNN.

96 **CNN poll revealed**: *Anderson Cooper 360°*, October 21, 2008.

97 **In the ad, spooky music**: "McCain Campaign Ad," October 24, 2008, C-SPAN, www.c-span.org/video/?281993-1/mccain-campaign-ad.

97 **"Senator Biden referred"**: *Anderson Cooper 360°*, "On the Trail," hosted by Anderson Cooper, aired October 21, 2008, on CNN.

97 **"How many times"**: Heilemann and Halperin, *Game Change*, 413.

97 **"Joe and Obama barely spoke"**: Ibid., 412.

97 **"Listen"**: Ibid., 413.

98 **"Look, as I said"**: "Senator Obama News Conference," October 22, 2008, video, C-SPAN, www.c-span.org/video/?281945-1/senator-obama-news-conference&start=13, 12:03.

98 **"Now in this crisis"**: *Saturday Night Live*, "Road to the White House," performed by Jason Sudeikis and Darrell Hammond, aired October 25, 2008, on NBC, www.nbc.com/saturday-night-live/video/road-to-the-white-house/n12332.

98 **"an estimated 200 interviews...are present"**: John M. Broder, "Hitting the Backroads, and Having Less to Say," *New York Times*, October 31, 2008, A20.

99 **"Now that the end...only a day left":** *Tell Me More*, "Candidates Make Aggressive Final Pitch on Eve of Election," hosted by Michel Martin, reported by Perry Bacon, aired November 3, 2008, on NPR, transcript, www.npr.org/templates/story/story.php?storyId=96490743.

99 **"There's something in the air":** "Minute by Minute, a Final Hectic Day on the Campaign Trail," *New York Times*, November 4, 2008, A21.

100 **"The actual power":** Biden, *Promise Me*, 4.

100 **60 percent of respondents:** Broder, "Hitting the Backroads."

100 **Evansville anecdote:** David Goldstein, "Biden Bids for Blue-Collar Voters Below the Media Radar," McClatchy News Service, November 2, 2008.

100 **"Hey, Hunter":** Broder, "Hitting the Backroads."

101 **"discipline...sort of a bore":** Peter Nicholas, "Confessions from the Campaign Trail," *Los Angeles Times*, October 28, 2008, A1.

101 **"something lithe and laid-back":** Christopher Hitchens, "Cool Cat," *The Atlantic*, January/February 2009, www.theatlantic.com/magazine/archive/2009/01/cool-cat/307224/.

102 **"They're saying now":** *American Morning*, "Polls Open in More States; Candidates Vote," hosted by John Roberts and Kiran Chetry, aired November 4, 2008, on CNN.

103 **"I voted":** Nedra Pickler, "Obama Unwinds with Basketball as He Awaits Returns," Associated Press, November 5, 2008.

103 **"All right, Mom":** Kristin Harty, "Election as VP Illuminates Stellar Career," *News Journal* (Wilmington, DE), November 5, 2008, A6.

103 **76,820 miles:** Kathy Kiely, "Obama Votes, Then Helps Man the Phone Banks," *USA Today*, November 5, 2008, 7A.

103 **"Hopefully I don't break my nose":** Michael McAuliff, "Family Time as Bam Votes...and Waits," *New York Daily News*, November 5, 2008, 4.

104 **"I sat next to her...first lady of the United States":** "President Obama Reflects on Election Night 2008," sound recording, "2008 Election Time Machine," Obama Foundation, www.obama.org/history/time-machine/.

105 **larger percentage of the electorate:** Laura McPhee, "Indiana's Historic Vote for Obama," *NUVO* (Indianapolis, IN), December 8, 2008.

106 **"Hello, Chicago!...Joe Biden":** Barack Obama, victory speech, Chicago, Illinois, November 4, 2008, CNN, transcript, http://edition.cnn.com/2008/POLITICS/11/04/obama.transcript/.

106 **"Joe Biden, thirty years ago...the Obamas and the Bidens":** *Decision 2008: Election Night*, 12 Midnight–1 a.m., NBC News Transcripts, hosted by Brian Williams, aired November 5, 2008, on NBC.

108 **"saw them cuddled together":** Melissa Chan, "Read the Full Transcript of President Obama Surprising Joe Biden with the Medal of Freedom," *Time*, January 12, 2017, http://time.com/4633826/joe-biden-obama-presidential-medal-freedom/.

108 **"My grandchildren...kidding":** "The Mondale Vice Presidency."

*Chapter Seven*

109 **"You're twelve...in dog years"**: Nedra Pickler, "Boss Gives Biden Cupcakes for His 66th Birthday," Associated Press, November 19, 2008.

110 **"I believe...you should hear"**: Walter F. Mondale to Jimmy Carter, memorandum, "The Role of the Vice President in the Carter Administration," December 9, 1976, Walter F. Mondale Papers, Minnesota Historical Society, http://www2.mnhs.org/library/findaids/00697/pdfa/00697-00034-1.pdf.

111 **"top staff person"**: James T. Wooten, "Califano, Sorensen, Schlesinger Named to Key Carter Posts," *New York Times*, December 24, 1976, 1.

111 **"The big breakthrough"**: "The Mondale Vice Presidency."

111 **"important impact"**: Leslie H. Gelb, "Mondale Is Expected to Have Real Power," *New York Times*, December 26, 1976, A1.

112 **"Jimmy is always saying"**: Ibid.

112 **"The first person...with the president"**: "The Mondale Vice Presidency."

112 **"The President likes to listen"**: Goldstein, *The White House Vice Presidency*, 142.

113 **"And then there's the incredible"**: David Ignatius, "Bumpy Road Ahead for a Traveler," *Washington Post*, November 20, 2008, A23.

113 **"You know, you've been...a certain period of time"**: Joe Biden, interview by George Stephanopoulos, *This Week*, ABC, December 21, 2008, transcript, VoteSmart, https://votesmart.org/public-statement/402047/abc-this-week-with-george-stephanopoulos-transcript#.XN3LdNNKjGI.

114 **"If you look back on it"**: "The Mondale Vice Presidency."

115 **"he had command"**: Barton Gellman, *Angler: The Cheney Vice Presidency* (New York: Penguin, 2009), 396.

115 **"so wide-ranging...apparent awareness"**: Ibid., 388.

115 **"I'm not a staffer"**: Stephen F. Hayes, *Cheney: The Untold Story of America's Most Powerful and Controversial Vice President* (New York: HarperCollins, 2007), 305.

116 **"a cautionary tale"**: Gellman, *Angler*, 388.

116 **"Above all else"**: Ibid., 397.

116 **"Cheney didn't crave"**: Jacob Weisberg, *The Bush Tragedy* (New York: Random House, 2008), 149.

116 **"Vice President Cheney"**: "Transcript: The Vice-Presidential Debate," *New York Times*, October 2, 2008, www.nytimes.com/elections/2008/president/debates/transcripts/vice-presidential-debate.html.

116 **"Those who allege"**: Vice President's Ceremonial Office, White House, "Interview of the Vice President by Jonathan Karl, ABC News," news release, December 15, 2008, https://georgewbush-whitehouse.archives.gov/news/releases/2008/12/20081215-8.html.

116 **"He was pretty...dead wrong"**: Joe Biden, interview by George Stephanopoulos, December 21, 2008.

117 **"He is not going to have...during my time"**: Vice President's Ceremonial Office, White House, "Interview of the Vice President by Chris Wallace, FOX

News," news release, December 19, 2008, https://georgewbush-whitehouse
.archives.gov/news/releases/2008/12/print/20081219-11.html.

117 **"I'm standing behind":** "The Mondale Vice Presidency."

117 **boarded a 1930s railcar:** Abdon M. Pallasch, "'I Will Not Be Traveling
Alone,'" *Chicago Sun-Times*, January 18, 2009; "Obama Rail Car Rolling in
History," *Washington Times*, January 17, 2009, www.washingtontimes.com/
news/2009/jan/17/obama-rail-car-rolling-in-history/.

118 **"Folks":** Joe Biden, rally at train station, Wilmington, Delaware, January
17, 2009, video, C-SPAN, www.c-span.org/video/?283431-1/wilmington
-inaugural-train-rally.

118 **"How long do you think he'll go?":** Lolita C. Baldor, "Biden Looks for
Allies' Support in Afghanistan," Associated Press, February 5, 2009.

119 **"some mechanical difficulty":** Pallasch, "'I Will Not Be Traveling Alone.'"

119 **Bamtrak:** Kenneth R. Bazinet, "Michelle Gets on Track for a Happy B'Day,"
*New York Daily News*, January 18, 2009.

120 **"Folks, in my family":** Joe Biden, remarks at preinaugural event, Washington, DC, January 18, 2009, CNN, transcript, http://transcripts.cnn.com/
TRANSCRIPTS/0901/18/se.02.html; see also "We Are One. The Obama Inaugural Celebration," YouTube video, 1:53:51, posted by Marc Schulz, December 30, 2012, www.youtube.com/watch?v=Lmq0hV_G3CY.

121 **"What a thrill":** "We Are One."

121 **"The president-elect was intently":** Plouffe, *The Audacity to Win*, 386.

121 **"For all our challenges...and patience":** Ibid., 387.

122 **"Hello, America":** "We Are One."

122 **"And Jill had...important to us":** Jill Biden, interview by Oprah Winfrey,
*The Oprah Winfrey Show*, January 19, 2009, "Jill: Joe Biden Had Choice of VP
or Sec. State," YouTube video, 4:16, posted by toron1970, January 20, 2009,
www.youtube.com/watch?v=lvEAamX30vk.

124 **"The sort of news...President Obama today":** Robert Gibbs, interview
by Harry Smith, *The Early Show*, CBS, January 20, 2009.

124 **"In the interest of transparency...No":** Robert Gibbs, interview by Meredith Vieira, *The Today Show*, NBC, January 20, 2009.

125 "**Certainly there were moments**": Liz Allen, interview by the author,
April 30, 2018.

*Chapter Eight*

126 **"You'll have them":** Remnick, *The Bridge*, 574.

126 **"I have to tell you...traveled":** Ibid., 573.

127 **"Dick Cheney in a wheelchair":** *Talk of the Nation*, "What Happened with
Obama's Oath of Office?," hosted by Neal Conan, aired January 21, 2009,
on NPR.

127 **"Are you prepared...so help me God":** "Jan. 20, 2009: Inaugural Ceremo-
nies for Barack Obama," YouTube video, 1:38:54, posted by US Presidential

Inauguration, December 29, 2012, www.youtube.com/watch?v=S4Vool vEsyQ.

128 **"It was announced":** "It's Really Contagious," *Laugh Lines* (blog), *New York Times*, January 23, 2009, https://laughlines.blogs.nytimes.com/2009 /01/23/its-really-contagious/.

129 **how he played gumshoe reporter:** *Anderson Cooper 360°*, "Oath of Office Do-over," hosted by Anderson Cooper, aired January 21, 2009, on CNN, transcript, http://edition.cnn.com/TRANSCRIPTS/0901/21/acd.01.html.

129 **"In golf…Congratulations, again":** Michael D. Shear, "Obama Sworn In Again, with Right Words," *Washington Post*, January 22, 2009, A4.

130 **"For those of us…Ohhh!":** "VP Joe Biden 'My Memory Is Not as Good as Justice Roberts,'" YouTube video, 0:45, posted by DemocraticMediaMKII, January 21, 2009, www.youtube.com/watch?v=JubjVCwr_PU.

131 **"Look at the president's":** *Anderson Cooper 360°*, "Oath of Office Do-over."

131 **"If we do everything right":** Joe Biden, remarks at House Democratic caucus annual retreat, Williamsburg, Virginia, February 6, 2009, "Joe Biden's Stimulus Stumble," video, "Top Ten Biden Gaffes," *Time*, http://content.time. com/time/specials/packages/article/0,28804,1895156_1894977_1846610,00 .html.

131 **"I don't remember…occurring again":** "Presidential News Conference," video, February 9, 2009, C-SPAN, www.c-span.org/video/?283922-1/presidential -news-conference.

132 **Barack and Joe resolved their spat:** Holly Bailey et al., "An Inconvenient Truth Teller," *Newsweek*, October 19, 2009.

132 **"Did Obama throw":** "Did Obama Throw Biden Under the Bus?," Fox News, February 10, 2009, www.foxnews.com/politics/did-obama-throw -biden-under-the-bus.

132 **"Come on":** Jimmy Orr, "Obama on Biden: I Don't Know What He's Talking About," *Christian Science Monitor*, February 10, 2009, www.csmon itor.com/USA/Politics/The-Vote/2009/0210/obama-on-biden-i-dont -know-what-hes-talking-about.

132 **"Stream of consciousness…'Odd Couple' parodies":** Maureen Dowd, "Oval Newlywed Game," *New York Times*, February 14, 2009, www.nytimes .com/2009/02/15/opinion/15dowd.html.

134 **"We will rebuild":** Barack Obama, address to joint session of Congress, Washington, DC, February 24, 2009, Office of the Press Secretary, White House, news release, February 24, 2009, https://obamawhitehouse.archives.gov/the -press-office/remarks-president-barack-obama-address-joint-session- congress.

134 **"She gazes up":** Michael Coleman, "Behind the Scenes at Obama's Big Speech," *Albuquerque Journal*, February 25, 2009, www.abqjournal .com/18470/behind-the-scenes-at-obamas-big-speech.html.

134 **"With a plan of this scale":** Obama, address to joint session of Congress, February 24, 2009.

135 **"Weird moment of humor":** Robin Abcarian, "Don't Mess with Joe!," *Top of the Ticket* (blog), *LA Times*, February 24, 2009, https://latimesblogs.latimes .com/washington/2009/02/dont-mess-with-joe.html.

135 **"It was Obama's one shot":** Michael Grunwald, *The New New Deal: The Hidden Story of Change in the Obama Era* (New York: Simon & Schuster, 2012), 12.

135 **"If he was for it":** Ibid., 19.

135 **"'It Would've Been Even Worse":** Ibid., 16.

136 **"As the White House point man":** Ibid., 15.

136 **"When I brief him":** Michelle Cottle, "Straight Man," *New Republic*, May 6, 2009, https://newrepublic.com/article/61661/straight-man.

136 **"This is the exciting part":** Grunwald, *The New New Deal*, 7.

137 **"We're going to follow the money…helpful to her":** Joe Biden, interview by Maggie Rodriguez, *The Early Show*, CBS, February 25, 2009.

137 **"They each had to let go":** Allen, interview.

137 **On Saturday evening:** "Gridiron Club," video, hosted by Steve Scully, reported by Dan Zak, aired March 22, 2009, on C-SPAN, www.c-span.org/video /?284773-3/gridiron-club&start=139; Elizabeth Kastor, "The Grand Old Gridiron," *Washington Post*, March 23, 1985; Dan Zak, "Skewers, but Not Much Sizzle, at Obamaless Gridiron Dinner," *Washington Post*, March 23, 2009, www.washingtonpost.com/wp-dyn/content/article/2009/03/22/AR2009 032200758_pf.html.

138 **"Obama's never really":** Toby Harnden, "No Thanks, Gridiron: Barack Obama Snubs the Washington Establishment," *Telegraph* (UK), March 17, 2009.

139 **"That's not exactly out of town":** Anne Schroeder Mullins, "Gridiron Singed by Obama No-Show," *Politico*, March 16, 2009, www.politico.com /story/2009/03/gridiron-singed-by-obama-no-show-020036?paginate=false.

139 **"Typical":** Zak, "Skewers, but Not Much Sizzle."

139 **"People feel uncommonly":** Mullins, "Gridiron Singed."

140 **"While there has always been":** Mark Leibovich, "Minutiae? In This White House, Call It News," *New York Times*, March 14, 2009, A10.

140 **"Frankly, the fact…dead wrong":** *Reliable Sources*, hosted by Howard Kurtz, aired March 22, 2009, on CNN, transcript, http://transcripts.cnn .com/TRANSCRIPTS/0903/22/sotu.02.html.

141 **"President Obama stiffed…say or think":** Elizabeth Sullivan, "Obama Is Unimpressed by the Press," *Plain Dealer* (Cleveland, OH), March 29, 2009.

141 **"Without Obama, the highest wattage":** Zak, "Skewers, but Not Much Sizzle."

142 **"You did such lovely work":** Ibid.

142 **"Biden steals the show at Gridiron":** Andrew Glass, "Biden Steals the Show at Gridiron," *Politico*, March 22, 2009, www.politico.com/story/2009 /03/biden-steals-the-show-at-gridiron-020322.

142 **"If your show's running long":** Zak, "Skewers, but Not Much Sizzle."

142 **"I'm going to be brief":** James Gordon Meek, "Biden Takes Geithner Joke to the Bank, as Obama's Busy Defending Him," *New York Daily News*, March 22,

2009, www.nydailynews.com/news/politics/biden-takes-geithner-joke-bank
-obama-busy-defending-article-1.359690.

142 **"on a really great speech"**: Glass, "Biden Steals the Show."

142 **"President Obama sends his greetings"**: Zak, "Skewers, but Not Much
Sizzle."

142 **"paper thin...letter F"**: Glass, "Biden Steals the Show."

143 **"To give you an idea"**: Linda Feldmann, "'Regular Joe' Plays a Key White
House Role," *Christian Science Monitor*, April 15, 2009, www.csmonitor.com
/USA/Politics/2009/0415/regular-joe-plays-a-key-white-house-role.

143 **"The gaffes weren't that important"**: Allen, interview.

*Chapter Nine*

145 **"who does a bunch"**: Mark Leibovich, "Speaking Freely, Sometimes, Biden
Finds Influential Role," *New York Times*, March 29, 2009, A1.

146 **"always seek Biden's counsel"**: Allen, interview.

146 **"peer, not a staffer"**: Feldmann, "'Regular Joe.'"

146 **"The dietary bar is set"**: Leibovich, "Speaking Freely."

146 **"settled into their own"**: Feldmann, "'Regular Joe.'"

146 **"It's like a couple"**: Ibid.

146 **"Faced with a vice president...this industry, no?"**: Michelle Cottle, "Straight Man," *New Republic*, May 6, 2009, https://newrepublic.com
/article/61661/straight-man.

147 **"There's, I think, an institutional"**: Leibovich, "Speaking Freely."

147 **"Whatever the outcome"**: Cottle, "Straight Man."

147 **"If Biden speaks the truth...Joe be Joe"**: Ibid.

148 **severe national flu outbreak:** Julie N. Chang, "Nearly 50 Hallyburton Ele-
mentary Students Call In Sick," *News Herald* (Morgantown, NC), March 4,
2009; Rob Carson, "Flu Outbreak Arrives Late, Hits Hard in Region's Schools,"
*News Tribune* (Tacoma, WA), March 19, 2009; "Flu Outbreak Hits Perkins
Co.," *North Platte (NE) Telegraph*, April 1, 2009; Robert Marchant, "Stomach
Virus Shuts Greeley High School," *Journal News* (Westchester County, NY),
April 18, 2009; Donald G. McNeil Jr., "Major Flu Strain Found Resistant to
Leading Drug, Puzzling Scientists," *New York Times*, January 8, 2009, A10.

148 **Commentators reached into history:** Centers for Disease Control and Prevention, "1918 Pandemic (H1N1 Virus)," Influenza (Flu), last modified May
7, 2018, www.cdc.gov/features/1918-flu-pandemic/index.html; John Long,
"A Worrisome Comparison," *Roanoke (VA) Times*, April 30, 2009; Centers for
Disease Control and Prevention, "Flu: 1957–1958 Pandemic," Influenza (Flu),
last modified January 2, 2019, www.cdc.gov/flu/pandemic-resources/1957
-1958-pandemic.html; Centers for Disease Control and Prevention, "Flu: 1968
Pandemic," Influenza (Flu), last modified January 2, 2019, www.cdc.gov/flu
/pandemic-resources/1968-pandemic.html.

148 **exotic strains were turning up in the far reaches of the world:** Shuang
Lewis, "Indonesia's Bird Flu Death Toll Reaches Four Since January," IHS

Global Insight, March 4, 2009; Shuang Lewis, "WHO Calls for Enhanced Efforts to Fight Bird Flu Threat in Vietnam," IHS Global Insight, March 3, 2009; Agence France-Presse, "HK and US Scientists Develop New Bird Flu Vaccine," March 2, 2009; Xinhua General News Service, "Hong Kong Bird Flu Outbreak Confirmed to Be H5N1," December 12, 2008; "Bird Flu Hits Darjeeling, Culling Begins," *Hindustan Times*, March 14, 2009.

148 **Kentucky reported an outbreak of bird flu:** Associated Press, "Bird Flu Found on Western Kentucky Poultry Farm," April 7, 2009; "Singapore Bans Poultry Imports from Kentucky," *Poultry News*, April 15, 2009, https://thepoul trysite.com/news/2009/04/singapore-bans-poultry-imports-from -kentucky.

149 **spread of swine flu:** Rachel Williams and Abigail Edge, "Swine Flu Cases Around the World," *Guardian*, April 29, 2009, www.theguardian.com /world/2009/apr/27/swine-flu-mexico1.

149 **swine flu hit Ohio:** Phillip Buffington, "Swine Flu Case Confirmed in Ohio," *Jackson County (OH) Times-Journal*, March 28, 2009.

149 **"You cannot catch swine flu":** Marianne White, "Spammed, Scammed, Jammed: Flu Outbreak Dominates Online Buzz," Canwest News Service, April 28, 2009, www.canada.com/entertainment/spammed+scammed+jammed +outbreak+dominates+online+buzz/1542857/story.html.

149 **"The truth is":** Philip Alcabes, "5 Myths About Pandemic Panic," *Washington Post*, March 15, 2009, B3.

149 **"That's unlikely":** Lindsey Tanner, "Paris Hilton Not Only One Confused About Swine Flu," Associated Press, May 1, 2009.

150 **ticked off the statistics:** *American Morning*, "Swine Flu Prompts EU Warning Against Travel to US," hosted by Alina Cho and John Roberts, aired April 27, 2009, on CNN, transcript, http://transcripts.cnn.com/ TRANSCRIPTS/0904/27/ltm.03.html.

150 **"Tonight":** *Anderson Cooper 360°*, "Swine Flu Spreads," hosted by Anderson Cooper, aired April 28, 2009, on CNN, transcript, http://transcripts.cnn.com /TRANSCRIPTS/0904/28/acd.01.html.

150 **"as a precautionary tool...cause for alarm":** Office of the Press Secretary, White House, "Remarks by the President at the National Academy of Sciences Meeting," news release, April 27, 2009, https://obama whitehouse.archives.gov/the-press-office/remarks-president-national -academy-sciences-annual-meeting.

150 **"Ed quickly...not from swine flu":** *The Situation Room*, "Obama Administration Tries to Ease Flu Fears," hosted by Wolf Blitzer, aired April 27, 2009, on CNN, transcript, http://edition.cnn.com/TRANSCRIPTS/0904/27 /sitroom.01.html.

151 **"This is obviously...potentially spread the virus":** "Presidential Press Conference," White House Archives, April 29, 2009, transcript, https:// obamawhitehouse.archives.gov/video/Presidential-Press-Conference -4/29/09?tid=108#transcript.

152 **"Closing a classroom...different things":** Joe Biden, interview by Matt Lauer, *Today*, NBC, April 30, 2009, "Biden Flu Advice: Avoid Airplanes and Subways," YouTube video, posted by TPM TV on April 30, 2009, www.you tube.com/watch?v=Rw1h2t355Bo.

154 **"The advice he is giving":** Office of the Vice President, White House, "Statement from Vice President Biden's Spokesperson Elizabeth Alexander," news release, April 30, 2009, https://obamawhitehouse.archives.gov/realitycheck /the-press-office/statement-vice-president-bidens-spokesperson-elizabeth -alexander.

154 **"If he could say that":** Nancy Benac, "Oh, Joe: VP's Off-base Flu Advice Needs Do-over," Associated Press, April 30, 2009.

154 **"The bottom line is":** *All Things Considered*, "Biden Clarifies Travel Comments," reported by Brian Naylor, aired April 30, 2009, on NPR, www.npr .org/templates/story/story.php?storyId=103675346.

154 **"I think what Joe Biden":** Benac, "Oh, Joe."

155 **"With all due respect":** *All Things Considered*, "Biden Clarifies."

155 **"extremely disappointing...public buildings:** Mark Memmott, "Biden Says He Wouldn't Fly Right Now," *Shots*, NPR, April 30, 2009, www.npr.org /sections/health-shots/2009/04/biden_says_he_wouldnt_fly_righ.html PUBLIC HEALTH.

155 **"I'm wondering if...what he meant to say":** Office of the Press Secretary, White House, "Press Briefing by Press Secretary Robert Gibbs," news release, April 30, 2009, https://obamawhitehouse.archives.gov/the-press -office/briefing-white-house-press-secretary-robert-gibbs-43009.

156 **"One thing the Obama administration...transportation industry in the United States":** *Hardball with Chris Matthews*, aired April 30, 2009, on MSNBC.

157 **"I have never...took you, Fritz":** "The Mondale Vice Presidency."

158 **"So there you have it...look terrific":** *The Daily Show with Jon Stewart*, "Snoutbreak 09," hosted by Jon Stewart, aired April 30, 2009, on Comedy Central, "Snoutbreak 09: What to Call the Swine Flu," video, Comedy Central, 3:44, www.cc.com/video-clips/zh325c/the-daily-show-with-jon-stewart-snoutbreak-09-what-to-call-swine-flu.

*Chapter Ten*

159 **"RACIAL BARRIER FALLS":** Adam Nagourney, "Obama: Racial Barrier Falls in Decisive Victory," *New York Times*, November 5, 2008, 1.

159 **"He now says":** *Larry King Live*, "Barack Obama's First Day in Office," hosted by Larry King, aired January 22, 2009, on CNN.

159 **"four little children":** Martin Luther King Jr., "I Have a Dream," speech, Washington, DC, August 28, 1963, Martin Luther King Jr. Research and Education Institute, Stanford University, https://kinginstitute.stanford.edu

/king-papers/documents/i-have-dream-address-delivered-march
-washington-jobs-and-freedom.

160 **"I understand there may"**: Barack Obama, address to the NAACP Centennial Convention, New York, New York, July 16, 2009, Office of the Press Secretary, White House, news release, https://obamawhitehouse.archives .gov/the-press-office/remarks-president-naacp-centennial-convention -07162009.

160 **"I said, 'Let's just push'"**: Krissah Thompson, "Scholar Says Arrest Will Lead Him to Explore Race in Criminal Justice," *Washington Post*, July 22, 2009.

161 **"Can you tell me...I'll wait"**: "Police Release 911, Dispatch Audio of Gates Arrest," sound recording, *Washington Post*, July 16, 2009, www.wash ingtonpost.com/wp-dyn/content/audio/2009/07/27/AU2009072701389 .html?sid=ST2009072703057.

162 **"No, I will not"**: Cambridge Review Committee, *Missed Opportunities, Shared Responsibilities: Final Report of the Cambridge Review Committee*, June 15, 2010, 56, https://www2.cambridgema.gov/CityOfCambridge_Content/documents /Cambridge%20Review_FINAL.pdf.

162 **"Instinctively, I knew...a gun"**: Thompson, "Scholar Says."

162 **"investigating a report...black man in America"**: Cambridge Review Committee, *Missed Opportunities*, 56.

162 **"I was thinking, this is ridiculous:** Thompson, "Scholar Says."

162 **"He...accused me...exhibited toward me"**: Cambridge Review Committee, *Missed Opportunities*, 56.

163 **"Who are you?"** Thompson, "Scholar Says."

163 **"very uncooperative...last of it"**: Cambridge Review Committee, *Missed Opportunities*, 56.

163 **"This is what happens"**: Ibid., 57.

163 **"Ya, I'll speak with"**: Ibid., 56.

163 **"This is what happens"**: Ibid., 57.

163 **"I warned Gates...under arrest"**: Ibid., 56.

164 **"exhibiting loud and tumultuous"**: Ibid., 55.

164 **"It took less than a day"**: Jesse Washington, "Scholar's Arrest Is a Bump on the Road to Equality," Associated Press, *Arizona Republic*, July 22, 2019, http://archive.azcentral.com/arizonarepublic/news/articles/2009/07/22 /20090722harvard-analysis0722.html.

164 **"I felt as if I were...deferred to sufficiently"**: Tracy Jan, "Racial Talk Swirls with Gates Arrest: Harvard Scholar Taken from Home," *Boston Globe*, July 21, 2009, A1.

165 **"I am appalled...rogue cops"**: Thompson, "Scholar Says."

165 **"I thought I was"**: Melody K. Hoffman, "Harvard Scholar's Arrest Sparks National Controversy," *Jet*, August 10, 2009, 11.

165 **"This incident should not be viewed"**: Cambridge Review Committee, *Missed Opportunities*, 54.

165 **"I think what went wrong":** Patrik Jonsson, "Gates Arrest: Racial Profiling or 'Tempest in a Teapot'?," *Christian Science Monitor,* July 21, 2009, sec. 2.

166 **"Recently Professor Henry…I'd get shot":** "President Obama's Primetime Press Conference on Health Reform," video, White House Archives, July 22, 2009, transcript, https://obamawhitehouse.archives.gov/video/President -Obamas-Primetime-Press-Conference-on-Health-Reform#transcript; "Obama: Police Acted 'Stupidly' in Scholar Arrest," YouTube video, posted by Associated Press on July 22, 2009, www.youtube.com/watch?v=LZYsW _PxWAM.

166 **"a very good joke":** *The Rachel Maddow Show,* aired July 22, 2009, on MSNBC, www.nbcnews.com/default.aspx?id=32104205&ns=msnbc-rachel _maddow_show&t=rachel-maddow-show-wednesday-july&print =1&displaymode=1098.

166 **"But so far…played in that":** "President Obama's Primetime Press Conference," July 22, 2009.

167 **"was personally outraged":** Peter Baker and Helene Cooper, "President Tries to Defuse Debate over Gates Arrest," *New York Times,* July 25, 2009, A1. This article provided significant detail on the incident.

167 **"But I think it's fair…progress that's been made":** "President Obama's Primetime Press Conference," July 22, 2009.

168 **"We're going to hear a lot":** *All Things Considered,* "Obama News Conference Examined," reported by Ron Elving, aired July 22, 2009, on NPR, www .npr.org/templates/story/story.php?storyId=106904093.

168 **"I think if he…happy to do that":** Peter Nicholas, "A Delicate Matter to Hash Out over a Beer," *Los Angeles Times,* July 28, 2009, A1.

168 **"I haven't heard":** *Anderson Cooper 360°,* "Harvard Professor," hosted by Anderson Cooper, aired July 22, 2009, on CNN, transcript, http://transcripts .cnn.com/TRANSCRIPTS/0907/22/acd.02.html.

168 **"There are not many certainties":** Melissa Trujillo, "Gates' Case Dropped, Debate over Blame Goes On," Associated Press, July 22, 2009.

169 **"I support the president":** "Cambridge Cops: Panel to Review Gates Case," CBSNews.com, July 23, 2009, www.cbsnews.com/news/cambridge -cops-panel-to-review-gates-case/.

169 **"deeply pained":** Beverly Ford and Rich Schapiro, "Sgt. James Crowley, Cop Who Arrested Harvard Professor Henry Louis Gates Jr., Denies He's Racist," *New York Daily News,* July 24, 2009, www.nydailynews.com/news/world/sgt -james-crowley-arrested-harvard-professor-henry-louis-gates-jr-denies -racist-article-1.427282.

169 **"The president's alienated":** "Obama Remark on Black Scholar's Arrest Angers Cops," Associated Press, July 23, 2009, www.recordnet.com/article /20090723/A_NEWS/907239988.

169 **"He rarely screws up":** Thomas M. Defrank, "President Obama Calls Sgt. James Crowley, Policeman Who Arrested Harvard Prof. Henry Louis Gates

Jr.," *New York Daily News*, July 24, 2009, www.nydailynews.com/news /politics/president-obama-calls-sgt-james-crowley-policeman-arrested -harvard-prof-henry-louis-gates-jr-article-1.426179.

169 **"Let me be clear":** Garance Franke-Ruta, "Obama Stands by His Criticism," *Washington Post*, July 23, 2009, voices.washingtonpost.com/44/2009/07/23 /gibbs_obama_has_no_regrets_ove.html?wprss=44.

170 **"The facts of this case":** Ibid.

170 **"I'm going to call Sergeant Crowley":** Ibid.

170 **"He said, 'Jesus Christ'":** Michael Daly, "Hello, Sgt. Crowley, It's the President Calling," *New York Daily News*, July 26, 2009, www.nydailynews.com /news/sgt-crowley-president-calling-article-1.426138.

170 **"No way!...Not a person breathed":** Ibid.

171 **"Hey, they're on...Obama's voice":** Marie Szaniszlo, "Prez's Mea Culpa Goes Over Smooth at Irish Pub," *Boston Herald*, July 26, 2009, www.boston herald.com/2009/07/26/prezs-mea-culpa-goes-over-smooth-at-irish-pub/.

171 **the crowd burst into cheers:** Daly, "Hello, Sgt. Crowley."

172 **"If you got to do...I told him that":** Office of the Press Secretary, White House, "Statement by the President," news release, July 24, 2009, https:// obamawhitehouse.archives.gov/realitycheck/the-press-office/statement -president-james-s-brady-briefing-room; "Clip: President Obama on Arrest of Henry Louis Gates," video, July 24, 2009, C-SPAN, www.c-span.org /video/?c4493233/clip-president-obama-arrest-henry-louis-gates.

172 **"The president was on TV":** Szaniszlo, "Prez's Mea Culpa."

172 **"Because this has been...press off my lawn":** Office of the Press Secretary, "Statement by the President," July 24, 2009.

173 **"Well," Axelrod said:** *Face the Nation*, hosted by Bob Schieffer, aired July 26, 2009, CBS, transcript, www.cbsnews.com/htdocs/pdf/FTN_072609.pdf.

173 **"He was very aggressive...rawest fears":** Obama, *Dreams from My Father*, 88–89.

174 **"trying to reconcile...good and bad whites":** Ibid., 85.

174 **"There are some big problems...needs to take place":** *Face the Nation*, July 26, 2009.

175 **"America's racial disparities":** Peniel E. Joseph, "Our National Postracial Hangover," *Chronicle of Higher Education*, July 27, 2009, www.chronicle.com /article/Our-National-Postracial/47462.

175 **"What beer's on tap":** Yael T. Abouhalkah, "What Beer's on Tap for Obama, Gates and Crowley?," *Kansas City Star*, July 25, 2009.

175 **"Since when did":** Susan Bourque, "Don't Promote Booze," letter to the editor, *Press Enterprise* (Riverside, CA), August 24, 2009.

175 **"Yes, Three Cans":** Dana Milbank, "It Wasn't One for the Guinness Book," *Washington Post*, July 31, 2009, A2.

175 **"Brew-ha-ha":** Clarence Page, "Obama's Brew-ha-ha," *Chicago Tribune*, August 2, 2009.

# Notes

175 **"Ale to the Chief":** *Anderson Cooper 360°*, "Beer at the White House," hosted by Anderson Cooper, aired July 30, 2009, on CNN, transcript, http://tran scripts.cnn.com/TRANSCRIPTS/0907/30/acd.01.html.

175 **"deep conversation or...personal situation":** *CNN Newsroom*, "Obama to Meet with Professor, Policeman," hosted by Kyra Phillips and Ed Henry, aired July 30, 2009, on CNN, transcript, http://transcripts.cnn.com/TRANSCRIPTS /0907/30/cnr.05.html.

176 **"If you said to me":** Peter Nicholas and Paul Richter, "Despite Fumbles, Biden's a Player," *Los Angeles Times*, August 18, 2009, A1.

176 **"was a fraught...relationship":** Kate Bedingfield, interview by the author, February 12, 2019.

177 **"Joe Biden," he wrote:** Alan Abelson, "The Great Beer Bash," *Barron's*, August 3, 2009, www.barrons.com/articles/SB124908131652898105?tesla=y.

177 **"news outlets were tipsy...and the puns":** Milbank, "It Wasn't One."

178 **"frank...what we discussed":** *Anderson Cooper 360°*, "Hot Topic, Cold Beer," hosted by Anderson Cooper, aired July 30, 2009, on CNN, transcript, http://transcripts.cnn.com/TRANSCRIPTS/0907/30/acd.02.html.

178 **"The vice president was":** "Obama Beer Summit James Crowley Press Conference," YouTube video, posted by Zennie62 Oakland News Now Today Commentary Vlog on July 31, 2009, www.youtube.com/watch?v=XwywZNPf8S8.

178 **"The national conversation":** Henry Louis Gates Jr., "'An Accident of Time and Place,'" The Root, July 30, 2009, www.theroot.com/an-accident -of-time-and-place-1790869916.

178 **"for a friendly, thoughtful conversation":** Barack Obama, "Statement on a Discussion with Professor Henry Louis Gates, Jr., and Sergeant James Crowley," July 30, 2009, in *Public Papers of the Presidents of the United States: Barack Obama 2009*, vol. 2 (Washington, DC: Government Printing Office, 2013), 1205, www.govinfo.gov/content/pkg/PPP-2009-book2/xml/PPP-2009 -book2.xml.

178 **survey by the Pew Research Center:** "Obama's Ratings Slide Across the Board," Pew Research Center, July 30, 2009, www.people-press.org/2009 /07/30/obamas-ratings-slide-across-the-board/.

179 **"Though this nation has proudly...understandable":** Eric Holder, speech on African American History Month, Washington, DC, February 18, 2009, Office of Public Affairs, Department of Justice, news release, February 18, 2009, www.justice.gov/opa/speech/attorney-general-eric-holder-department -justice-african-american-history-month-program.

179 **"Quite simply...hubris":** "The Chilling and Cowardly Words of Eric Holder," editorial, *Washington Examiner*, February 18, 2009, www.washing tonexaminer.com/the-chilling-and-cowardly-words-of-eric-holder.

179 **"inexcusable":** Michelle Levi, "Conservatives Hammer Holder for 'Cowards' Comment," CBSNews.com, February 19, 2009, www.cbsnews.com/ news/conservatives-hammer-holder-for-cowards-comment/.

179 **"hackneyed and reprehensible":** Ibid.

179 **"I think it's fair to say…flare-up or conflict":** Helene Cooper, "Attorney General Chided for Language on Race," *New York Times*, March 8, 2009, A26.

180 **"Race is an…tinged by race":** Ta-Nehisi Coates, "Fear of a Black President," *The Atlantic*, September 2012, www.theatlantic.com/magazine/archive/2012/09/fear-of-a-black-president/309064/.

181 **"The irony of Barack Obama":** Ibid.

182 **"More important than…white was subordinate":** Michael Eric Dyson, interview by the author, June 2, 2018.

## Chapter Eleven

185 **one hundred thousand NATO:** Tom VanDen Brook, "US Needs to Revise Afghan Strategy, General Says," Gannett News Service, August 31, 2009.

186 **"The only senior official":** Ben Rhodes, *The World as It Is: A Memoir of the Obama White House* (New York: Random House, 2018), 65.

186 **"serious…education for females":** General Stanley McChrystal, "Special Address," International Institute of Strategic Studies, London, October 1, 2009, Institute of World Politics, www.iwp.edu/docLib/20131125_Gen-McCrystalAddress1012009.pdf, 4; "General McChrystal Speech Part 2," YouTube video, posted by SewYouKnow on October 6, 2009, www.youtube.com/watch?v=tXx_8Jp_TWs.

186 **"We need to reverse":** McChrystal, "Special Address," 5; "General McChrystal Speech Part 2."

187 **"we use a plan":** McChrystal, "Special Address," 2; "General McChrystal Speech," YouTube video, posted by SewYouKnow on October 6, 2009, www.youtube.com/watch?v=F1KGnacqfMc.

187 **"we need patience":** McChrystal, "Special Address," 4; "General McChrystal Speech Part 2."

187 **"an appealing earnestness…he looks gaunt":** Evan Thomas, "General McChrystal's Plan for Afghanistan," *Newsweek*, September 25, 2009, www.newsweek.com/general-mcchrystals-plan-afghanistan-79551.

187 **"McChrystal had a mythical":** Rhodes, *The World as It Is*, 66.

187 **"The short, glib answer":** General Stanley McChrystal, question-and-answer session, International Institute of Strategic Studies, London, October 1, 2009, "Gen. Stanley McChrystal Comments That Have Angered the White House," YouTube video, posted by FreedomsLighthouse on October 6, 2009, www.youtube.com/watch?v=VEhHxzuTssQ.

188 **"The top American commander":** John F. Burns, "Top U.S. Commander in Afghanistan Rejects Scaling Down Military Objectives," *New York Times*, October 2, 2009, A12.

188 **"If the president sided":** Jonathan Alter, *The Promise: President Obama, Year One* (New York: Simon & Schuster, 2010), 378.

188 **"Although Vice President Biden":** General Stanley McChrystal, *My Share of the Task: A Memoir* (New York: Portfolio, 2013), 349.

188 **"Stan's speech was innocuous":** Robert M. Gates, *Duty: Memoirs of a Secretary at War* (New York: Vintage, 2015), 368.

188 **President Obama had authorized:** Bob Woodward, "Key in Afghanistan, Economy, Not Military," *Washington Post*, July 1, 2009, A1.

189 **"Just let me take":** Bob Woodward, *Obama's Wars* (New York: Simon & Schuster, 2010), 101.

189 **"we're just prolonging":** Ibid., 102.

189 **announcing the troop decision in March:** Office of the Press Secretary, White House, "Remarks by the President on a New Strategy for Afghanistan and Pakistan," news release, March 27, 2009, https://obamawhitehouse .archives.gov/the-press-office/remarks-president-a-new-strategy -afghanistan-and-pakistan.

190 **"Officials involved in the deliberations":** Mark Leibovich, "Speaking Freely, Sometimes, Biden Finds Influential Role," *New York Times*, March 29, 2009, A1.

190 **forty-seven US troops:** Department of Defense, *Report on Progress Toward Security and Stability in Afghanistan*, October 2009, https://dod.defense.gov /Portals/1/Documents/pubs/October_2009.pdf.

190 **"Can I just clarify...strategic sense":** Holly Bailey et al., "An Inconvenient Truth Teller," *Newsweek*, October 19, 2009.

191 **"What I found...positive manner":** Julie Smith, interview by the author, April 27, 2018.

192 **"we run the risk...lead to failure":** Woodward, *Obama's Wars*, 176.

192 **"The president has...open-ended engagements":** Axelrod, *Believer*, 393.

192 **"The word-on-the-streets":** Rosa Brooks, interview with the author, April 18, 2009.

192 **"After I left office":** Gates, *Duty*, 368.

192 **"The president has been taken hostage":** Mark Ambinder, "Boxed into a Corner on Afghanistan, the President Resists," *The Atlantic*, September 21, 2009, www.theatlantic.com/politics/archive/2009/09/boxed-into-a-corner-on -afghanistan-the-president-resists/26959/.

193 **"What was supposed to have been":** Axelrod, *Believer*, 394.

193 **"Neither is justifiable...was furious":** Ibid.

193 **"taken aback...rejected his advice":** Thomas, "General McChrystal's Plan."

194 **"The goals need to be":** Axelrod, *Believer*, 394.

194 **"The president would...military leadership":** Witcover, *Joe Biden*, 459.

194 **"At sixty-six":** Rhodes, *The World as It Is*, 65.

195 **"wound up being the difference":** Nicholas and Richter, "Despite Fumbles."

195 **"And yes Mr. Vice President":** Josh Earnest (@PressSec44), "And yes Mr. Vice President, you're right...," Twitter, March 23, 2010, 9:49 a.m., https:// twitter.com/PressSec44/status/10933796367.

195 **"We all have to have our words":** Nicholas and Richter, "Despite Fumbles."

195 **"Just How Wrong...his mouth again":** Thomas Ricks, "Just How Wrong Can Joe Biden Be?," *Best Defense* (blog), *Foreign Policy*, December 28, 2009, https://foreignpolicy.com/2009/12/28/just-how-wrong-can-joe-biden-be/.

196 **"When was the last time"**: Thomas E. Ricks, "Dave Does Dull: Storm Warnings on the Petraeus-ometer," *Best Defense* (blog), *Foreign Policy*, September 24, 2009, https://foreignpolicy.com/2009/09/24/dave-does-dull-storm-warnings-on-the-petraeus-ometer/.

196 **"From nuclear arms control"**: Peter Baker, "Biden No Longer a Lone Voice on Afghanistan," *New York Times*, October 14, 2009, A1.

196 **"We got to stop"**: Woodward, *Obama's Wars*, 194.

196 **"was whisked to Denmark"**: Michael D. Shear, "McChrystal Flown to Denmark to Discuss War with Obama," *Washington Post*, October 3, 2009, A4.

197 **"In both our initial greeting"**: McChrystal, *My Share*, 350.

197 **"neither [Obama nor McChrystal]...carry it out"**: Woodward, *Obama's Wars*, 194.

197 **"productive...lead the war"**: Shear, "McChrystal Flown."

197 **"I like him"**: Woodward, *Obama's Wars*, 194.

197 **"refused to say"**: Shear, "McChrystal Flown."

197 **"One of the things"**: Frank James, "Obama Disappointed by Chicago's Failed Olympics Bid; Congratulates Brazil," *The Two-Way* (blog), NPR, October 2, 2009, www.npr.org/sections/thetwo-way/2009/10/obama_disappointed_for_chicago.html.

198 **"There's going to be a...counterinsurgency strategy"**: Woodward, *Obama's Wars*, 325.

198 **"We're going to begin"**: Ibid.

198 **"Our overarching goal"**: Office of the Press Secretary, White House, "Remarks by the President," news release, December 1, 2009, https://obamawhitehouse.archives.gov/the-press-office/remarks-president-address-nation-way-forward-afghanistan-and-pakistan.

198 **"Sir, we have a problem...*have been a problem*"**: McChrystal, *My Share*, 387.

199 **"troublemaker"**: Mark Leibovich, *This Town* (New York: Blue Rider, 2013), 129.

199 **"handpicked collection of...Bite Me?'"**: Michael Hastings, "The Runaway General," *Rolling Stone*, July 8, 2010, 92–93.

201 **"staff...dumb PR move"**: Leibovich, *This Town*, 129–130.

202 **"For a number of minutes"**: McChrystal, *My Share*, 387.

202 **"Regardless of how I judged"**: Ibid.

202 **"about McChrystal that...mocking the vice president"**: Gates, *Duty*, 487.

202 **"For once I couldn't...'No excuses, sir'"**: Ibid.

203 **"disgusted president didn't"**: Alter, *The Promise*, 444.

203 **"The *Rolling Stone* interview...chain of command"**: Ibid.

203 **"the White House...a classic understatement"**: Ibid.

204 **"Anticipation built over"**: Leibovich, *This Town*, 130.

204 **In a statement, the defense secretary**: US Department of Defense, "Gates Issues Statement on McChrystal Profile," news release, June 22, 2010, http://archive.defense.gov/news/newsarticle.aspx?id=59723.

204 **"We'll have more to say...if you saw it"**: Office of the Press Secretary, White House, "Press Briefing," news release, June 22, 2010, https://

obamawhitehouse.archives.gov/realitycheck/the-press-office/press-briefing
-press-secretary-robert-gibbs-6222010.

205 **"rather defensively...national security staff]":** Gates, *Duty*, 487, 491.

205 **"Biden snarling":** Packer, *Our Man*, 519.

205 **"I'm leaning...Biden's credibility":** Gates, *Duty*, 487–488.

206 **"He didn't tell me...good guy,' he said":** Rhodes, *The World as It Is*, 84.

206 **"McChrystal...had handed":** Gates, *Duty*, 491.

207 **"the same personalities":** Rhodes, *The World as It Is*, 85.

207 **"brothers in arms...underpinned the relationship":** Bedingfield, interview.

208 **"General McChrystal was relieved":** "Leno: 'Rethinking Its Boycott,'" *Laugh Lines* (blog), *New York Times*, June 24, 2010, https://laughlines.blogs .nytimes.com/2010/06/24/leno-rethinking-its-boycott/.

*Chapter Twelve*

210 **"If people ask you...first and foremost":** Barack Obama, speech at campaign rally, Columbus, Ohio, May 5, 2012, Office of the Press Secretary, White House, news release, May 5, 2012, https://obamawhitehouse.archives.gov/the -press-office/2012/05/05/remarks-president-and-first-lady-campaign-event.

210 **Ohio race looked tight:** Federal Election Commission, *Federal Elections 2008: Election Results for the U.S. President, the U.S. Senate and the U.S. House of Representatives*, July 2009, https://transition.fec.gov/pubrec/fe2008/federalelections 2008.pdf, 36.

210 **"Today our auto industry":** Obama, speech at campaign rally, Columbus, Ohio.

210 **"There were a lot":** Jim Provance, "Obama Makes Pitch for Another 4 Years," *The Blade* (Toledo, OH), May 6, 2012.

211 **"This morning...for the ticket":** Joe Biden, interview by David Gregory, *Meet the Press*, NBC, May 6, 2012, transcript, www.nbcnews.com/id/47311900 /ns/meet_the_press-transcripts/t/may-joe-biden-kelly-ayotte-diane-swonk -tom-brokaw-chuck-todd/#.XGV3VpNKjGI, video, www.nbcnews.com/meet -the-press/video/flashback-bidens-2012-endorsement-of-same-sex -marriage-471856195543.

211 **presidents had switched out sitting vice presidents:** Rob Manker, "The Veeplacements," *Chicago Tribune*, October 23, 2011.

212 **"Swapping Clinton for Biden":** Axelrod, *Believer*, 449.

212 **"A lot of people think...out of the question":** Bob Woodward, interview by John King, *John King, USA*, CNN, October 5, 2010.

212 **"No one in the White House":** Ed Henry, "White House Denies Obama-Clinton Ticket in the Works," CNN.com, October 6, 2010, www.cnn .com/2010/POLITICS/10/06/obama.clinton/index.html.

212 **"We sincerely suggest...much of a future":** William Kristol, "Why Not the Best?," *Weekly Standard*, May 28, 2012.

213 **"No question about...President Obama":** Biden, *Meet the Press*, May 6, 2012.

# Notes

214 **"Joey, you're so handsome":** Biden, *Promises to Keep*, 5.

215 **"I think—look...beyond that":** Biden, *Meet the Press*, May 6, 2012.

216 **"We were completely shocked":** Abrams, *Obama: An Oral History*, 259.

216 **"Thing was":** Cramer, *What It Takes*, 252.

217 **"Joe Biden had balls":** Ibid., 251.

217 **"Let me ask you...what this is about":** Biden, *Meet the Press*, May 6, 2012.

217 **"WHAT THE FUCK...":** Mark Halperin and John Heilemann, *Double Down: Game Change 2012* (New York: Penguin, 2014), 296.

218 **Obama's journey on the issue:** Peter Wallstein and Scott Wilson, "Obama's Evolution on Gay Marriage," *Washington Post*, May 11, 2012; Jim Kuhnhenn and Lisa Lerer, "For Obama and Clinton, Twisty Paths to 'Yes' on Gay Marriage," Associated Press, June 27, 2015.

218 **"He has liberal instincts":** Randall Kennedy, *The Persistence of the Color Line: Racial Politics and the Obama Presidency* (New York: Vintage, 2012), 274.

218 **"It seems rather obvious":** Ibid., 28.

218 **"Don't Ask, Don't Tell" policy:** Charlie Savage and Sheryl Gay Stolberg, "In Shift, U.S. Says Marriage Act Blocks Gay Rights," *New York Times*, February 23, 2011.

219 **Mehlman, who had come out as gay:** Edward-Isaac Dovere, "Book: W.H. Scrambled After Biden Gay Marriage Comments," *Politico*, April 16, 2014, www.politico.com/story/2014/04/joe-biden-gay-marriage-white-house -response-105744, quoting Jo Becker, *Forcing the Spring: Inside the Fight for Marriage Equality* (New York: Penguin, 2014).

220 **"I was just maniacal":** Abrams, *Obama: An Oral History*, 260.

220 **"I wanted it to be":** Ibid., 259.

220 **"I think you may have":** Becker, *Forcing the Spring*, 288.

220 **"I'm grateful that":** Julie Pace, "Biden OK with Equal Rights for Married Gay Couples," Associated Press, May 6, 2012.

221 **"entirely consistent":** Mike Lillis, "Pressure Grows from Democrats for Obama to Back Same-Sex Marriage," *The Hill*, May 9, 2012, https://thehill .com/homenews/house/226255-pressure-grows-for-obama-to-back-same -sex-marriage.

221 **"I don't understand":** Halperin and Heilemann, *Double Down*, 299.

221 **"I didn't go out volunteering":** Dovere, "Book: W.H. Scrambled."

222 **"We're going to start...we made news":** *Morning Joe*, "Teacher Appreciation Week," featuring Joe Scarborough, Mark Halperin, and Mika Brzezinski, aired May 7, 2012, on MSNBC.

222 **"Oh, that interview":** Duncan, interview.

223 **"I did it without thinking...had my back on this":** Ibid.

224 **"I have no announcements...same-sex couples":** Office of the Press Secretary, White House, "Press Briefing by Press Secretary Jay Carney, 5/7/12," news release, May 7, 2012, https://obamawhitehouse.archives.gov/the-press -office/2012/05/07/press-briefing-press-secretary-jay-carney-5712.

224 **"I've got to put Jay":** Halperin and Heilemann, *Double Down*, 299.

225 **"No guidelines"**: *Good Morning America*, "President in Favor of Gay Marriage," hosted by Robin Roberts and George Stephanopoulos, aired May 10, 2012, on ABC.

225 **"The act of contrition"**: Halperin and Heilemann, *Double Down*, 299.

225 **"in this thing together"**: Ibid., 300.

225 **"'a Biden gaffe'...cared about deeply"**: Biden, *Promise Me*, 67–68.

226 **"Mr. President, are you"**: Barack Obama, interview by Robin Roberts, ABC News, May 9, 2012, https://abcnews.go.com/Politics/transcript-robin-roberts-abc-news-interview-president-obama/story?id=16316043.

226 **"Big breaking news"**: ABC News Special Report, hosted by Diane Sawyer and George Stephanopoulos, May 9, 2012, "President Obama—Gay Marriage: Gay Couples 'Should Be Able to Get Married,'" YouTube video, posted by ABC News on May 9, 2012, www.youtube.com/watch?v=kQGMTPab9GQ.

226 **"I have to tell you"**: Obama, interview by Robin Roberts.

227 **"Truly historic and potentially watershed"**: *The Situation Room*, "President Obama Publicly Supports Same-Sex Marriage," hosted by Wolf Blitzer, aired May 9, 2012, on CNN, transcript, http://transcripts.cnn.com/TRANSCRIPTS/1205/09/sitroom.01.html.

227 **"Did he jump the gun...generosity of spirit"**: *Good Morning America*, "President in Favor."

228 **"It has always taken strong"**: "President Obama's Moment," editorial, *New York Times*, May 10, 2012, A28.

228 **"For the first time, the millions"**: "A Laudable Stance on Gay Marriage," editorial, *Kansas City Star*, May 9, 2012.

228 **Gallup found:** Frank Newport, "Half of Americans Support Legal Gay Marriage," Gallup, May 8, 2012, https://news.gallup.com/poll/154529/half-americans-support-legal-gay-marriage.aspx.

228 **"So you're not...ends well"**: *Good Morning America*, "President in Favor."

## Chapter Thirteen

230 **"Good evening, I'm Beau Biden"**: "Introduction of Joe Biden," YouTube video, posted by Democratic National Convention on August 27, 2008, www.youtube.com/watch?v=CEtbBSwR7SE.

230 **"The types of words"**: Nora Caplan-Bricker, "The Biden Dynasty," *National Journal*, June 18, 2014.

230 **"there's less theater"**: Maureen Milford and Cris Barrish, "In Times of Crisis, Bidens Rally for Beau," *News Journal* (Wilmington, DE), August 26, 2013.

230 **his father's swearing-in at the hospital:** Witcover, *Joe Biden*, 98.

231 **"The first thing I said"**: Edward-Isaac Dovere, "In Biden's Tragedy, Americans See Their Own," *Politico*, June 1, 2015, www.politico.com/story/2015/06/joe-bidens-tragedy-is-a-death-in-the-american-family-118517.

231 **"I was sitting"**: Axelrod, interview.

231 **"People say this guy"**: Halperin and Heilemann, *Double Down*, 73.

# Notes

232 **"He simply wasn't attending":** Axelrod, interview.

233 **"I was glad no one":** Biden, *Promise Me*, 30.

233 **"Doc, promise you're…your dad, Beau":** Ibid., 27.

233 **"Why not Beau?":** Ibid., 31.

234 **"successful procedure":** Office of the Vice President, White House, "Statement from the Vice President and Dr. Jill Biden," news release, August 21, 2013, https://obamawhitehouse.archives.gov/the-press-office/2013/08/21/statement-vice-president-and-dr-jill-biden.

234 **"On our way home":** Beau Biden Foundation (@BeauBidenFdn), "On our way home! Can't wait to get back. Thank you, Houston. -bb," Twitter, August 22, 2013, 8:53 a.m., https://twitter.com/BeauBidenFdn/status/370574526167273472.

234 **"I just want you all":** Joe Biden, remarks at Lackawanna College, Scranton, Pennsylvania, August 23, 2013, Doug Denison, "'My Son Beau Is Fine,'" *News Journal* (Wilmington, DE), August 24, 2013.

234 **"Barack was the first person":** Biden, *Promise Me*, 75.

235 **"I wanted to reassure him":** Ibid., 69.

235 **"I wanted to do anything I could":** Steve Ricchetti, interview by the author, May 14, 2018.

235 **"I love Scranton…five years ago":** Barack Obama, remarks at Lackawanna College, Scranton, Pennsylvania, August 23, 2013, Office of the Press Secretary, White House, news release, August 23, 2013, https://obamawhitehouse.archives.gov/the-press-office/2013/08/23/remarks-president-and-vice-president-college-affordability.

236 **"The docs have given me":** Jonathan Starkey, "Biden Remains Mum on Health," *News Journal* (Wilmington, DE), November 21, 2013.

236 **"What are you going…pay me back whenever":** Biden, *Promise Me*, 76.

237 **"It's what I say about Joe…hurt Obama was":** Kaufman, interview.

237 **"It wasn't about the money":** Duncan, interview.

237 **"They're polar opposites":** Smith, interview.

238 **"As the day goes on":** Ibid.

238 **"The news could not have been":** Biden, *Promise Me*, 123.

239 **"I felt an obligation":** Ibid., 126.

239 **"I was tired and worried":** Ibid., 135.

240 **"He is not a demonstrative…hear it from Barack":** Ibid., 159.

241 **"We need to see each other":** Donald James, "60th Annual Fight for Freedom Fund Dinner Keynoted by Vice President Joe Biden," *Michigan Chronicle*, May 6, 2015, A2.

242 **"seemed to figure out each other":** Office of the Press Secretary, White House, "Remarks by the President Honoring the NASCAR Sprint Cup Champion Kevin Harvick," news release, April 21, 2015, https://obamawhitehouse.archives.gov/the-press-office/2015/04/21/remarks-president-honoring-nascar-sprint-cup-champion-kevin-harvick; "President Obama Honors NASCAR's Kevin Harvick," video, April 21, 2015,

C-SPAN,www.c-span.org/video/?325509-2/president-obama-honors-nascars
-kevin-harvick.

242 **"You know what, let me…they're like magic":** Office of the Press Secretary, White House, "Remarks by the President at White House Correspondents'
Association Dinner," news release, April 25, 2015, https://obamawhitehouse
.archives.gov/the-press-office/2015/04/25/remarks-president-white-house
-correspondents-association-dinner; "President Obama Complete Remarks
at 2015 White House Correspondents' Dinner (C-SPAN)," YouTube video,
posted by C-SPAN on April 25, 2015, www.youtube.com/watch?v=NM6d0
6ALBVA.

243 **"Smile, I'd say to myself":** Biden, *Promise Me*, 174.

243 **"May 30. 7:51 p.m.":** Ibid., 189.

244 **"Make fun of Joe Biden":** Joe Battenfield, "Tragedy Puts Petty Politics in Perspective," *Boston Herald*, May 31, 2015, www.bostonherald.com
/2015/05/31/battenfeld-tragedy-puts-petty-politics-in-perspective/.

244 **"He's Uncle Joe":** Dovere, "In Biden's Tragedy."

244 **"I never said this publicly":** Duncan, interview.

244 **"The Bidens have more family":** Office of the Press Secretary, White House,
"Statement by the President on the Passing of Beau Biden," news release, May
30, 2015, https://obamawhitehouse.archives.gov/the-press-office/2015/05/30
/statement-president-passing-beau-biden.

245 **"Five years in the Biden family…decamped to Delaware":** Allen,
interview.

245 **"There will come a day":** Joe Biden, speech at the TAPS National Military Sur-
vivor Seminar and Good Grief Camp, Arlington, Virginia, May 25, 2012, "Video
and Transcripts: How Joe Biden Has Coped with Loss," *Washington Wire* (blog),
*Wall Street Journal*, June 1, 2015, https://blogs.wsj.com/washwire/2015/06/01/
video-and-transcripts-how-joe-biden-has-coped-with-loss/.

246 **"His words did perfect justice":** Allen, interview.

246 **"President Obama loves Joe Biden":** *CNN Newsroom*, "President Obama
to Give Eulogy for Beau Biden," featuring Michael Smerconish, Victor Black-
well, and Christi Paul, aired June 6, 2015, on CNN, transcript, www.cnn
.com/TRANSCRIPTS/1506/06/cnr.01.html.

247 **"As I look for the perfect words":** *CNN Newsroom*, "Funeral for Beau Biden,"
aired June 6, 2015, on CNN, transcript, www.cnn.com/TRANSCRIPTS
/1506/06/cnr.03.html; "Funeral for Beau Biden," YouTube video, posted
by *Washington Post* on June 6, 2015, www.youtube.com/watch?v=UaRK
ekOwl5o.

247 **"We are here…admire you more":** *CNN Newsroom*, "Funeral of Beau Biden."

250 **"No assassin in his right mind":** Francis X. Clines, "Spiro T. Agnew,
Point Man for Nixon Who Resigned Vice Presidency, Dies at 77," *New York Times*,
September 19, 1996, www.nytimes.com/1996/09/19/us/spiro-t-agnew-point
-man-for-nixon-who-resigned-vice-presidency-dies-at-77.html.

250 **"It was a very, very good relationship":** Axelrod, interview.

250 **"the revelation…sublime of human emotions"**: *Hardball with Chris Matthews*, aired June 8, 2015, on MSNBC, www.msnbc.com/transcripts /hardball/2015-06-08.

251 **"Long after the last partisan battle…old-fashioned love"**: George E. Condon Jr., "This Is How America Will Remember Barack Obama," *nationaljournal.com*, June 6, 2015, www.theatlantic.com/politics/archive/2015/06 /this-is-how-america-will-remember-barack-obama/442641/.

252 **"Remember, Mr. President"**: Biden, *Promise Me*, 73.

252 **"That bled into the office…angry at each other"**: Smith, interview.

252 **"This was not a president"**: Duncan, interview.

*Chapter Fourteen*

254 **"So why is there a podium?"**: Allen, interview.

254 **"To have the impact"**: Ibid.

254 **"The loop was incredibly small"**: Bedingfield, interview.

254 **"This just wasn't done"**: Allen, interview.

255 **"Nobody's told me anything"**: Ibid.

255 **"It felt like the end"**: Bedingfield, interview.

256 **"Just to make sure"**: Allen, interview.

256 **"You're going to want to be live"**: Ibid.

257 **"So here we go…a way that he rarely is"**: Bedingfield, interview.

257 **"I was petrified"**: Ricchetti, interview.

257 **"May none but honest and wise"**: "State Dining Room," White House Historical Association, www.whitehousehistory.org/white-house-tour/state -dining-room.

258 **"I think this is the most extraordinary"**: John F. Kennedy, "Remarks at a Dinner Honoring Nobel Prize Winners of the Western Hemisphere," April 29, 1962, *Public Papers of the Presidents of the United States: John F. Kennedy, 1962* (Washington, DC: Office of the Federal Register, National Archives and Records Administration), 161.

258 **"I don't want to embarrass…"**: All quotations from the Medal of Freedom ceremony from Office of the Press Secretary, White House, "Remarks by the President and the Vice President in Presentation of the Medal of Freedom to Vice President Joe Biden," news release, January 12, 2017, https:// obamawhitehouse.archives.gov/the-press-office/2017/01/12/remarks -president-and-vice-president-presentation-medal-freedom-vice; see also "President Obama Awards the Presidential Medal of Freedom to Vice President Biden," video, January 12, 2017, White House Archives, https://obamawhite house.archives.gov/photos-and-video/video/2017/01/12/president-obama -awards-presidential-medal-freedom-vice-president-0?tid=93.

258 **"welcoming and warm"**: Bedingfield, interview.

261 **"Think where man's glory"**: William Butler Yeats, "The Municipal Gallery Revisited," 1937, in *Selected Poems and Two Plays of William Butler Yeats*, ed. M. L. Rosenthal (New York: Collier, 1977), 175.

264 **"I was tearing up…somebody you care about"**: Kaufman, interview.

265 **"I remember everybody"**: Ricchetti, interview.

268 **"You carried your own burden"**: Seamus Heaney, "From the Republic of Conscience," 1985, in *The Haw Lantern* (New York: Farrar, Straus and Giroux, 1987), 12.

270 **"I don't care"**: Jimmy Kimmel (@jimmykimmel), "I don't care which side you're on, the tribute @POTUS just paid @JoeBiden was one of the most touching I've ever seen. Watch it," Twitter, January 12, 2017, 1:07 p.m., https://twitter.com/jimmykimmel/status/819651945203834880.

270 **"I want a man who looks at me"**: Angel Gray, comment on "A Look at Barack Obama's Close Relationship with Joe Biden," YouTube video, posted by CBS News on January 13, 2017, www.youtube.com/watch?v=h-zTcphloNM.

*Epilogue*

273 **"He had been subtly weighing in…to my chances"**: Biden, *Promise Me*, 77.

273 **"The president was convinced…cast in stone"**: Ibid., 78.

274 **Barack Obama was my friend"**: Ibid., 79.

274 **"The president was urging"**: Ibid, 88.

274 **"I found myself saying"**: Ibid., 207.

274 **"the president was not encouraging"**: Ibid., 233.

275 **"I don't think you should"**: Ibid., 246.

275 **"lending me the"**: "Vice President Biden Rose Garden Statement," video, October 21, 2015, C-SPAN, www.c-span.org/video/?328803-2/vice-president -biden-passes-presidential-bid; "Full Text: Biden's Announcement that He Won't Run for President," *Washington Post*, October 21, 2015, www.washington post.com/news/post-politics/wp/2015/10/21/full-text-bidens -announcement-that-he-wont-run-for-president/?utm_term=.df902d 53d9bf.

275 **"to be upbeat"**: Biden, *Promise Me*, 247.

275 **"It may very well be"**: "Vice President Biden Rose Garden Statement."

275 **"Joe Biden looked a little less"**: Biden, *Promise Me*, 247.

276 **"You've got to run"**: Ibid., 22.

276 **"tried to make his father"**: Maureen Dowd, "What Would Beau Do?," *New York Times*, August 2, 2015, SR1; Biden, *Promise Me*, 22.

276 **"Biden had known for years…assuage the dis"**: Maureen Dowd, "Uncle Joe's Family Web," *New York Times*, February 24, 2019, SR11.

277 **"upset—not specifically"**: Chris Smith, "Democrats Don't Like to Be Told Who to Vote For," *Vanity Fair*, December 28, 2018, www.vanityfair.com /news/2018/12/obama-has-flirted-with-beto-and-biden-is-not-happy.

277 **"new blood"**: Ashley Nagaoka, "Former President Obama Speaks at UH Manoa for Launch of Foundation's Asia-Pacific Leadership Program," Hawaii News Now, January 4, 2019, www.hawaiinewsnow.com/2019/01/04

/obama-foundation-launches-asia-pacific-leadership-program-with-series
-workshops-hawaii/.

277 **"a blow to Joe Biden...that hurts Joe":** Amie Parnes, "Obama 'New Blood'
Remark Has Different Meaning for Biden," *The Hill*, January 13, 2019, http://
thehill.com/homenews/administration/424987-obama-new-blood-remark
-has-different-meaning-for-biden.

278 **"President Obama has long":** Jennifer Epstein, "Obama Holds Off on
Endorsing Biden, His Vice President," Bloomberg, April 25, 2019, www
.bloomberg.com/news/articles/2019-04-25/obama-holds-off-on-endorsing
-biden-his-vice-president.

278 **"Whoever wins the nomination":** Michael Scherer and John Wagner,
"Former Vice President Joe Biden Jumps into the White House Race," *Washington Post*, April 25, 2019.

278 **"The expectation that he":** Marc Caputo and Natasha Korecki, "Joe Biden Is
Running as Obama's Heir. The Problem: He's Not Obama," *Politico*, April 25, 2019,
www.politico.com/story/2019/04/25/biden-obama-2020-relationship-1287353.

279 **in his electrifying speech in 2004:** Obama, keynote speech at the Democratic National Convention.

279 **"Beauty," Harvard professor of aesthetics:** Elaine Scarry, *On Beauty and
Being Just* (Princeton, NJ: Princeton University Press, 1999), 29.

279 **"the most beautiful man":** Robert Boyers, "A Beauty," in *The Best American
Essays 2012*, ed. David Brooks (New York: Mariner, 2012), 52–53.

279 **"Beauty quickens":** Scarry, *On Beauty,* 24.

279 **"It is the very way":** Ibid., 23.

# Bibliography

Abrams, Brian. *Obama: An Oral History 2009–2017*. New York: Little A, 2018.

Allen, Jonathan, and Amie Parnes. *HRC: State Secrets and the Rebirth of Hillary Clinton*. New York: Crown, 2014.

———. *Shattered: Inside Hillary Clinton's Doomed Campaign*. New York: Broadway, 2017.

Alter, Jonathan. *The Center Holds: Obama and His Enemies*. New York: Simon & Schuster, 2013.

———. *The Promise: President Obama, Year One.* New York: Simon & Schuster, 2010.

Axelrod, David. *Believer: My Forty Years in Politics*. New York: Penguin, 2015.

Badhwar, Neera Kapur, ed. *Friendship: A Philosophical Reader*. Ithaca, NY: Cornell University Press, 1993.

Balz, Dan. *Collision 2012: The Future of Election Politics in a Divided America*. New York: Penguin, 2014.

Becker, Jo. *Forcing the Spring: Inside the Fight for Marriage Equality*. New York: Penguin, 2014.

Belcher, Cornell. *A Black Man in the White House: Barack Obama and the Triggering of America's Racial-Aversion Crisis*. Healdsburg, CA: Uptown Professional, 2016.

Biden, Joe. *Promise Me, Dad: A Year of Hope, Hardship, and Purpose*. New York: Flatiron, 2017.

———. *Promises to Keep: On Life and Politics*. New York: Random House, 2007.

Boyers, Robert. "A Beauty." In *The Best American Essays 2012*, edited by David Brooks, 52–62. New York: Mariner, 2012.

Bradlee, Benjamin C. *Conversations with Kennedy*. New York: W. W. Norton, 1975.

Branch, Lessie B. *Optimism at All Costs: Black Attitudes, Activism and Advancement in Obama's America*. Amherst: University of Massachusetts Press, 2018.

Brooks, David, ed. *The Best American Essays 2012*. New York: Mariner, 2012.

Brower, Kate Andersen. *First in Line: Presidents, Vice Presidents, and the Pursuit of Power*. New York: Harper, 2018.

Chait, Jonathan. *Audacity: How Barack Obama Defied His Critics and Created a Legacy That Will Prevail*. New York: Custom House, 2017.

Chambers, Veronica, ed. *The Meaning of Michelle: 16 Writers on the Iconic First Lady and How Her Journey Inspires Our Own*. New York: St. Martin's, 2017.

Coates, Ta-Nehisi. *Between the World and Me*. New York: Spiegel & Grau, 2015.

———. *We Were Eight Years in Power: An American Tragedy*. New York: One World, 2018.

Collins, Philip. *When They Go Low, We Go High: Speeches That Shape the World and Why We Need Them*. New York: Overlook, 2018.

Cramer, Richard Ben. *What It Takes: The Way to the White House*. New York: Vintage, 1993.

Dorey-Stein, Beck. *From the Corner of the Oval: A Memoir*. New York: Spiegel & Grau, 2018.

Dyson, Michael Eric. *The Black Presidency: Barack Obama and the Politics of Race in America*. New York: Mariner Books, 2017.

Eizenstat, Stuart E. *President Carter: The White House Years*. New York: Thomas Dunne, 2018.

Falk, Avner. *The Riddle of Barack Obama: A Psychobiography*. Santa Barbara, CA: Praeger, 2010.

Firstbrook, Peter. *The Obamas: The Untold Story of an African Family*. New York: Crown, 2011.

Gans, John. *White House Warriors: How the National Security Council Transformed the American Way of War*. New York: Liveright, 2019.

Garfield, Robert. *Breaking the Male Code: Unlocking the Power of Friendship*. New York: Gotham, 2015.

Garrow, David J. *Rising Star: The Making of Barack Obama*. New York: William Morrow, 2017.

Gates, Robert M. *Duty: Memoirs of a Secretary at War*. New York: Vintage, 2015.

Gellman, Barton. *Angler: The Cheney Vice Presidency*. New York: Penguin, 2009.

Goldstein, Joel K. *The White House Vice Presidency: The Path to Significance, Mondale to Biden*. Lawrence: University Press of Kansas, 2016.

Goodwin, Doris Kearns. *Lyndon Johnson and the American Dream*. New York: St. Martin's, 1991.

Greif, Geoffrey L. *Buddy System: Understanding Male Friendships*. Oxford: Oxford University Press, 2008.

Grunwald, Michael. *The New New Deal: The Hidden Story of Change in the Obama Era*. New York: Simon & Schuster, 2012.

Halperin, Mark, and John Heilemann. *Double Down: Game Change 2012*. New York: Penguin, 2014.

Harfoush, Rahaf. *Yes We Did: An Inside Look at How Social Media Built the Obama Brand*. Berkeley, CA: New Riders, 2009.

Hayes, Stephen F. *Cheney: The Untold Story of America's Most Powerful and Controversial Vice President*. New York: HarperCollins, 2007.

Heaney, Seamus. *The Haw Lantern*. New York: Farrar, Straus & Giroux, 1987.

# Bibliography

Heilemann, John, and Mark Halperin. *Game Change: Obama and the Clintons, McCain and Palin, and the Race of a Lifetime*. New York: HarperPerennial, 2010.

Jamieson, Kathleen Hall, ed. *Electing the President 2008: The Insiders' View*. Philadelphia: University of Pennsylvania Press, 2009.

Joseph, Peniel E. *Dark Days, Bright Nights: From Black Power to Barack Obama*. New York: Basic Civitas, 2010.

Kamarck, Elaine C. *Why Presidents Fail and How They Can Succeed Again*. Washington, DC: Brookings, 2016.

Kantor, Jodi. *The Obamas*. New York: Back Bay, 2012.

Kennedy, Randall. *The Persistence of the Color Line: Racial Politics and the Obama Presidency*. New York: Vintage, 2012.

Kloppenberg, James T. *Reading Obama: Dreams, Hope, and the American Political Tradition*. Princeton, NJ: Princeton University Press, 2011.

Laskas, Jeanne Marie. *To Obama: With Love, Joy, Anger, and Hope*. New York: Random House, 2018.

Lawrence, John A. *The Class of '74: Congress After Watergate and the Roots of Partisanship*. Baltimore, MD: Johns Hopkins University Press, 2018.

Lawrence-Lightfoot, Sara. *Respect: An Exploration*. Cambridge, MA: Perseus, 2000.

Leaver, Kate. *The Friendship Cure: Reconnecting in the Modern World*. New York: Overlook, 2018.

Leibovich, Mark. *This Town: Two Parties and a Funeral—Plus Plenty of Valet Parking!—in America's Gilded Capital*. New York: Blue Rider, 2013.

Lewis, C. S. *The Four Loves*. San Diego, CA: Harvest, 1988.

Litt, David. *Thanks, Obama: My Hopey, Changey White House Years*. New York: HarperCollins, 2017.

Maclay, William. *Journal of William Maclay*. Edited by Edgar S. Maclay. New York: Appleton, 1890.

Mann, James. *George W. Bush*. The American President Series. New York: Times Books, 2015.

———. *The Obamians: The Struggle Inside the White House to Redefine American Power*. New York: Viking, 2012.

Maraniss, David. *Barack Obama: The Story*. New York: Simon & Schuster, 2012.

Mastromonaco, Alyssa, and Lauren Oyler. *Who Thought This Was a Good Idea?* New York: Twelve, 2017.

McChrystal, General Stanley. *My Share of the Task: A Memoir*. New York: Portfolio, 2013.

Mendell, David. *Obama: From Promise to Power*. New York: Amistad, 2007.

Miller, Stuart. *Men and Friendship*. Los Angeles: Jeremy P. Tarcher, 1992.

Mina, An Xiao. *Memes to Movements: How the World's Most Viral Media Is Changing Social Protest and Power*. Boston: Beacon, 2018.

Nehamas, Alexander. *On Friendship*. New York: Basic, 2016.

Obama, Barack. *The Audacity of Hope: Thoughts on Reclaiming the American Dream*. New York: Three Rivers, 2006.

———. *Dreams from My Father: A Story of Race and Inheritance*. New York: Broadway Paperbacks, 2004.

Obama, Michelle. *Becoming*. New York: Crown, 2018.

Offner, Arnold A. *Hubert Humphrey: The Conscience of the Country*. New Haven, CT: Yale University Press, 2018.

Packer, George. *Our Man: Richard Holbrooke and the End of the American Century*. New York: Knopf, 2019.

———. *The Unwinding: An Inner History of the New America*. New York: Farrar, Straus & Giroux, 2013.

Pfeiffer, Dan. *Yes We (Still) Can: Politics in the Age of Obama, Twitter, and Trump*. New York: Twelve, 2018.

Plouffe, David. *The Audacity to Win: The Inside Story and Lessons of Barack Obama's Historic Victory*. New York: Viking, 2009.

Raghavan, Gautam, ed. *West Wingers*. New York: Penguin, 2018.

Remnick, David. *The Bridge: The Life and Rise of Barack Obama*. New York: Alfred A. Knopf, 2010.

Rhodes, Ben. *The World as It Is: A Memoir of the Obama White House*. New York: Random House, 2018.

Rotundo, E. Anthony. *American Manhood: Transformations in Masculinity from the Revolution to the Modern Era*. New York: Basic, 1993.

Sanger, David E. *Confront and Conceal: Obama's Secret Wars and Surprising Use of American Power*. New York: Crown, 2012.

Scarry, Elaine. *On Beauty and Being Just*. Princeton, NJ: Princeton University Press, 1999.

Schlesinger, Arthur M., Jr. *Robert Kennedy and His Times*. Boston: Houghton Mifflin, 1978.

Sharpley-Whiting, T. Denean, ed. *The Speech: Race and Obama's "A More Perfect Union."* New York: Bloomsbury, 2009.

Slevin, Peter. *Michelle Obama: A Life*. New York: Alfred A. Knopf, 2015.

Souza, Pete. *The Rise of Barack Obama*. Chicago: Triumph, 2008.

Strozier, Charles B., and Wayne Soini. *Your Friend Forever, A. Lincoln: The Enduring Friendship of Abraham Lincoln and Joshua Speed*. New York: Columbia University Press, 2016.

Suri, Jeremi. *The Impossible Presidency: The Rise and Fall of America's Highest Office*. New York: Basic, 2017.

Trilling, Lionel. *Sincerity and Authenticity*. Cambridge, MA: Harvard University Press, 1997.

Watts, Steven. *JFK and the Masculine Mystique: Sex and Power on the New Frontier*. New York: Thomas Dunne, 2016.

Weisberg, Jacob. *The Bush Tragedy*. New York: Random House, 2008.

Welty, Eudora, and Ronald A. Sharp, eds. *The Norton Book of Friendship*. New York: W. W. Norton, 1991.

White, Theodore H. *The Making of the President 1960*. New York: Atheneum, 1961.

# Bibliography

Willis, Deborah, and Kevin Merida. *Obama: The Historic Campaign in Photographs*. New York: Amistad, 2011.

Wilser, Jeff. *The Book of Joe: The Life, Wit, and (Sometimes Accidental) Wisdom of Joe Biden*. New York: Three Rivers, 2017.

Witcover, Jules. *The American Vice Presidency: From Irrelevance to Power*. Washington, DC: Smithsonian, 2014.

———. *Joe Biden: A Life of Trial and Redemption*. New York: William Morrow, 2010.

Wolffe, Richard. *Renegade: The Making of a President*. New York: Three Rivers, 2010.

Woodward, Bob. *Obama's Wars*. New York: Simon & Schuster, 2010.

Wright, Lawrence. *The Terror Years: From al-Qaeda to the Islamic State*. New York: Alfred A. Knopf, 2016.

Yeats, William Butler. *Selected Poems and Two Plays of William Butler Yeats*. Edited by M. L. Rosenthal. New York: Collier, 1977.

Zelizer, Julian E., ed. *The Presidency of Barack Obama: A First Historical Assessment*. Princeton, NJ: Princeton University Press, 2018.

# Index

# Index

# Index

# Index

Index

# Index